MW00780416

ELEUSIS

Archetypal Image of Mother and Daughter

BOLLINGEN SERIES LXV · 4

Carl Kerényi

E L E U S I S

Archetypal Image of Mother
and Daughter

Translated from the German by Ralph Manheim

BOLLINGEN SERIES LXV · 4

PRINCETON UNIVERSITY PRESS

PRINCETON, NEW JERSEY

Published by Princeton University Press,
41 William Street, Princeton, New Jersey 08540

Copyright © 1967 by Bollingen Foundation
All Rights Reserved

THIS IS VOLUME FOUR IN A GROUP OF STUDIES OF
Archetypal Images of Greek Religion WHICH CONSTITUTE
THE SIXTY-FIFTH PUBLICATION IN THE BOLLINGEN SERIES.
TRANSLATED FROM THE AUTHOR'S MANUSCRIPT BY RALPH MANHEIM,
THIS BOOK WAS FIRST PRINTED IN 1967 BY PANTHEON BOOKS
FOR THE BOLLINGEN FOUNDATION.
EARLIER VERSIONS APPEARED IN DUTCH,
Eleusis: de heiligste mysteriën van Griekenland, © 1960,
N. V. SERVIRE, THE HAGUE; AND IN GERMAN, *Die Mysterien von Eleusis,*
© 1962, RHEIN-VERLAP AG, ZURICH.

Library of Congress Cataloging-in-Publication data
will be found on page 258.

ISBN 0-691-01915-0 (paperback)
First paperback printing, in the Mythos Series, 1991

Princeton University Press books are printed on acid-free paper,
and meet the guidelines for permanence and durability of the
Committee on Production Guidelines for Book Longevity
of the Council on Library Resources

3   5   7   9   10   8   6   4

Printed in the United States of America
by Princeton Academic Press

DIS MANIBUS

Ioannis Huizingae

Non semel quaedam sacra traduntur: Eleusin servat, quod ostendat revisentibus.

There are holy things that are not communicated all at once: Eleusis always keeps something back to show those who come again.

—SENECA, *Quaestiones naturales* VII 30 6

Contents

LIST OF ILLUSTRATIONS

Photographs are ascribed to museums unless otherwise accredited. The following abbreviations refer to photographic sources:

DAI Deutsches archäologisches Institut.

JIAN *Diethnes ephemeris tes nomismatikes archaiologias: Journal international d'archéologie numismatique.*

ACKNOWLEDGMENTS

Acknowledgment is gratefully made to Cornell University Press for permission to use a quotation from Lane Cooper's translation of Plato's *Phaedrus,* copyright 1938 by Lane Cooper; to Harcourt, Brace & World, Inc., and Faber and Faber Ltd., for quotations from Robert Fitzgerald's translation of *Oedipus at Colonus* in the Harvest edition of Sophocles, *The Oedipus Cycle;* to Harvard University Press and William Heinemann Ltd. for quotations from translations by Frank Cole Babbitt of Plutarch's *Moralia,* vol. I, by Clinton W. Keyes of Cicero's *De legibus,* and by W. R. Paton of *The Greek Anthology,* vols. III and V, all in the Loeb Classical Library; to Princeton University Press for quotations from George E. Mylonas' *Eleusis and the Eleusinian Mysteries,* copyright © 1961 by Princeton University Press; and to The Soncino Press Limited for quotations from a translation by Jacob Schachter and H. Freedman of the tractate Sanhedrin in *The Babylonian Talmud,* vol. VI.

Thanks are due also to John Travlos for making his plans of Eleusis available for this publication, in newly revised form, and for helping in the procurement of an air view of the site. His large plan of the site (fig. 17) has been slightly modified by the addition of a reference to the Anaktoron, with consequent revision of numerals, and by the placing of arrows for location.

T H I S B O O K is identical with none of the earlier works I have published on the same subject. Issued in a pocketbook series, the Dutch volume *Eleusis: de heiligste mysteriën van Griekenland* was necessarily limited in length. Similar considerations led me to limit the scope of the German volume *Die Mysterien von Eleusis*. Even so, it contained more than an attempt at reconstruction. Unfortunately, it was already in print when G. E. Mylonas' book *Eleusis and the Eleusinian Mysteries* appeared. This publication for the first time made possible a complete survey of the results of excavations and a discussion of their interpretation by archaeologists. It called for an enlargement of my book. Another difference followed from my conviction that the Eleusinian gods should be numbered among the "Archetypal Images." This point of view was stressed neither in the Dutch nor in the German volume, but is expressed in my earlier essay on the Divine Maiden. It is developed in the present work, which treats the problem of the Mysteries more fully, from the standpoint not only of Greek existence—this was the central theme of the German version—but also of *human nature.*

It is *human nature,* man as a whole, in his concrete reality, that is sometimes helped by outward means to achieve an inner light. Such a means at Eleusis was fasting. In addition to hunger, there was another undeniable condition for the accomplishment of the Mysteries, which may be termed the pharmaceutical preparation for them: the drinking of the *kykeon.* My investigations have now been extended in this direction, which was not considered in the previous versions. I have gained a measure of certainty in this new field from a correspondence with the Basel pharmacologist Dr. Albert Hofmann, to whom I wish to give thanks for his help in this still incomplete inquiry.

From the very beginning of this work, I have aimed to take exact account of the results of the archaeological research carried on at the site of the *epopteia:* in the Telesterion. This research has achieved a high degree of precision thanks to the work of John Travlos. In May, 1964, I had the privilege of visiting Eleusis with Travlos, who is still carrying on excavations [1] and may be expected to provide a new reconstruction of the Telesterion. The hypothesis that a small rise in the rocky ground of the Telesterion was regarded as an "omphalos," and formed the center of the cult, struck us both as erroneous. While I was on the spot, I had occasion to reflect on another question also. It concerns the building which had the form of a temple and whose tympanum was probably decorated with a representation of the rape of Persephone, surrounded by figures known to us from the west tympanum of the Parthenon. Laid out parallel to the north side of the Telesterion, it was situated on the site—outside the entrance of the Telesterion—which several archaeologists formerly believed to have been occupied by the temple of Demeter. Travlos has worked out a theoretical reconstruction of this building. He regards it not as a temple but as a treasure house (*thesauros*), where the most valuable gifts of the Athenians were kept.[2]

An answer to this question has no great significance for a reconstruction of the Mystery ceremony. I consider it possible that this building was the sacrarium, which apart from the Hierophants only the Emperor Marcus Aurelius was permitted to enter and of which we shall speak in this book. This would offer a third possibility, in addition to the two others discussed below (pp. 110 f.), of identifying the Megaron, which the Eleusinians may also have designated as a *thesauros*. Fortunately such uncertainties, which cannot be obviated entirely, have no bearing on anything that is essential from our standpoint. The reader should not expect this book to take a position on controversies having little to do with the Eleusinian religion. Nor should he expect the archaeologists to supply an answer as to the content of the Mysteries. Sound solutions can be arrived at only if the two sciences, archaeology and the history of religions, are properly co-ordinated.

*

Below the reader will find a reproduction of the cup which I now assume to be the earliest extant representation of Persephone. It is from the beginning of the Middle Minoan period (shortly after 2000 B.C.) and was found by Professor Doro Levi in 1955 in his excavation of the first palace of Phaistos. He describes it as follows: "A low cup, the inner surface of which shows a religious scene. Two women are seen dancing in most lively attitudes around the Snake Goddess. The head of the Goddess rests on the top of an elongated triangular body with no arms but with a series of arcs running along each of the sides. The body of the goddess and the snakes immediately remind us of the very similar tubular clay idols, or sacrificial tubes,

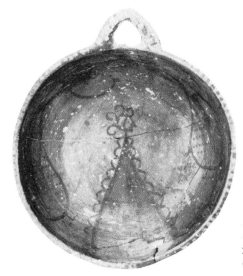 

Persephone with two companions, in a cup of the Middle Minoan period from the first palace at Phaistos (with transcript). Archaeological Museum of Heraklion, Crete

found at Prinias and in other early-Hellenic sites of more than 1000 years later." [3]

The tubular clay idols, or sacrificial tubes, assuredly served for communication with the subterranean realm. This realm is indicated by the snake, which figures prominently in one version of the myth of Persephone: Zeus, in the form of a snake, seduces her, his own daughter.[4] Snake and incest are archaic motifs in mythology.[5] The number three (a triad of personages) can also be regarded as an archaic element. It occurs in the Greek myth of Persephone: her two companions are most often Artemis and Athena.[6] The Homeric Hymn to Demeter mentions an indefinite number of Okeanidai who play with Persephone and pick flowers: this fits in with the Homeric style, which effaces and excludes the archaic elements. But we recognize the same scene preceding the abduction of the goddess in the hymn (15; cf. below, p. 34) and in the Phaistos cup: Persephone admiring the flower.

*

After all, the continuing excavations of John Travlos and my Appendixes—especially Appendix I—serve to show how little one can speak of an end of Eleusinian research. Nothing is further from my mind than to give the impression that with this book all difficulties and contradictions of the known facts are resolved and that the last word has been said. To the contrary. I have intentionally left open the possibility of new conclusions and continued investigation. My book should act as the *kykeon* of Eleusis in all probability did: as a stimulant—indeed, as an agent rousing other students to seek a more complete historical vision of what Eleusis really *was*.

C. K.

Ascona, Switzerland
May 27, 1966

[I

FEW SUBJECTS in the science of religion lend themselves so well to an attempt at reconstruction on the basis of on-the-site archaeological findings as Eleusis and its Mysteries. In view of the mystical core of the subject, such archaeological treatment will give the reader a feeling of standing on firmer ground. But it has also been a pleasure for the author, at least in the first part of this work, to employ this method of exposition and to attempt a reconstruction based on archaeological and other material. Like the re-narration employed in my *Gods of the Greeks* and *Heroes of the Greeks,* this too is a scientific method. What makes both methods scientific is that in both cases the resistance of the material must be scrupulously respected. In this respect they are superior to other methods, which can offer only a schematic cross section of the historical material, and this only from a single standpoint. In an attempt at reconstruction, the implications of the existing material must be examined and tested over and over again.

It must always be asked—this is our criterion in the present case—whether each new statement is not in such contradiction to other facts, belonging to the reliable tradition concerning the Mysteries, that they cannot be used together in a reconstruction. Let us assume, for example, that the total context of a great ceremony of the Catholic Church, such as High Mass, has been lost. Only fragments from liturgical books and ruins of churches have been preserved. We cannot assume that the Mass has been the same from the start. The preserved fragments may date from different periods. A reconstruction can, nevertheless, be undertaken, because there is one thing we do not doubt, namely, that at every stage in its development the liturgy somehow formed a coherent whole with its own inner logic. This inner logic can be grasped even if we do not know what the liturgy as a whole *was* for the participants who still understood it thoroughly. We are able to judge what elements conflict with this logic and hence cannot fit into the context.

In the present book such an attempt at reconstruction occupies the foreground. But if I go so far as to call the first part "Reconstruction," this only means that in this section I try to provide a reconstruction of the Mysteries without reflecting on what their content may have been for the religious man of antiquity; hermeneutical reflection and investigation are reserved for the second part. This "hermeneutical essay," however, does not aim at re-creating the *emotional* experience of the devotees of the cult. Let us suppose that the content of the Mysteries of Eleusis—as certain scholars suppose to this day—was a drama. We shall see that this cannot have been the case. But even if it had been and the participants in the Mysteries had been deeply moved by a drama, even then we should be able, without undergoing a similar emotional experience, to ask on what human grounds the drama can have been so moving. The task of hermeneutics is to penetrate these grounds.

The evidence is not of the same kind in reconstruction and in hermeneutics. In the first case we can content ourselves with evidence that fragments of the Mysteries, which have not come down to us in context, fit together as we have supposed. In the second case we shall have such evidence if we find that our interpretation accords with human experience, even of an unusual kind. No field of human experience is excluded from scientific investigation, and this also goes for religious experience. If historical investigation should shrink back from fields making demands on the investigator's capacity for experience or at least openness to the experience of others, it would not cease to be "academic"; it would cease to be science.

[2

IN MY earlier study on the subject [1] I attempted to lay the foundations of a hermeneutics extending beyond Eleusis and the Greeks. "The central problems connected with these Mysteries will always be among the most essential problems of the history of ancient religions." In these words Samson Eitrem,[2] the great Norwegian historian of religions, who has himself made a noteworthy contribution to the study of the Mysteries, stressed the importance of the subject. My first attempts to reconstruct small or larger parts of the sacred action date back to the twenties. At first they were mere reflections, which even when written down were not published. Later on, I spoke of my ideas while guiding students at Eleusis and in my Budapest lectures. My thinking on the subject was stimulated by F. Noack's *Eleusis*, dealing with the architectural history of the sanctuary of Eleusis,[3] and by the excavations of Konstantinos Kuruniotis, which I followed in the course of frequent excursions to Eleusis from Athens.

In 1939, while I was preoccupied by a not unrelated mythological theme, that of the "Primordial Child," an ethnological work of the utmost importance appeared.[4] Quite unexpectedly, it showed me a new approach to the "central problems" of Eleusis [5] and provided me with the broader base to which I have just referred. Similarities between the sacred actions of Eleusis—or the preparations for them—and the initiation rites of primitive peoples had been stressed at an earlier date. But no one had found mythological and ritual material coinciding in so many details with the content, that is, the myth of the Eleusinian religion, as that now discovered among the Wemale of western Ceram. The editor of the book, the head of the Ceram expedition of the Frobenius Institute, did not yet suspect that his discoveries would be of any relevance to the history of Greek religion.

I myself had no idea, when in the summer of 1939 I conceived my study[6] on the island of Elba and committed it to writing in San Gimignano with no thought of Jungian ideas, that it would appear in the same year with a psychological commentary by C. G. Jung, in Albae Vigiliae, the series of humanistic studies that I had just founded.[7] Apart from the study of classical antiquity, I was at that time in contact with no research activity except for that of the Frobenius Institute. It was the Frobenius Institute that discovered and collected the myths which helped crystallize my ideas about the "Primordial Maiden," a figure providing a parallel to the "Primordial Child." My first published study on the Eleusinian Mysteries was built up around Kore-Persephone, the "Divine Maiden," and the Ceramese Kore figure, whom I considered as two polarities which cast light on each other.[8]

When I now look back at this stage of my approach to the Eleusinian secret—for that was my concern from the very start—I find a part of its value in the fact that it was my study which first led Jung to a psychological appraisal of the Eleusinian Mysteries and the parallels they presented to the findings on Ceram and which later led Jensen, the ethnologist who compiled *Hainuwele* (with a collaborator), to elucidate these parallels from *his* point of view, that of the historical ethnologist.[9] He attributed to the Eleusinian Mysteries the same role as I had in my study: to his mind, they constitute a Greek example of the ritual embodiment of a myth which is also clearly embodied in rites that have survived down to our own times on the remote Indonesian island of Ceram. The myth is related to the nourishment men derive from plants. The context can be characterized most suggestively with the help of Greek words: *zoë* means not only the life of men and of all living creatures but also what is *eaten*. In the Odyssey (XVI 429), the suitors wish to "eat up" the *zoë* of Odysseus. The same meaning attaches to *bios*, the characteristic life of men.[10] Where men draw their nourishment chiefly from plants, the nutritive plants—not only grain but the tuberous and fruit-bearing plants as well—are individually perishable, destructible, edible, but taken together, they are the eternal guarantee of human life.

Jensen reconstructed the world view of an early culture which had this very foundation, the nutritive plant, a world view which bore within it at least the germ of tragic myths and rites. Whether, as Jensen assumed, this world view possessed the same inner cohesion among all peoples of like culture and whether these myths and rites follow logically, as it were, from this cohesion is not demonstrable. All that can be demonstrated is that among archaic peoples there are myths and rites based on the belief that plant nourishment and procreation—which are seen to be closely related—first came into being through the violent death of a divine being. The original myth, I should like to intercalate, speaks rather of an *apparent* death, which resulted in the dissemination and procreation of life, but in the imitation of the myth, in the cult, this seeming death is reflected in actual sacrifices. In view of the abundant examples from many widely separate regions, one can justly assume that the common features of the Eleusinian and the Ceramese myths and rites had their source in a historical or, rather, prehistorical conception of this kind. But this conception was already far removed from the Greeks who fashioned the myth that presided over the Eleusinian

Mysteries, much farther than from the Wemale of western Ceram. Historical ethnology has shown, or at least helped us to perceive, not only the common prehistoric source of similarities but also the *distance* separating the examples in question from that source.

Jensen criticized in detail Jung's explanation of these similarities, namely, his derivation of them from common human foundations, the "archetypes" which Jung believed to have been at work both in Greece and in Indonesia. It must be recognized, however, that this criticism is based on a criterion that a psychologist cannot accept as valid in his field. Jensen insists that dreams should disclose a completeness, an inner logic and coherence, such as the ethnologist himself can find only approximatively in his own material and is obliged to construct. C. G. Jung never held that archaic contents rise up in modern man with all their original coherence and consistency, like a massive and fully visible mountain, but only that enduring elements of forgotten myths emerge, like the summits of sunken mountain ranges. Jensen's book did not decide the question of this possibility, even in connection with the Eleusinian Mysteries. There still remained two equally justifiable explanations of the parallels between the myths of western Ceram and the Eleusinian mythology, one based on the transmission of a prehistoric view of the world, the other stressing a common human foundation. But even if the first theory should prove to be likely on historical grounds, we should still have to accept the second; for the assimilation of foreign conceptions always presupposes a common human foundation, without which no transmission would be possible. Thus we cannot speak of an absolute alternative between the archetypal explanation and an explanation based on the historical transmission. The question is, rather: spontaneous acquisition on an archetypal foundation or transmission on the same foundation. The term "archetypal" seems to contain implications which compel one to accept it but which, for that very reason, make it a commonplace that arouses no particular interest. We must take care not to attach too much importance to the *word*.

[3

I M U S T once again point out, as I did in the Introduction to my *Prometheus: Archetypal Image of Human Existence* (pp. xviii f.), that in my first studies, which Jung later commented on from the standpoint of his theory of "archetypes," I managed quite well without the terms "archetype" and "archetypal." Also, in connection with the mythologies of Eleusis and of western Ceram, I spoke only of a "primordial figure." By this I meant that such a figure is "typical" not only of a particular culture—in this case the culture of Greece or Ceram—but in far greater degree of human nature in general. Thus from the very start the simpler term "archetypal" was applicable to my idea.

Jung was the first writer of our day to revive this old term from the common language of Western culture. But at the time when he wrote his commentaries on my essays he was still using it with caution. He preferred to speak of "types," which recur over and over again in dreams. For such types he found examples and arguments, but not for special "archetypes," working in the human soul and common to all mankind, such as his theory finally came to require. The "primordial figures" in the form of the "Divine Child" and the "Divine Maiden," which I found in various mythologies widely remote from one another, were very welcome to him as examples of the "archetypes" he was looking for. The source of my association with him was not that I took any of his theses as a foundation but, rather, that he believed he could take my investigations as a foundation. This spurred me to further research. For it meant that insights which I had gained in the purely historical field of religious and mythological tradition could be of help to the suffering human beings with whom physicians and psychotherapists deal.

Thus the connection was far from being purely verbal. But I should never have chosen the term "archetypal images" in place of "primordial figures" and "primordial images" if it had not offered advantages for the phenomenological definition of mythology. I have already discussed this in the Introduction to my *Prometheus* (p. xix). Also, in the development of my own ideas, I have begun to prefer "image" to "figure." Both figures and images occur in mythology. But "image" gives rise at once to the challenging, commanding question: Image of whom or of what? With "figure," on the other hand, the question lies dormant. Of course, one can always ask: What *is* this or that figure? But this question leads rather to description, as in the case of Walter Friedrich Otto, than to such penetration as I attempted in my *Hermes der Seelenführer: Das Mythologem vom männlichen Lebensursprung* and am attempting in the present series.

If such statements as "That is archetypal" or "That is an archetype" made further investigation seem superfluous or unnecessary, one would have to discard this terminology in a scientific work. Its use would be tantamount to word magic, even if in this case the magic word happens to be a technical term employed by physicians and psychologists. Why extend the field of inquiry beyond the limits of Eleusis or even of the ancient world if our only conclusion is to be: "An archetypal action was performed," or "The initiates busied themselves with archetypes"? Nothing could be more trivial than such simplistic, schematic truths. Our questions must be very concrete: What was the content of the Mysteries? Whose images is it that we, the noninitiate, still encounter at Eleusis? They are the images of Mother and Daughter—as it were, a holy duality. But what *are* mother and daughter? what are Demeter and Persephone?

[4

S I N C E   T H E method of reconstruction aims at something particular and concrete, not at mysteries in general, but at the Eleusinian Mysteries, a hermeneutical approach should also be concerned with what is particular and in a certain sense concrete in these Mysteries. Our quest must be for this particular and not for the archetype in general. The position I take in this respect is pre-Jungian, as in my studies on the Primordial Child and the Primordial Maiden—hence not influenced by the conclusions which Jung drew from my findings. Of course, my present position is also post-Jungian, and not only in a temporal sense, for on the basis of my study Jung did concern himself with the theme. And yet, in respect of Eleusis, my post-Jungian position is not very different from my pre-Jungian view of the Primordial Child and the Primordial Maiden.

Jung's contribution—his commentary—to the "Primordial Child" was fundamentally different from his contribution to the "Primordial Maiden." In commenting on the "Primordial Child" for the benefit of those who wished to gain a psychological understanding and evaluation of this motif common to a number of mythologies, he worked with the motif itself. On the basis of the phenomenology of the mythological primordial child, which I had developed, he was able for the first time to describe the phenomenology of one of his archetypes, namely, the child archetype. This unexpected collaboration and amplification of the field of my research was to me enormously stimulating. Jung seems, for his part, to have been very much inspired by my second study, in which I attempted to apply the method of the first to the Eleusinian theme. He attempted a commentary similar to the first, and it was not successful.

The principal archetypes which he *then* proposed—and, as I have said, he often referred to them only as "types"—were: "the Shadow, the Wise Old Man, the Child (including the Child-Hero), the Mother ('Primordial Mother' and 'Earth Mother') as a superordinate personality ('daemonic' because superordinate), and her counterpart the Maiden, and lastly the Anima in man and the Animus in woman." [11] Although, for the sake of the theme, he added the "Maiden" to the series as a "counterpart," the "Primordial Maiden," the "Kore," whose phenomenology I have described, cannot, with all her manifestations, be reduced to a single type. Jung writes: "The 'Kore' has her psychological counterpart in those types which I have called the Self or superordinate personality on the one hand, and the Anima on the other." [12] But just this twofold parallel presents a difficulty, not one of a logical nature, which Jung would discard as a matter of principle, but a difficulty inherent in the theme itself. The Anima, to employ the Jungian terminology, is man's idealized image of the feminine, while the superordinate personality of the woman is something very different.

Another objective difficulty arises when Jung tries to find a psychological parallel to the "Kore" in the "Self," and equates her with the superordinate personality of the Woman. According to Jung, as he insists also in the present context, the "Self" is "the total man, that is, man as he really is, not as he appears to himself. To this wholeness the unconscious psyche also belongs, which has its requirements and needs just as consciousness has." [13] This "Self" cannot be one thing in the man and something else in the woman. But then he goes on to describe a very particular amplification of the feminine consciousness, which can have no application to the man: "A woman lives earlier as a mother, later as a daughter. The conscious experience of these ties produces the feeling that her life is spread out over generations—the first step towards the immediate experience and conviction of being outside time, which brings with it a feeling of immortality. The individual's life is elevated into a type, indeed it becomes the archetype of woman's fate in general. This leads to restoration or apocatastasis of the lives of her ancestors, who now, through the bridge of the momentary individual, pass down into the generations of the future. An experience of this kind gives the individual a place and a meaning in the life of the generations, so that all unnecessary obstacles are cleared out of the way of the life-stream that is to flow through her. At the same time the individual is rescued from her isolation and restored to wholeness. All ritual preoccupation with archetypes ultimately has this aim and this result." [14]

Thus the "archetype of feminine destiny," into which only a *woman* can be amplified, cannot be the "Self," but only a step on the way to the Self. These are the ideas of a great psychologist concerning the mythological presuppositions of the Eleusinian Mysteries (the presuppositions are as far as I got in my study on the "Kore") but not an explanation of the "Eleusinian emotions" (as Jung calls them) from the standpoint of the theory of the archetypes, in so far as emotions may be presumed to have occurred also in the *male* initiates. Jung himself at the end stresses the failure of his purely psychological explanation and resorts to the history of culture: "The Demeter-Kore myth is far too feminine to have been merely the result of an anima-projection. Although the Anima can, as we have said, experience herself in Demeter-Kore, she is yet of a wholly different nature. She is in the highest sense *femme à homme,* whereas Demeter-Kore exists on the plane of mother-daughter experience, which is alien to the man and shuts him out. In fact, the psychology of the Demeter cult has all the features of a matriarchal order of society, where the man is an indispensable but on the whole disturbing factor." [15]

In this way Jung left the last word on the question of origins to the ethnologist, who for his part knows nothing of so generalized a matriarchal order, in which men are regarded as a mere disturbing factor. But he knows of several concrete matriarchal orders. The Wemale, who are here the chief example invoked, are not thoroughly and consistently matriarchal. [16] That is why I have said that the situation in this respect is pre-Jungian, that is, in every respect open to further investigation. This is also true from the standpoint of psychology, unless an explanation is built up on the basis of the suggestions with which Jung himself was not satisfied and of general notions concerning a matriarchal period in human history. This was attempted by his disciple Erich Neumann, [17] who, in addition, took undue liberties in interpreting the ancient monuments.

The position which I took independently of Jung in my "Primordial Child" and "Primordial Maiden" still strikes me as tenable. From this point of view it would not be necessary to develop a new terminology. To sum up as briefly as possible, I employ two words, one of which had been appropriated by Jungian psychology and the other by existentialist philosophy—a fact which bears witness to their intelligibility in the Western cultural sphere—though neither of these trends can claim exclusive rights to them. From my point of view, I speak of *archetypal facts of human existence*, of realities which cannot be mere realities of the psyche and which, of course, are also not concrete in the manner of tangible objects. They are concrete in the same sense as *bios*, the historical existence of the individual man. [18] An archetypal element of *bios,* the individual human existence, is first of all human existence itself; another is life, *zoë,* which in the Greek language is distinguished from *bios* and which is proper not to man alone but to all species. Accordingly, the first volume of this series deals with Prometheus, considered as an archetypal image of human existence, and another with Dionysos, the archetypal image of indestructible life.[19]

Another archetypal element is the "beginning," the *arche* in every *bios,* in the life of every man. Its archetypal image is the Primordial Child. The source of life lies deeper than the beginning of life, though it is no less an archetypal element of human existence. But every life has both a masculine and a feminine origin. In my study *Hermes der Seelenführer,* I have dealt with the archetypal image of the *masculine source of life.* We are entitled and indeed obliged to speak of a feminine origin of life in the same sense. Erich Neumann's formulation: "The woman experiences herself first and foremost as the source of life," [20] is meaningful also from the standpoint of a hermeneutics of the Eleusinian Mysteries. But it is one-sided and inadequate if taken to mean that the "self-understanding" of the feminine provides an understanding of the Mysteries. On the contrary, we are confronted with the historical fact that in the Mysteries both men and women seem to envisage the *feminine source of life,* but not in an intellectual way. In what way, then? Only a reconstruction can provide an answer. And on what foundation? If an answer is possible, only hermeneutics can be expected to provide it.

[5

T H U S F A R all attempts at a psychological approach to the secret of Eleusis have failed. In his attempt Jung prudently confined himself to

observations "on the psychological aspect of the Kore figure" (this was
the title of his contribution to my study); Erich Neumann's approach
was far more susceptible to ethnological criticism. In Jung's case, such
criticism may be termed superfluous. Outside the realm of psychology,
two different approaches have been attempted: one on an archaeological, the other on a philological and a human plane.

On the archaeological plane the excavations begun by Konstantinos
Kuruniotis were carried on with the utmost thoroughness by his asso-
ciate and successor, the architect John Travlos. G. E. Mylonas, also an
archaeologist, busied himself more than thirty years ago, likewise
under the guidance of Kuruniotis, with the excavation of the deepest
prehistoric strata of Eleusis, and has since then repeatedly gone back
to this activity. His researches at Eleusis developed into a life work, and
in so far as his book relates to the general archaeological picture, it is
indispensable.[21] However, the discovery and restoration of the Hierophant's throne, which was of the utmost importance for the reconstruction of the most secret ceremony, was the work of Travlos and was
not sufficiently taken into account by Mylonas. Another reason why his
study of the Mysteries could not be satisfactory is that, in surveying the
relevant works of philologists and historians of religion, he confined
himself to the authorities most quoted today. He failed to take note of
the important work of the great French scholars Charles and François
Lenormant on the content of the Mysteries, or of Walter Friedrich
Otto's daring theory and the document on which it is based, the
papyrus fragment containing an allusion to the vision of the initiate in
Eleusis.[22]

On the philological and the human planes, Otto offers a very
different approach from those just mentioned; but, unfortunately, his
novel theory did not help his reputation as a scholar. Otto made

so bold as to assume in his study [23] that true miracles were performed in the Mystery Night of Eleusis. This contention was tantamount to a challenge. He called upon his readers to consider the scattered allusions to the experiences—the *pathe*—of the initiate at Eleusis from a new standpoint and to experiment with the idea, which Otto took very seriously, that those who participated in the Mysteries may have *experienced* what they believed to be an authentic divine epiphany. Otto may be said to have had a precursor in the Dutch scholar K. H. E. de Jong, who had already interpreted the classical passage in Plato's *Phaedrus* (250 C) [24] as indirect evidence that spirits were made to appear at Eleusis.[25] De Jong followed in the footsteps of the French archaeologist Charles Lenormant,[26] who took the passage in the *Phaedrus* literally, although he had in mind a false epiphany, produced by some technical contrivance. The archaeological findings contain nothing to substantiate the existence of a special contrivance of this sort in the sanctuary. Otto, for his part, did not make his thesis any more plausible by suggesting that, in addition, an ear of grain may have grown and ripened miraculously during the Mystery Night.[27] This notion seemed too close to the miracle of St. Januarius in Naples. I myself was provided with a new approach to Eleusis by an interpretation of the final scene of *Oedipus at Colonus* and by the tradition concerning the trial of Aischylos for alleged betrayal of the Mysteries.[28]

The perspectives, and in particular the mythological dimension, that were opened up by my study on the "Divine Maiden" have not been abandoned in the present study. Where it has been necessary to correct any of the statements I then made, I have done so tacitly, and the same applies to my treatment of other learned literature. If I have not referred to a work in my footnotes, this does not mean that I did not take it into consideration or esteem it. I have always tended more to value the work of other scholars than to disparage it. In the first twenty years of my preoccupation with the Eleusinian Mysteries I lived so close to that literature that it would have been hard for me to break with it. Excavators take the greatest care in removing the earth that covers the temples and go so far as to pass it through a sieve. I have been obliged to treat the mass of books and articles on Eleusis in almost the same way. And how delighted and grateful I have been when even the merest fragment of ancient evidence that had not previously been taken into consideration was caught in my sieve. A complete compilation of the literature concerning the Mysteries that I have read in the course of half a century would be ostentatious.

I dedicate this book as well as the works (mentioned in the Preface) leading up to it to the serene genius, the Erasmian spirit, of the Dutch historian of culture Jan Huizinga. His investigations of "play" show points of contact with my study of festivals in *The Religion of the Greeks and Romans.* There can be no feast without play and certainly no mystery festival.

Many scholars still adhere to the commonplace that the secret of the Eleusinian Mysteries was so well kept that we can know *nothing* about them. This is not true. Our knowledge cannot be complete, but it is perhaps more than a mere beginning. What we know surely deserves, at the very least, to be taken into consideration. And if this is so, we shall have regained not only an element of the Greek religion but also a feature of Greek culture. Our picture of Greek existence will be enriched by a trait to which little attention has thus far been accorded: by a *natural* capacity to see visions. This capacity could occasionally be stimulated. A statement that might be an axiom of the Eleusinian religion occurs in Kallimachos' Hymn to Apollo (10): "He who sees the god is great, he who does not see him is small." The trait is one to which some readers will be more attracted than others—the friends of initiations more than the friends of Greek philosophy—but this can be of no concern to the historian. It would only detract from the clarity of the picture if, disregarding such sharply contoured and plastic manifestations as ceremonies and their objects, we were to replace this trait with the general concept of the irrational. It would be an unjust simplification to term these investigations a contribution to our knowledge of the irrational among the Greeks.[29] This, too, no doubt. But to do them full justice one would have to say that they are an attempt to investigate a concrete historical fact, the Mysteries of Eleusis. Through them we shall know a little more about Greek culture also.

ELEUSIS:

Archetypal Image of Mother and Daughter

Part One Reconstruction

1. *Excavation and industry in present-day Eleusis*

2. *The excavated area near the Great Propylaia. At the far right, a bust of the Emperor Antoninus Pius*

I. THE GEOGRAPHICAL AND CHRONOLOGICAL SETTING

The Sacred Road

MODERN DEVELOPMENTS have dealt kindly with the natural settings of nearly all the most celebrated holy places of the ancient Greek religion. Cleared many years ago from the last vestiges of the medieval and Turkish periods, the Akropolis at Athens stands there as though it had sprung from the rocky soil and from the marble mountains of Attica. A whole village and its predecessor, a Byzantine city, have been removed from the ruins of the temple of Apollo at Delphi, and once more the high mountains hold uncontested sway over the sacred precinct. The resinous scent of Aleppo firs envelops the grove of Zeus at Olympia and the sanctuary of Asklepios at Epidauros in an atmosphere of natural enchantment. Delos and Samothrace give the impression of remote islands of the gods, cut off from the world. Only poor Eleusis, so easily reached from Athens, lies disenchanted beneath the yellow-gray film of dust and smoke that seldom departs from it. Cement factories are gradually eating away its crenelated romantic backdrop [1].

In the late twenties buses were already running on the former Sacred Road, the route of the processions between Athens and the site of the Mysteries [2]. At that time, one would sometimes meet, as early as April, the season of the first harvest, a throng of reapers on the highway. A meaningful encounter on that road, for it suggested the fertility of the Rharian Plain, the farmland between Thria and Elcusis, where in ancient days grain was sown according to the instructions of Demeter. It was here, the Eleusinians believed, that the goddess bestowed grain

5

on their hero Triptolemos and through him on all mankind. In the late twenties one could still discern some of the river beds and watercourses crossed by Theseus, founder of the Athenian state, as he came from Eleusis and also by the annual procession from Athens to Eleusis. It was here that the procession of the mystai passed each year on its way to undergo the highest degree of initiation.

Not only has this road lost all air of sanctity today; it has almost ceased to be a country highway. The city is spreading up the mountain slope over the stony soil whose hardness for the pedestrian of ancient times is still remembered. Already urban enterprise has reached the lofty cypresses and the sparse woods near the cloister church of Daphni, erected on the site of a temple of Apollo. New houses have been built overlooking the Bay of Eleusis. The path leading through the pass between Mount Aigaleos and Mount Poikilon has been widened into an asphalt highway, and the plain that lies before us is no longer as it was. It was formerly one of those where two harvests were gathered each year. If the inroads of industry continue, there will soon be no harvest at all.[1]

In the distance we can see the cloud of dust and smoke that lies over Eleusis, while in the foreground we behold, its contours quite unchanged, the scene of a glorious episode in the history of the world, the battle of Salamis. The Greeks made this battle into an incomparable performance, not only with the movements of their ships but also with their songs, the early morning hymns to the gods and heroes of the country.[2] To be sure, it was not the Greeks who looked upon the battle as a spectacle for the benefit of an audience but Xerxes, king of the Persians. Across from the island of Salamis, on the southern slope of the Aigaleos, Xerxes had a throne of rock erected, in order that he might look on, missing no detail, at the victory of his fleet, which he expected to be an easy matter: as we look down on the scene from a still higher vantage point, we are led to reflect not only on the past and now dwindling fertility of the plain of Thria which we can already glimpse, or on the bravery of the Greek warriors shut up in the bay, but also on the Mysteries of Eleusis which on this occasion—according to the story handed down to us by Herodotos—revealed their extraordinary importance in so striking a way.

The Mysteries at the Time of Xerxes (480 B.C.) and of Valentinian (A.D. 364)

O N   T H E 27th or 28th of September of the year 480 B.C., another event in addition to the battle of Salamis is said to have taken place in the geographical and historical setting I have described—some twelve miles west of ancient Athens. And this other event is fully as illuminating as the victory of the blockaded Greeks. Regardless of whether it was a later invention or a vision actually beheld and believed at the time, it is of the utmost importance for our knowledge of historical Greek existence. This, to be sure, was no empirical happening but an "act of the human spirit," as were, in the words of Bachofen, the legends that made a place for themselves in the historical tradition, the narratives of events which never took place or which at least cannot be verified but which can, if clarified and faithfully interpreted, throw light on the historical reality.[3]

There were two Greek renegades in the retinue of the Persian king. One was the Athenian Dikaios, son of Theokydes, who having been banished from Athens had won the esteem of the Persians. It was he who gave an eyewitness report of the event, which is recorded by

Herodotos. The other renegade was Demaratos, banished king of the Spartans. Before the battle of Salamis the two of them, probably with a part of the Persian army, were on the plain of Thria, through which ran the Sacred Road. The whole countryside around Athens had been laid waste. The Athenians had all taken to the ships or else withdrawn with their women and children to the mountains of the mainland. The day of the Mysteries came. Ordinarily the initiates left Athens on the 19th of the month of Boëdromion—according to our time reckoning, the 27th or 28th of September—for Eleusis, there to celebrate the mysterious holy night. On this day of the year 480, Dikaios and Demaratos, standing on the plain of Thria, witnessed the following scene. I take the story almost literally from Herodotos (VIII 65).

A great cloud of dust rose from Eleusis, as though stirred up by a crowd of some thirty thousand men. The two onlookers were amazed and wondered what men could raise such dust. Immediately afterward they heard voices that seemed to be crying, "Iakchos! Iakchos!" as at the Feast of the Mysteries. Demaratos was unfamiliar with the ceremonies performed at Eleusis and asked what the cries were. Dikaios, who later told the story, replied: "Demaratos, it can only be that the king's army will suffer a great defeat. For this is clear: since all Attica has been abandoned by its inhabitants, those sounds must be a divine host that has come from Eleusis to help the Athenians and their allies. If it makes for the Peloponnese, it will endanger the king and his army on the mainland; if it turns toward the fleet at Salamis, the king is in danger of losing his fleet. For this is the feast that the Athenians celebrate each year in honor of the Mother and the Daughter. At this festival all the Athenians, as well as those other Greeks who so desire, are initiated. The voices you hear are the cries of 'Iakchos!' that resound at the feast." Whereupon Demaratos said: "Be silent and mention this to no one else. If your words came to the king's ears, you would lose your head. Neither I nor anyone else could save you. Just keep your peace. The gods will decide the fate of the host." This was Demaratos' warning. From the dust and voices a cloud arose and drifted toward Salamis, where the Greeks were encamped. Seeing this, the two men knew that Xerxes' fleet was doomed.

This is the story as recorded in Herodotos. In it the cloud of dust and smoke that is always over Eleusis appears in a strangely transfigured light. In any case, one element of the miraculous tale is the nature of the soil at the site of the Mysteries. Another is the knowledge that at the time of the Persian Wars roughly thirty thousand initiates took part in the Mysteries when not prevented from so doing: a round number which Herodotos elsewhere cites for the whole population of Athens (V 97). On this occasion the festive throng was replaced by something divine. In a chorus of his tragedy *Ion* (1079–86),[4] Euripides makes the sea and the sky reply to the dance of the throng arriving at Eleusis along the Sacred Road for the Mystery Night. Then: "the starry ether of Zeus takes up the dance, the moon goddess dances, and with her the fifty daughters of Nereus dance in the sea and in the eddies of the ever flowing streams, so honoring the Daughter with the golden crown and the holy Mother. . . ." The leader of the dance on earth was held to be the youthful torch-bearing god whose statue the procession bore from Athens and to whom it cried "Iakchos! Iakchos!" In *The Frogs* (316) of Aristophanes, the cry resounds in the underworld, in the abode of the blessed who in their lifetime had been initiated at Eleusis and now continue to dance in the Elysian Fields. Thus heaven, earth, and underworld are drawn into the dance.

Here we touch upon a third and perhaps the most important element of the story, which, if we suppose that the renegades each in fact experienced a hallucination, may well have been its source. This element is the general conviction that the Mysteries with all their rites, including the torchlight procession and dance, *had to be celebrated* when the time came. They were more than a common festival, they encompassed the world. A later version of the miraculous tale, recorded in Plutarch's life of Themistokles (15), adds the characteristic sign of the secret rite, lest anyone suppose that the essential part of the Mysteries was not observed on this occasion. At the very moment when the cries were heard, a light flashed across the bay from Eleusis: the light from the sanctuary, the one feature of the Mysteries that is not kept secret but mentioned in almost all the accounts. The profane could be excluded from the procession, but the fire that issued from the sanctuary could not remain a secret.

If this mysterious rite which encompassed and concerned the whole world could not be performed by men, the gods had to attend to it. A reason need scarcely be given since the Mysteries concerned the whole world, but an answer is provided by the victory at Salamis. Apparently what happened was that a divine host, a procession of spirits which could not be seen but only heard, replaced the festive throng of the Athenians with their cries of "Iakchos," joined the battling Greeks, and helped them to victory. This miracle has no known parallel, no analogy, in the history of Greek religion. When the Dioskouroi or Herakles appear in battle, they help as they are expected to. Their epiphany derives from their well-known helpful nature. The procession of spirits was an expression of perplexity, if you will, springing from the perplexity of the soul and not only of man's conscious mind—it was an expression of a profound awareness that all Greek existence was inseparably bound up with the celebration of the Mysteries at Eleusis. What would have happened if, in those days when the existence of the Greeks was so threatened, Eleusis had ceased to be the theater of the ceremonies which had never once been neglected since their founding? It was unthinkable. The Greeks as a whole and the people of each city looked upon themselves as "mankind," as the representatives of the whole human race. Certain philosophers, it is true, taught that the human race was immortal.[5] But we should not underestimate the Greeks' knowledge to the contrary: they knew that whole cities and tribes had perished, on the mainland and on the islands, and that, as Hesiod says [6] earlier, happier races of men had passed away. But nowhere was it stated that those who had perished had been in possession of the Eleusinian rites. At the time of the battle of Salamis, in the days when the country was occupied and laid waste by the enemy, they were not celebrated—or were they, perhaps, after all? They must have been. They and the victory that brought salvation—the salvation of Greek existence—could be thought of only as one.

A later witness very clearly expresses the knowledge, bordering on certainty, of the Greeks that their own existence was bound up inseparably with the Eleusinian Mysteries. He was not himself a Greek, but he was a devout worshiper of the gods; he was initiated at Eleusis and even held the rank of a hierophant, though not of Eleusis. His name was Vettius Agorius Praetextatus. His religious offices—as well as his high political honors—are recorded in an inscription in Rome.[7] In the year A.D. 364 the Catholic Emperor Valentinian prohibited all nocturnal celebrations with a view to abolishing, among other rites, the Mysteries of Eleusis. He began "at the hearth"—so runs the record of the Greek historian Zosimos, a pagan author of the fifth century, clearly alluding to the Eleusinian custom that a boy who had been initiated "at the hearth" was always sent by the Athenian state to take part in the Mysteries. "But," Zosimos' report continues,[8] "after Praetextatus, who held the office of proconsul in Greece, declared that this law would make the life of the Greeks unlivable, if they were prevented from properly observing the most sacred Mysteries, which hold the whole human race together, he permitted the entire rite to be performed in the manner inherited from the ancestors as if the edict were not valid."

This late testimony throws a highly significant light on the meaning of the Mysteries of Eleusis. They were thought to "hold the entire human race together," not only because people continued, no doubt, to come from every corner of the earth to be initiated, as they had in the days of the Emperor Hadrian, but also because the Mysteries touched on something that was common to all men. They were connected not only with Athenian and Greek existence but with human existence in general. And Praetextatus clearly stated just this: *bios*, life, he declared, would become "unlivable" (*abiotos*) for the Greeks if the celebration were to cease. Beyond a doubt the "Greeks" are here contrasted with the Christians. The sharpness of this formulation of the significance of Eleusis, which has no parallel in earlier documents, springs from the conflict between Greek religion and Christianity. Nevertheless, it suffices to give the Mysteries a special significance for us, which goes beyond any concern for the history of religions. If life was unlivable for the Greeks without the annual celebration at Eleusis, it means that this celebration was a part not merely of non-Christian existence but also of Greek life, of the Greek form of existence; and this is another reason why it is of concern to us. Despite the enormous amount of literature devoted to them, the Eleusinian Mysteries have not been studied from the standpoint of Greek existence, nor has Greek existence ever been considered in the light of Eleusis.

Testimonies to the Beatitude of the Initiates

THE EARLIER statements on the significance of the Eleusinian Mysteries are not distinguished by the same precision as the last, but they do stress something of existential importance. I do not employ the word "existential" in the strict sense employed in existential philosophy. I speak of "Greek existence" in the sense of a historical *fact*—"existential" designates the highest and most universal degree of importance, for it concerns the possibility of precisely this fact: that it *could* endure precisely as it was, and not otherwise. This importance was clearly manifested in the events of 480 B.C. and A.D. 364. The extreme importance of the Mysteries for the survival of personal existence, regardless of death, is already stressed by the Homeric Hymn to Demeter,[9] a poem of the archaic period, perhaps from as early as the eighth century B.C., which tells how the goddess Demeter inaugurated the Mysteries.

The style of this hymn in honor of the two goddesses, Demeter the Mother and Persephone the Daughter, is Homeric, and this in itself called for the omission of certain mythical details which other poets and storytellers do not pass over in silence. After Mother and Daughter are united, it is very briefly related how Demeter restored to mankind the fruit she had withdrawn in her grief, the grain which in antiquity grew so abundantly on the Rharian Plain at Thria, and the other plants and flowers. But—and this should be stressed at the very outset—this blessing with which she expressed her joy over what she herself had gained at Eleusis was not her essential gift to man; the essential gift was the ceremonies which no one may describe or utter. At this point the poet falls silent, not for reasons of Homeric style but because—these are his words (479)—"great awe of the gods makes the voice falter."

What he is permitted to add is a message whose *form* is still discernible in the Beatitudes of Christ's Sermon on the Mount. Here the word *olbios*, which I render as "blessed," bears no reference, as it often does elsewhere, to material wealth. Intentionally the poet leaves his meaning unclear to the profane (480–82). "Blessed is he among men on earth"—so runs this beatitude—"who has beheld this. Never will he who has not been initiated into these ceremonies, who has had no part in them, share in such things. He will be as a dead man in sultry darkness." The existential emphasis lies on the blessedness. It was achieved through participation in a rite. Thus an inequality was created between the initiate and the profane, a division here and now, by virtue of which *one* group is blessed while the others go to their death in imperfection and uncertainty. The end of existence has taken on two faces. The one shines back on men, lending their existence a special radiance. The other—the end awaiting the vast uncharacterized multitude—is luster-less. The grammatical context of "such things" [10] is clear: other men, in the darkness of death, will not share in "such things" as those of which the initiates have partaken. As the reader will see from Chapter IV, the Homeric hymn refers to the secret of the Mysteries in circumlocutions that must have been perfectly clear to the initiate.

Sophokles put the same beatitude into the mouth of a character probably in his tragedy *Triptolemos;* but here the statement is even more exalted and deals more explicitly with the end of life, whose whole character depends on participation or nonparticipation in the Myster-ies: "Thrice blessed are those among men who, after beholding these rites, go down to Hades. Only for them is there life; all the rest will suffer an evil lot." [11] But of the poets who speak of the Mysteries in the form of a beatitude, it is only Pindar who tells us something about their content. He speaks in such a way that the initiate could recognize the secret in the words that cloaked it: "Blessed is he who, after beholding this, enters upon the way beneath the earth: he knows the end of life and its beginning given by Zeus!" [12] "End" and "beginning" are seemingly colorless words. But they reminded the initiates of a vision in which the two were united.

The initiate possessed a knowledge which conferred blessedness and not only in the hereafter; both knowledge and beatitude became his possession the moment he beheld the vision. Both gifts of Eleusis, a happiness both here and hereafter, are praised by the poet Krinagoras of Lesbos.[13] His older contemporary, the Roman Cicero, in his treatise *On the Laws*,[14] attaches the highest importance to the radiance which Eleusis cast on all life. "We have been given a reason," he writes, "not only to live in joy but also to die with better hope" (*neque solum cum laetitia vivendi rationem accepimus sed etiam cum spe meliore moriendi*). Three centuries earlier, the Attic orator Isokrates was able, thanks to his calculated ambiguity, to do justice not only to the personal hopes conferred by the Mysteries but also to their implications for the whole human race. In his Panegyric on Athens (IV 28), he mentions the two gifts of Demeter: the grain and the Eleusinian rites (see also p. 121). And in speaking of the latter he again distinguishes two blessings: "Those who take part in them," he says, "possess better hopes in regard to the end of life and in regard to the whole *aion*."

The ambiguity lies in the word *aion*. It *can* refer to the life span, the personally characterized life of the individual man, though everywhere else in Isokrates it means the duration of the world.[15] Participation in the Mysteries offered a guarantee of life without fear of death, of confidence in the face of death. That is why the poets looked upon the initiates as so superior to other mortals. All Greeks—actually all Greek-speaking persons, the language was the criterion—could share in this gift. It conferred on Greek existence a characteristic sense of security, and because it was able to do this, it responded to a spiritual need which, it was not unreasonable to suppose, formed a bond uniting the whole human race: this was the need for a bulwark against death. Thus, as the story related by Herodotos shows, though the Greeks never said so explicitly, the Mysteries were of fundamental importance to the community, to existence in common. But the threat of death faced all men and each man personally. Would life have been worth living without the hope inspired by the Mysteries of Eleusis? Both to the community and to the individual, they supplied confidence in the face of all-devouring death.

The End of the Mysteries

THE ELEUSINIAN Mysteries provided such confidence throughout their existence, which probably extended over a period of two thousand years. Before we attempt to penetrate their sacred precinct, it would be of the utmost interest to consider their historical destinies. But very few historical details have come down to us, and we know nothing at all of the inner history, the transformations in the spiritual content and forms, of the cult. Archaic secret cults are not ordinarily susceptible of inner change. The Eleusinian Mysteries may, it is true, be termed the classical mysteries of Greece. But even so, even if an archaic cult became classical, we cannot without proof speak of transformation; at most we can note certain changes in outward form. It is in connection with the last days of the cult that we possess the most detailed information.

The end of the sanctuary of Eleusis is reported to us in the fifth century after Christ by Eunapios, historian and biographer of the last Greek philosophers and orators, in the form of a prophecy which was fulfilled when Alaric, king of the Goths, invaded Greece in A.D. 396. Eunapios was initiated into the Mysteries by the last legitimate Hierophant of Eleusis, who had been commissioned by the Emperor Julian to restore the cult, which had already fallen into considerable neglect. He was followed by a last high priest, who usurped the office and title of Hierophant. The prophecy which Eunapios records in his biography of Maximos the Neoplatonist relates to him and to the final destruction of the sanctuary. His story follows:

"I may not mention the name of the Hierophant of the time. Suffice it to say that he was the same who had initiated the writer and who traced his descent back to the Eumolpidai. It was he who foresaw the destruction of the sanctuary and the end of all Greece. He said clearly, in the writer's presence, that after him there would be a Hierophant who had no right to approach the Hierophant's throne because he was dedicated to other gods and had sworn unspeakable oaths never to preside over other ceremonies. And yet he would preside, although he was not even a citizen of Athens. The sanctuary—so far-reaching was his prophecy—would be destroyed and laid waste in his own lifetime, and the other would live to look on, despised for his boundless ambition. The worship of the Two Goddesses would come to an end even before his death, and he, shorn of his honor, would neither remain Hierophant nor live long. And so it was: scarcely had the man from Thespiai who held the rank of Father in the mysteries of Mithras become Hierophant . . . than Alaric with his barbarians poured through the Pass of Thermopylai, as though running down a racecourse, a field stamped by horses: the gates of Greece had been opened to him by the godlessness of those who in their dark garments entered with him unhindered and by the dissolution of the hierophantic rules and of the bond they embodied." [16]

There were Eleusinian rules which defined who might be Hierophant and who might not. These were included in the written laws of the Eumolpidai; hence they were no part of the secret. One such rule, for example, was that the Hierophant's name must not be mentioned.[17] These were probably the ordinances which Cicero wished to receive from Atticus.[18] Eunapios also looked upon them as the bond that holds the world together. He mentions neither the true nor the false Hierophant by name. The two Hierophants whose rivalry shattered the bond witnessed the collapse not only of the Mysteries but of the whole world. The men in dark garments who moved in with Alaric were monks. A new form of existence began for Greece. The identification of Greek existence with the Mysteries is manifested clearly and movingly by their common fate.

The Question of the Origins

T H U S   T H E end of the Mysteries is clear. Not so their beginning. The question is not merely since when the region of Eleusis shows traces of a human settlement. To this archaeology provides a clear answer.[19] But before we can even suggest a hypothetical date for the inception of the Mysteries, we must answer another question: When did the place [3] become the site of a cult exceeding in scope and importance the small household cults or tribal cults and cults of the dead which may be presumed to have existed everywhere? The earliest settlement to have been excavated in the region of Eleusis and its Mystery sanctuary is older than the era commonly known as "Mycenaean." In the so-called Middle Helladic period—the eighteenth and seventeenth centuries B.C.—the unimpressive stone houses of this settlement covered the whole mountain slope on which the sanctuary

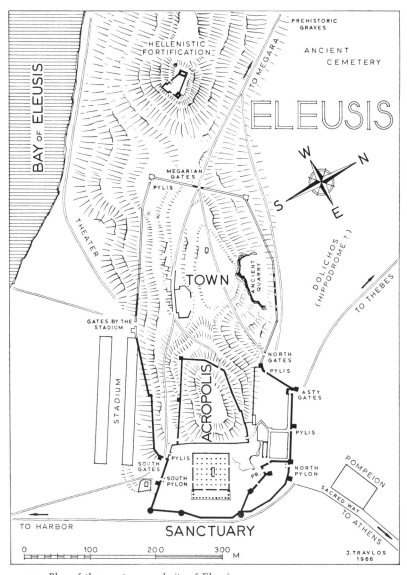

PREHISTORIC
GRAVES

ANCIENT
CEMETERY

HELLENISTIC
FORTIFICATION

TO MEGARA

BAY OF ELEUSIS

ELEUSIS

MEGARIAN
GATES

PYLIS

THEATER

W
S
N
E

TOWN

ANCIENT
QUARRY

DOLICHOS
(HIPPODROME ?)

TO THEBES

GATES BY THE
STADIUM

NORTH
GATES

PYLIS

STADIUM

ACROPOLIS

ASTY
GATES

PYLIS

SOUTH
GATES

PYLIS

SOUTH
PYLON

PR.

NORTH
PYLON

POMPEION

SACRED WAY

TO HARBOR

SANCTUARY

TO ATHENS

0   100   200   300   M

J. TRAVLOS
1966

3.   *Plan of the sanctuary and city of Eleusis*

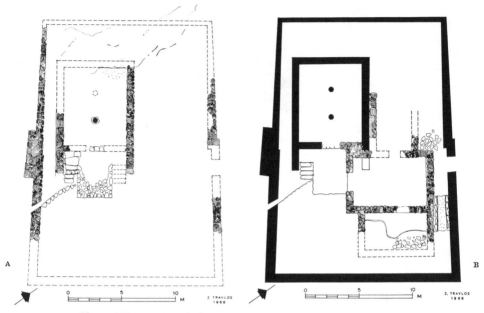

A   B

4. *Plans of Megaron B and of its extension*

was later built. On the strength of fire marks Professor Mylonas con-
jectures that the village was destroyed at the end of the above-
mentioned period. The excavations have yielded no indication that any
of the buildings was a temple. Or, as Mylonas puts it (p. 32), we have
no evidence of a cult of the grain goddess at that time at Eleusis.
Obviously this observation applies equally well to a cult of Rhea, the
Great Mother Goddess, or of Persephone, goddess of the underworld,
which in that early period would seem far more likely than a cult of
Demeter.

    This makes it all the more interesting to note that in the settlement
which replaced the first village on the mountain slope in the first Late
Helladic or Early Mycenaean period, roughly from 1580 to 1500 B.C., the
place on the mountain later occupied by the Mystery sanctuary was left

empty. The cult which was to be characteristic of Eleusis must have made its appearance at this time. The empty space on this particular spot offers a negative indication of some significant cult. For it was here that the historical Mystery sanctuary was subsequently built, and as early as the second Late Helladic period, roughly in the fifteenth century B.C., this was the site of the building which the archaeologists call "Megaron B" [4a]. From the transformations undergone by this building we can, I believe, infer that it was specially intended for use in a Mystery cult.

It was originally a single room, its roof supported by two inner columns. In other respects it resembled a Greek temple without columns outside the entrance. It opened out upon a projecting platform, with steps to one side, as though intended for the public appearance of a priest or god. Those privileged to witness this event could gather in front of the platform, in a courtyard surrounded by high walls. In the third Late Helladic period, between 1400 and 1100 B.C., this edifice was extended by three rooms situated between the gate leading to the courtyard and the main building. If there was no other entrance to the court, the addition of the three new rooms made it necessary to pass around or through them to the main building [4b]. Such indications argue in favor of a Mystery cult or a way of initiation. Before the construction of the buildings, the way of initiation may have taken the form of a dance. To judge by all these indications, the Eleusinian Mysteries would seem to have been inaugurated toward the middle of the second millennium B.C. This was a period of mutual influence, religious and otherwise, between Crete and continental Greece, then ruled over by "Mycenaean" kings.

But we do not know whether Eleusis ever existed independently as a small city or whether, as early as the sixteenth century B.C., it owed its existence predominantly to the cult which was to make it famous. Possibly it was ruled by its priests rather than by "Mycenaean" kings. This would not have been usual for Greece, but something very particular, related perhaps to the tradition that the inhabitants of Eleusis were Thracians, originally hostile to the Greeks. On the Athenian stage Eumolpos,[20] the mythical ancestor and predecessor of the Hierophants, was represented as the enemy of Erechtheus, like him, a warlike king, and in this form assuredly a poetic invention in the style of the ancient Mycenaean heroic legend. But also, according to his mythical genealogy, Eumolpos was a Thracian.[21] This is confirmed by the name of the hero Immarados, whom the genealogists gave him as a son. "Immarados" is related to the Thracian place name Ismaros [22] and reflects a phonetically more advanced Thracian language, perhaps a southern dialect. The tomb of the Thracian hero Tereus in Megara [23] proves that Thracian tribes had pressed beyond Eleusis to the Isthmus. In the second millennium these Thracian tribes, like the Albanians today, lived side by side with the Greeks in wild mountainous regions and were completely Hellenized. They were no less open to Cretan influence than the Greeks.[24]

The Homeric Hymn to Demeter seems to argue directly against the possibility that Eleusis, like the other important cities of the Mycenaean age, once had a dynasty of its own. Aside from Keleos, in whose palace the events leading up to the founding of the Mysteries took place, the poet enumerates many kings of Eleusis in the Homeric style. Keleos himself, to judge by his name, which means "woodpecker," is a mythological being, a forest king of the same race as the primordial inhabitants of the earth, on whom Demeter had bestowed her gift of grain. He is not a figure in the Homeric style, nor a real ancestor of a race such as might have been called Keleidai. It is characteristic, however, that the noblest families of Eleusis, when it already belonged to the Athenian state, derived their lineage from ancestors who, instead of real names, bore names connected with sacred offices. A family of this kind were the Eumolpidai. Their ancestor was the just-mentioned Eumolpos, "he who sings beautifully"; in his mythological transfiguration he was a swan among men, son of Poseidon the sea-god and of Chione the snow virgin, while in reality he was the priest whose voice resounded in the rites of the holy nights.[25] As we have seen, the high priests of the Mysteries, the Hierophants, had to be descended from his line. A second family of priests was that of the Kerykes, descended from Keryx, "herald," a son of Hermes, the divine herald. From this family were appointed the Dadouchos, the second priest of the Mysteries, known as the "torch bearer," also the Hierokeryx, "herald of the ceremonies," and finally the priest who officiated at the altar.

The name Eleusis is also no usual Greek place name. We are told that the place had formerly been called Saisaria.[26] Perhaps a poet had referred to Eleusis by this name on the basis of some old story. Saisara was the name of an Eleusinian heroine. Her name, "the grinning one," assuredly denotes an aspect of the underworld goddess. The name Eleusis is still more transparent. It refers to the underworld in the favorable sense and may be translated as "the place of happy arrival." Grammatically, it is differentiated by accent and inflection from *eleusis*, "arrival," but, like it, is related, according to the rules of Greek vowel gradation, to Elysion, the realm of the blessed. No superficial adaptation of a foreign name could have fallen in with this striking grammatical regularity. The name of Eleusis appealed to the throngs of those who strove for a happy arrival and gave itself to be recognized as the goal of human life.

According to the sacred history of Eleusis, the first to "arrive" was Demeter herself. The Homeric hymn tells us that she came from Crete (123), but this does not absolutely mean that the Mysteries themselves were of Cretan origin. The goddess was the first initiate and also the founder of the Mysteries; her initiation was the finding of her daughter. This did not happen in Crete. Nevertheless, as with so many of the characteristic elements of Greek cultural history, there are indications pointing to an origin in Crete, the great island whose advanced civilization had been shared by Greeks since the fifteenth century B.C.

Ancient literature contains a single explicit mention of Crete in connection with the Eleusinian Mysteries. A learned historian of the first century B.C., Diodorus of Sicily, tells us that the Cretans laid claim to these Mysteries, as well as to the Orphic mysteries and those of Samothrace. Claims of this kind were frequently raised in antiquity without justification. Diodorus does not name his authority. It was probably a historian from Crete. His proof of the Cretan origin of the Mysteries, cited in Diodorus (V 77 3), is of interest: elsewhere—these are the exact words—such rites are communicated in secret, but in Crete, in Knossos, it had been the custom since time immemorial to speak of these ceremonies quite openly to all and, if anyone wished to learn of them, to conceal none of the things which elsewhere were imparted to the initiate under a vow of silence. Whoever wrote this may have generalized and drawn overhasty comparisons: but he may perfectly well have been referring to elements of the cult which in his day still survived in Knossos and which are unknown to us.

Of course, there could be different degrees of secrecy in connection with cults of like content. The Greek language itself draws a distinction between the *arrheton*, the ineffable secret, and the *aporrheton*, that which was kept secret under a law of silence. Those admitted to the Mysteries, even to the true secret, the *arrheton*, may originally have included the whole collectivity, the tribe or the community. The *arrheton* was by its very nature ineffable. Here we may speak with Goethe of a "holy open secret." [27] Certain rites in themselves imposed secrecy on those who partook of them. But this direct effect could have its source only in the ineffable center of the rites. Around the center were grouped elements less charged with emotion, concerning which it was necessary to order silence. At Eleusis these included the festive procession and many of the things that were carried in it. The moment the participants in the procession gathered at the Poikile in Athens, the prohibition proclaimed by the Hierophant and the Dadouchos forbidding all barbarians and murderers to take part came into effect: [28] they alone were not permitted to take part in the holy open secret. This was not very different from the situation prevailing in Crete, according to Diodorus' source: the moment in the ceremonies when strict secrecy came into force seems to have varied.

There is an Orphic hymn which points, not explicitly to Crete, but only in a southern direction, toward the sea which bordered the route of the procession and the place where the initiates danced. I have quoted the words from the chorus of Euripides which says that even the goddesses of the sea, the daughters of Nereus, participated in the dance of the initiates. Presenting a mythological transfiguration of the remote origins, the Orphic Hymn to the Nereids tells us that the sea-goddesses were the first to reveal the holy Mysteries (24 11)—the Mysteries of the "most holy Bakchos and of the pure Persephone." This was a way of saying that the most important mysteries of the Greeks came from the sea. In the Bay of Eleusis they were received by Thracian priests. Their original language broke through in the song of the Hierophant, in the strange names for the gods, long after the initiations had become Greek and indeed the most sacred mysteries of Greece. Herein lies a possible answer to the question of origins.

II. THE MYTHOLOGICAL SETTING

No Drama Was Presented at Eleusis

THE ACTUAL secret, the *arrheton* of Eleusis, was connected with the goddess Persephone—indeed she, the *arrhetos koura*, the "ineffable maiden," the only one of all the divine beings to be given this epithet in the tradition,[1] *was* the secret. This becomes comprehensible only as we gradually penetrate to the core of the Mysteries. The secret was surrounded by many other minor secrets of which one was not permitted to speak. And all these secret elements were set in a framework of mythological tales, which were subject to no law of silence and were merely regarded as a preparation for the Mysteries. The most incomprehensible of the many false theories that have been put forward in connection with the Eleusinian Mysteries is the notion that in them one of the well-known mythological tales—the story of the rape of Persephone, for example—was presented in dramatic form. One can only agree with the English commentators on the Homeric Hymn to Demeter [2] who declared that to attempt to trace anything that was ever publicly related or represented back to the Mystery rites is a naïve waste of time.

Mythos means word, statement, originally a true, uttered happening.[2a] It is not credible that the Eleusinian *myths,* which were presented to all in word and image, should even have had anything to do with the *aporrheton,* the forbidden, not to mention the innermost secret, the *arrheton.* Forbidden sacred tales have existed everywhere and at all times. They are often hinted at in connection with various secret cults. They were even represented as dramas, in theaters which have been excavated in the sacred precincts of the Kabeirian mysteries in Samo-

26

thrace and Thebes, or close by the temple of the Arcadian mystery goddess at Lykosoura. This was not the case at Eleusis. The shrine itself
contained nothing resembling a stage, nor was there a second building
resembling a theater. The myths form a public introduction to the
Mysteries—an introduction indeed for us, who must steep ourselves in
them if we are to arrive at an understanding of the forbidden element.
Apparently only a very few tales and carved or painted representations
were concealed; these were recounted and displayed to the initiates in
the sanctuary. They served not so much to instruct as to foster the
pleasure people took in storytelling and in the physical appearance of
the gods. Such tales and representations moved from the inside out—
from the bud, as it were, to the unfolded flower.

Through them, through myths in word and image, the path leads
beyond words and images. Before we take it, we must attempt to form
an idea of what this possibility of a sphere "beyond word and image"
meant in Greek religion.

The Two Goddesses

THE GREEK word for god, *theos*, corresponds to a predicative
concept.[3] Used by itself, without article, it designates a divine happening: the god as event. The article removes the emphasis from the event
and introduces a more personal view of the god. Provided with the
masculine or feminine article, but still unchanged in form, *theos* points
to a definite god or goddess, a deity whom the speaker does not wish to
name: either because he *may not* or because he *need not*. Consequently
Theos or the feminine Thea, rather than a name, is very much in place
when mystery gods are to be spoken of. Between the usage with article

and that without article there often lies the proper name, which the profane were not permitted to utter. To the *arrheton* corresponded at most *theos*. The proper name belonged to the *aporrheta*. In public—but not openly—one spoke of "the god" or "the goddess."

This state of affairs is adequately demonstrated by inscriptions, by letters on vases, and by a recent find, the scribbling of an initiate of the Kabeirian mysteries in Thebes.[4] At Eleusis the Mystery godhead—I select at first this general form of expression, indeterminate in respect to number and gender—was known to the public as "the two deities" in a dual form which can mean either "the two gods" or "the two goddesses." Persons of particular piety continued long after the classical period to employ this indefinite designation.[5] Everyone knew that the two deities were *goddesses*. The stress, as far as the public was concerned, was more on the dual. As soon as the initiates entered the sphere of the *aporrheta*, they actually encountered even more deities. And it is not theoretically excluded that in the *arrheton* the *Two* became *One*. In Herodotos the Athenian who explained the miracle to the Spartan before the battle of Salamis mentions no names but says "the Mother and the Daughter" (see p. 8). The tradition has come down to us that it was Homer and allegedly before him Pamphos, the writer of hymns, who first put "Persephone," the name of the daughter, into a poem.[6] The poets always preferred to speak of her without a name as the Kore, the "Maiden." The different ways of writing her name on Attic vases may disclose a fluid situation somewhere between utterance and concealment.

The member of the pair who was turned outward was Demeter. The name identifies her as "Mother" and as De, in an older form Da, a female deity whose succor and assistance were evoked in archaic formulas by the use of this syllable. In the Mycenaean script the same syllable—in the language already connected with *meter*—meant perhaps a measure for grainfields.[7] It was therein that Demeter differed from Gaia or Ge, the Earth: Earth she was, too; not, however, in its quality of universal mother but as mother of the grain; as mother not of all beings, both gods and men, but of the grain and of a mysterious daughter, whom one did not willingly name in the presence of the profane.

Nothing connected with Demeter, mother of the grain, was a secret, not even her daughter in so far as she was only a maiden, stolen from her mother and restored to her. Still less was the gift of Demeter, the ear of grain, which grew out of the earth and ripened before the eyes of all, a secret. It, too, was shown in the Mysteries. But grain in sheaves would scarcely have adorned the visible architecture of the Mystery shrines, at Eleusis and probably wherever else there was an Eleusinion, a temple devoted to the cult of the Eleusinian deities, if *it* had been the secret. Nor was there any secret about Demeter's celebrated grief. Because of it, the goddess was looked upon in modern times as a kind of Greek *mater dolorosa*, although she had no other Madonna-like traits. One came closer to the truth when she was painted as a buxom Ceres (Ceres was her name among the Romans, one name among others in ancient Italy). And because it was no secret, we are perfectly aware of the reason for her grief, the story of the rape of Kore. I have no need to tell it in detail.[8] I shall assemble only the most important traits of the myths of Mother and Daughter, first in a wider frame than Eleusis or Attica.

The Myths concerning Demeter

T H E S U R P R I S I N G thing about the myths of Demeter, when we consider the image of the tranquilly enthroned goddess in so many monuments, is her restless search for her daughter. In these tales the grain mother comes to resemble such divine women as Io, Europa, or Antiope, with their moonlike wanderings.[9] Her figure undergoes metamorphoses which cannot be wholly explained by the different times and places in which the stories originated. The Cretan story of Demeter, it is true, differs from the Arcadian story. But the latter itself contains a transformation of the goddess who has two faces but nevertheless remains one.

The Cretan myth of Demeter is pre-Homeric. The Odyssey refers to it (V 125), and it is quite possible that the Homeric Hymn to Demeter is alluding to the same story when it quotes the goddess as saying that she came from Crete (123). Not only Demeter's grief seems to have been well known but also her love for, and union with, the Cretan hunter Iasios or Iasion in the furrow of the thrice-plowed field. It is Ovid who first tells us that her lover was a hunter.[10] But we know from other sources of a great hunter on Crete who "captured the living" and was therefore named Zagreus—and who was none other than the Lord of the Underworld.[11] Homer's contribution to the story, to the effect that Zeus struck Iasios with his thunderbolt, may very well be related to the hunter's subterranean character. What happened to Demeter is not very different from what happened to Persephone. The difference is that Demeter was willing. We are not surprised to learn that the fruit of her love was Ploutos, "riches."[12] What else could have sprung from the willingness of the grain goddess? But just this was repeated at Eleusis.

After the rape of Persephone a child was born, the little Ploutos, who resembled the ravisher, Plouton—Latinized as Pluto. That *wealth* was born was no secret of the Mysteries. In two representations of the Eleusinian goddesses intended for the general public, two magnificent vase paintings in late Attic style, we see the child: once as a little boy standing with a cornucopia before the enthroned Demeter [50a], and once in the cornucopia being handed to Demeter by a goddess rising out of the earth [51] (cf. below, p. 165)—as though he had been born down there in the realm to which Kore had been carried away. These are not the only examples. Names and images of wealth—the name Plouton is one of them—surround the Mysteries of Eleusis. In an Athenian drinking song [13] and in Koan sacred law [14] Demeter, the mother of Ploutos, is called "the Olympian"—an epithet distinguishing her from the Mystery goddess "the Eleusinia," who was worshiped at Eleusis and elsewhere. As Eleusinia she was the same goddess and yet another: Persephone's mother.[15]

Demeter's lot was much harder in barbaric Arcadia than it was on Crete. There the wandering goddess has the same adventure as the Kore of Eleusis: she is ravished.[16] Her persecutor and ravisher was a god whose name means "husband of Da": Poseidon.[17] The goddess turns herself into a mare and hides in a stud, whereupon the god, in the form of a stallion, begets upon her not only a mysterious daughter whose name no one was permitted to utter but also a famous mythical steed.[18] In the same story the face of the goddess changes. As one ravished, she was the wrathful one and, along with her angry face, bore also the evil name of Erinys. But when she was reconciled and had bathed in the river Ladon, she grew mild: the statues of both forms, Demeter Erinys and Demeter Lousia, were to be seen in her temple at Thelpousa.[19] In Arcadia she was also a second goddess in the Mysteries of her daughter, the unnamable, who was invoked only as Despoina, the "Mistress." [20] But in the mysteries of Lykosoura, as in those of Eleusis, the greater of the two was surely the daughter. Was the Arcadian Persephone really different from her mother, who had also suffered the fate of the Kore?

In these figures, one may ask, was the universal fate of women merely raised to a purely divine plane—what the mothers have suffered, the daughters also must suffer? Or were mother and daughter two only for the profane? For a Great Goddess could do just that: in a single figure which was *at once* Mother and Daughter, she could represent the motifs that recur in *all* mothers and daughters, and she could combine the feminine attributes of the earth with the inconstancy of the wandering moon. As mistress of all living creatures on land and sea she could reach up from the underworld to heaven. The mystery goddess of Lykosoura wore a cosmic mantle adorned with representations of the inhabitants of earth and sea, and she also held in her lap the *cista mystica*, the closed basket holding the instruments of the secret rites. [21] Her mother sat beside her on the same throne. At Thelpousa, however, Demeter *alone* possessed two statues in the same temple, one of angry countenance, which bore the Mystery basket.

Here there were two possibilities: either the one goddess had two faces, as at Thelpousa, or two goddesses, who may be regarded as different aspects of a single one, met coming from different directions. This would signify that Demeter and Persephone, though of different origin, had become an inseparable unity. Or did Demeter take the place of a greater mother of Persephone with whom she was associated in earlier times? This question will be taken up in our final analysis of duality at Eleusis (see pp. 144 ff.). The unity of the Eleusinian pair is expressed in an inscription on Delos. [22] It was found in the sacred precinct of the Egyptian gods, where Demeter was honored side by side with Isis, a foreign Great Goddess who also grieved and wandered. On the sacred island where, beginning in the third century B.C., foreign cults also were celebrated, the worshipers were particularly sensitive to such matters. They attached more importance to the unity of the goddesses than to the differences between them. The inscription runs: "[Property] of Demeter the Eleusinian, maiden and woman." The Greek wording leaves no room for doubt: maiden and woman (or wife) are two simultaneous attributes of the Eleusinian goddess. This again was not the whole secret of the Eleusinian Mysteries, or else it would not be graven on stone. Yet there is something beyond the outward appearance. The mythological traditions become transparent, disclosing a human fact, which always and everywhere permits the soul to hold mother and daughter together and causes them to be identified with one another. Seldom has this been expressed in such timeless and suprapersonal terms as in the mythologem of Demeter and Persephone.

In the duality which was always retained at Eleusis, Demeter represented the earthly aspect, Persephone another, rather ghostly and transcendent. Of the two, Demeter was always the accessible one, a mythological figure into which a man desirous of approaching Persephone could enter more easily. And the Eleusinian version of the mythologem, as recorded in the Homeric Hymn to Demeter, shows that just this, a kind of self-identification with her, the mourning goddess, was expected of the initiates at Eleusis. The hymn describes particulars of Demeter's mourning, which we know to have been imitated by the mystai. We must now turn our attention to this poem and attempt, with the help of other ancient sources, to understand its most important elements.

Rape and Mourning

WITH GREAT art the Homeric hymn tells the story of the rape of Persephone. Her mother is far away. Or, rather, it is the daughter who has gone off to some remote place, where she is playing and picking flowers with the daughters of Okeanos, the older generation of sea-goddesses. In accordance with the will of Zeus, Gaia, the Earth, has lured her thither and surprised her with a wonderful flower that had never been seen before. Only as the ground is beginning to open—to "gape"—is the name of the meadow mentioned (17), as though incidentally and yet with great emphasis. It is the *Nysion pedion*, the Nysan Plain, so named after the Dionysian mountain of Nysa, which the poet placed near the ocean. In general, Nysa was regarded as the birthplace and first home of the wine god. But there was also a city in Asia Minor by the name of Nysa, a later Greek colony formed in Caria of three smaller cities. There the divine marriage of Plouton and Kore was celebrated on "the Meadow" [23]—here the word is employed as a place name—and the underworld deities were worshiped in a nearby cave. It was a "Nysan Meadow" or "Nysan Plain," selected and prepared for the cult. This cult was probably instituted on the basis of the Homeric hymn and provides us with an interpretation of the *Nysion pedion*. The name occurs in the hymn and was taken as a form of Nysa. The Nyseïon of which the Iliad speaks (VI 133) and the "plain" known as the "Garden of Dionysos" near a cave at Brasiai in Laconia [24] must have been similar cult sites. All these, including the Thracian Nyseïon of Homer and the plain and cave near Brasiai, were dedicated to the cult of Dionysos. The story to the effect that Demeter's daughter was ravished in a place called the "Nysan Plain" probably has to do with this same cult.

It was a dangerous region to which Kore let herself be lured in her search for flowers, but in all likelihood it was not originally connected with the name Plouton. Dionysos himself had the strange surname of "the gaping one," [25] formed from the very word employed by the poet of the Homeric hymn (16). The notion that the wine god in his quality of Lord of the Underworld was the girl's ravisher does not appear on the surface in the hymn. We should hardly have been able to detect it in the background if an archaic vase painter had not shown us Persephone with Dionysos [5].[26] It was not always forbidden to narrate or depict this version. The vase painters of the classical period adopted a different one, which was the official version at Eleusis: in their representations of the Eleusinian myth, they give the old wine god the gentler features of Pluto, the underworld god in his aspect as giver of wealth.[27] The Homeric poet has Hades, the underworldly brother of Zeus, drive his horses out of the gaping earth in heroic style. He lifts the girl into his chariot and takes his ravished bride on a long journey over the earth before turning back to his subterranean realm. The place where this happened was pointed out by the river Kephisos near Eleusis. It was called Erineos [28] after a wild fig tree (*erineos*) which stood nearby. In general, there was a close tie between the wild fig tree and the subterranean Dionysos: his mask was cut from its wood in Naxos.[29] To this day the Greeks have a superstitious fear of sleeping under a fig tree. A wild

5. *Demeter, Hermes, Persephone, Dionysos. Transcript of the painting on one side of the Xenokles cup. London, British Museum*

fig tree designated the entrance to the underworld in places other than Eleusis.[30]

The girl's lamentations are heard not by the moon but by Hekate in her cave—for the Athenians she, too, was a daughter of Demeter, invoked as such in the Eleusinian chorus of Euripides (*Ion* 1048)—but she does not see the ravisher. Helios, the Sun, hears and sees all. The last to hear Persephone's voice is Demeter. She tears her diadem from her head, wraps herself in garments of mourning, and wanders about for nine days, without eating or bathing, bearing two burning torches. On the tenth day she meets Hekate, who also bears a light in her hand, and the two of them go to Helios. From the sun-god they learn who the ravisher was. Demeter's grief turns to anger. She leaves the gods and goes among mankind, taking on an ugly form to avoid being recognized. Thus she comes to Eleusis and sits down by the Virgin's Well [17: 2], to which the inhabitants come for water.

It was a mythological well, known by different names in the different versions of the holy story. It was called Parthenion, "virgin's well," [31] no doubt because it was connected with the destiny of a virgin, and Anthion, "well of flowers," [32] presumably because a flowering from the depths was thought to take place here. It is a waste of time to try to identify it with other wells in the region or to situate it anywhere except where it was put by the planners and builders of the sanctuary in the sixth century B.C. and where it stands today [6]. Provided with a round margin, it was the Kallichoron, "well of the beautiful dances," as it is also called in the hymn (273). On the stone pavement round about, circles, which it seemed to the excavators could still be seen, indicated the basic figure of the dance that was at one time performed by the initiates. After the fifth century B.C., the wall of the sacred precinct broke up the dance ground but did not infringe on the well, and it is thus that we find it today. In the Homeric hymn the goddess sits down to rest by a well, the mythological prototype of the present one, in the shade of an olive tree (100). But the poet has previously indicated that he does not mean to tell the story of Kore's disappearance by this same well. This is the interpretation we must put on the passage to the effect that not even the olive trees had heard her lamentations (23). They would have heard if the rape had not occurred in the Nysan Fields. But there are instances in Greek mythology of virgins disappearing with a well while dancing round it.[33] And vase paintings originating in the South Italian cult of Persephone show that a flowering was expected from the depths. They represent the event in the form of sprouting flowers, plants, or ears of grain [39] (see below, p. 131).[34]

By the well sits Demeter—so the hymn continues—in the form of an old woman who expects no more children but is still able to perform the duties of a nurse. A little further on, according to the poet's conception, lie the palaces of the kings who then inhabited Eleusis with their households. The nearest is the palace of Keleos. Soon his four daughters come to draw water. At home, with their mother Metaneira, they have left a little brother who still needs a nurse. This the goddess has foreseen and offers the girls her services. They are accepted, and she moves into

6. *The archaic well by which the Goddess sat, walled around as it is to-day*

the women's quarters of the palace. She is received by Metaneira with her baby at her breast. As the goddess enters, the doorway is filled with divine light. The queen is stricken with awe, although she has not recognized the goddess. She stands up from her easy chair and offers it to the goddess. But Demeter takes only a simple chair and lets her veil fall across her face. Iambe, the serving maid, has spread a white sheep's skin over the chair. Upon it Demeter remains seated for a long while (198).

These were the signs of her grief, and all those undergoing initiation had to imitate them before entering the Telesterion. The palace of Keleos was not a telesterion. The house of the Mysteries was not yet standing. The rites had not yet been established. The poet describes nothing of which it was forbidden to speak. It was thus that the participants prepared for the Mysteries in their own homes or in the place where the sacrificial beast on whose skin they would sit fasting was immolated: in Athens no doubt in the Eleusinion, the city's Eleusinian temple. But not every version of the holy story puts Demeter's act of mourning—her sitting in silence—in the palace of Keleos. There was another and perhaps older version according to which the goddess sat on a rock [7].[35] There she sat "without laughing." This "laughless rock"—*agelastos petra*—was seen only by those who entered the sacred precinct. Warned in a dream not to mention anything he saw in the inner sanctum, the pious Pausanias omitted to mention this rock in his description (I 38 7). The present-day visitor must look for it within the Lesser Propylaia [17: 5], to the right of the Sacred Road. There, according to an old story, sat the goddess, not far from the Well of the Beautiful Dances, near the hollowed-out place in the mountain slope which was dedicated to the god of the underworld and sheltered the little temple of Pluto. It was said that Theseus also sat on the

7. *Demeter, seated on the ground, receives a small procession. Fragment of a votive relief at Eleusis*

agelastos petra before descending to the underworld.[36] In various periods the Eleusinians knew of, and pointed out, at least three entrances to Hades: one through the well, a second here, and a third near the wild fig tree by the Kephisos.

As the goddess sat there unlaughing, in Metaneira's quarters or on the rock, Iambe, the hearty serving maid, stepped into her role. Her name was Iambe, like the meter of iambic, that is, satirical, poems, but in the feminine rather than masculine form. Her role was to make Demeter laugh by jests and mockery, to turn her grief into tenderness (200–4). This she succeeded in doing by means of obscene gestures, which the Homeric poet's style forbids him to describe. But there is another version, something of which has come down to us.[37] The atmosphere of the festivals of Demeter allowed of coarse games and tales. According to this version, there was then no king in Eleusis but only a poor peasant with his family. His name was Dysaules, "he in whose hut it was not good to live." His wife Baubo also had an eloquent name: it meant "belly." She did not hesitate to perform an obscene dance before the goddess and to throw herself on her back. In this way she made Demeter laugh.

In the Homeric hymn Iambe did the same with her jests. The blond goddess grows mild and tender, as in the old Cretan love story. But she is not consoled. A motif is now introduced which makes everything clear and which even the Homeric poet could not veil. The queen fills a beaker with sweet wine and offers it to Demeter, who refuses it, saying that for her to partake of the red wine would be contrary to *themis,* the order of nature (207). We readily understand her words once we know the identity of the ravisher who had snatched her daughter off into the realm of the dead, once we know to whom the cover name of Hades or Pluto refers. According to the hymn, the rape occurred on the Nysan Plain, where the Dionysian ground opened. A philosophical critic of all mysteries, the severe Herakleitos declared: "Hades is the same as Dionysos." [38] The subterranean wine god was the ravisher. How could the maiden's mother have accepted *his* gift? And so she invented another beverage, which was not one of the secrets of the Mysteries but which was drunk before initiation and became a sign of the Mysteries.

It was called *kykeon,* "mixture," and was made from barley, water, and mint. It was a special brew. Anyone wishing to be initiated at Eleusis had to drink of it.[39] That is why the vessel in which it was prepared and carried could become a symbol of initiation [59].[40] Demeter's mixture was taken after long fasting [41] and was also—as the poet expressly says (211)—compatible with *hosia*, the religious decorum that the mother had to observe in the period of mourning after the rape, an act of violence, an abduction to the realm of the dead. But now we are approaching something that appears incomprehensible.

Demeter takes the little Demophoön under her care. And the child grows and thrives like a god (235), though he is given nothing to eat and his mother does not nurse him. Each night the goddess lays him in the fire like a log. This she does secretly; the parents notice nothing and only marvel at their son's godlike appearance. But the queen cannot resist her curiosity. She surprises the strange action of the goddess and cries out in horror (248–49): "My son Demophoön, the strange woman is putting you into the fire. I must mourn and lament for you." Demeter turns round in anger. She takes the child out of the hearth fire, lays him on the floor, where he is picked up by his sisters who have rushed into the room, and makes herself known. Her admonition is addressed not only to the queen but to all mankind. The narrative is interrupted by her announcement (256): "Unknowing are ye mortals and thoughtless: ye know not whether good or evil approaches." Metaneira is an example. By her strange action Demeter would have made her son immortal. Now he would remain mortal like all other men. For herself the goddess demands a temple above the Well of the Beautiful Dances. It is built. Thither Demeter withdraws and lets no plants grow on earth. The gods receive no more sacrifices until Zeus sends Hermes to the underworld to bring the Kore back to her mother (335).

Demeter's Journey to Hades

W E H A V E come to a part of the story which the poet of the Homeric hymn not only veils—as he veiled Dionysos the ravisher in the Nysan Fields—but omits altogether. Perhaps a geometrical figure will help me to sum up my first two chapters. Round the ineffable secret of the Eleusinian Mysteries we may draw three concentric circles. The three zones they mark off can be defined or at least localized with precision. The ineffable, the *arrheton*, was enacted in the Eleusinian sanctuary, the Telesterion. With the story of Demophoön and the "big fire" (248), the hymn has brought us, as it were, to the threshold of the sanctuary. No secrecy attached to the great fire that rose from the Telesterion. The innermost circle surrounded the palace in which burned this fire which thoughtless, ignorant mortals, the profane, could not understand. The second circle encompassed everything that occurred in Athens in the so-called Lesser Mysteries of Agrai and everything that happened after the procession formed in Athens, on the march, and in the *aule* or courtyard of the sanctuary.[42] Here every detail was *aporrheton*, subject to the law of silence. In regard to the procession itself, to be sure, the silence was less strict. Chapter III will deal with what we know of this zone.

The Homeric hymn skips over the first two zones and remains within the third: the homes of the initiands and the temple where they sacrifice to the goddesses. Thus it is only natural that the poet should shrink back from the sanctuary and circle round it, so to speak. He leads us now to the "temple of Demeter." The temple is a poetical simplifi-cation of the more complex sanctuary, including a way to the underworld. There, in the temple, the goddess waits, angry and resentful, for Zeus to alter his decision and restore her daughter. We do not learn from the hymn but only from hints supplied by other poets that Demeter went elsewhere during this period of waiting.

In a hymn by Philikos, who was a priest of Dionysos in Alexandria in the third century B.C., we read this plea to Demeter: "Lead Persephone back beneath the stars" (48).[43] Since this hymn is preserved only in fragments on a papyrus, we do not know whether in it Demeter responded to the plea, whether Philikos described her descent to the underworld and meeting with her daughter, or whether he, too, held back from the ultimate revelation. An Orphic hymn addressed to Demeter as Meter Antaia, the "Ghostly Mother," says more and yet not everything. This hymn is based on the more primitive version of the sacred tale according to which only Dysaules and his peasant family were then living at Eleusis. Eubouleus, the son of Dysaules, was a swineherd. When the earth opened and swallowed up Persephone, his pigs were swallowed up with her. The Orphic hymn begins at this point: ceasing to fast at Eleusis, Demeter goes down to Persephone in the underworld after "the sacred son of Dysaules" has shown her the way (41 6; cf. p. 171).

In the Homeric hymn it is Hermes, messenger of the gods, who carries the commands of Zeus down to Hades and Persephone, rulers of the underworld. What now occurs points beyond the great secret of the Mysteries and lies outside the realm of the Eleusinian Mysteries. The fact that the Homeric hymn describes the rise of the Kore in as great detail as the rape provides strong support for this observation. For however the rise of the Kore may have been described, the mere fact that it was described and even represented shows that it cannot have been an element in the Mysteries.

In the Homeric hymn the Kore is carried back to her mother, just as she was ravished, in Hades' chariot. When Hades hears Zeus' decision from Hermes, he feigns wholehearted obedience. But secretly he gives Persephone a tiny pomegranate seed to eat, knowing that this will make her return to him for a third of the year and during this period reign over all living creatures as Queen of the Underworld. A third of the year is a period without significance in the life of the grain. No seed remains beneath the earth for four months. As the Great Goddess over all mortal beings (365), a true ruler of the world, Persephone is now permitted to mount the chariot of Hades. Hermes guides her to the temple of Demeter. Demeter springs to meet her like a maenad (386) worthy of her own mother, Rhea, the ecstatically wandering Great Mother, who in another form of the myth is as closely connected with Persephone as herself (cf. p. 133). She, too, appears in the hymn and persuades Demeter to make the plants grow again on earth (459). Hekate, who had helped in the search, also joins in celebrating the reunion between mother and daughter.

We need concern ourselves no further with the mythological frame-work. After Demeter has seen her daughter, she hastens to the kings of Eleusis to initiate them and to show them the sacred rites by which they are to solemnize the ineffable secret. The hymn concludes with the praise of the two blessings of the goddesses: the inner blessing, the vision which confers beatitude, and the outer blessing of wealth, which the Two Goddesses pour forth on those who love them.

III. THE LESSER MYSTERIES
AND THE PREPARATIONS
FOR THE GREAT MYSTERIES

Myesis and *Epopteia*

GREAT GREEK philosophers like Plato and Aristotle—and before them, no doubt, Sokrates—often illustrated spiritual experiences by examples drawn from religious high points of Greek life.[1] Plato shows us Sokrates taking a walk with the handsome but sickly Phaidros by the banks of the Ilissos near Athens, not far from the sanctuary of Agrai. Agrai was the scene of the Lesser Mysteries, which served as a preparation for the Great Mysteries of Eleusis. Plato says not a single word about the proximity of the Mystery site. Young Phaidros first reads a discourse on love by Lysias, the fashionable stylist. Then Sokrates, with playful irony, improvises a discourse of his own. Only at the climax of his second, serious discourse on love does Sokrates employ terms which in the Mysteries designate two levels of initiation (*Phaedrus* 250 c; cf. below, p. 98): the first rite, the *myesis*, which was enacted here on the banks of the Ilissos, and the second and highest, the *epopteia*, which took place at Eleusis.

Similar terms are employed in the speech of the priestess Diotima in Plato's *Symposium*. In explaining the nature of love to Sokrates, she distinguishes the physical from the spiritual sphere with the words: "These are the Lesser Mysteries of love, the *myesis* into which even you, Sokrates, may enter; but as to the greater and more hidden ones, the *epoptika* . . ." (209 E). Neither Sokrates in the *Phaedrus* nor Diotima in the *Symposium* is actually speaking of the Mysteries of Agrai and Eleusis. But to their contemporaries it was perfectly clear that they were referring to those mysteries when they spoke of the mysteries of spiritual life, which must begin on the level of physical love and which lead finally to the great vision of the Ideas. In these philosophical dialogues the allusions to the two ceremonies are *figurative,* but it is certain that the original *tone* of the rites was faithfully reproduced. The tone of Agrai and the *myesis* was more physical, that of Eleusis and the *epopteia* more spiritual.

Myesis can be rendered by the Latin word *initia,* "beginnings," or its derivative *initiatio,* or initiation, signifying introduction into the secret. For *myesis* comes from the verb *myeo* (μυέω) which denotes the action. The simpler verb *myo* (μύω), from which the noun derives, implies the element of secrecy. It means nothing other than "to close," as the eyes do *after seeing.* The self-evident first object of this verb is the subject itself: he closes *himself* after the manner of a flower. But a second object is also possible, which must be very close to the subject, his very own possession. Such an object is the secret. In German this close connection between the secret and the holder of the secret is expressed by the derivation of the noun *Geheimnis* (secret) and the adjective *heimlich* (secret) from *Heim* (home), the most private precinct. In Greek a number of composite words can be traced back to the hypothetical verbal adjective *myston,* which can signify only that which is shut up within itself: *mysto-dotes* is one who gives out such a secret (Apollo in Mesomedes' Hymn to the Muse),[2] *mysto-graphos,* one who writes down secrets. These are late words: old are *mystes,*[3] and *mysteria,* the festival at which the secret is communicated.

The Mysteries, those that imparted the greatest secret, were those of Eleusis. They were celebrated in the autumn month of Boëdromion. The *mystai,* "initiates," came in ritual procession to this festival of "vision," at which *epopteia,* the state of "having seen," was attained. No one who had not been initiated was permitted to enter the precinct where something higher than *myesis,* the first rite, was solemnized. Even for this introduction into the secret, absolute secrecy was prescribed. Nothing more was made public than where and when the *myesis* was to take place and what had to be done in preparation for it. It is only of these elements that we can speak in any detail.

In the first half of the fifth century before Christ the *myesis* was still held each month in the courtyard of the house of the highest initiation, the Telesterion of Eleusis,[4] so called because here the goal, the *telos,* was attained. *Teleo,* "to initiate," is derived from this noun, and *telete,* a general term for the celebration of mysteries or similar rites, is related to the same root. Originally the *myesis* which preceded participation in the *telete* of Eleusis was not connected with the mysteries celebrated by the Ilissos. However, a connection was established in time, and accordingly the mysteries of Agrai came to be called the Lesser or Little Mysteries in contradistinction to the Great Mysteries of Eleusis. In Plato's *Gorgias,* Sokrates says that this had been regulated by a holy law (497 c), and the same relationship between the rites is reflected in the *Phaedrus* and the *Symposium,* where the physical rites are represented as a preparation for the spiritual ones. In our investigation we, too, shall have to begin with the mysteries of Agrai and only then proceed to the Great Mysteries.

What Happened by the Ilissos?

I T M U S T have been toward the middle of the fifth century B.C. that the men at Eleusis who administered the Great Mysteries, the Eumolpidai and Kerykes, became convinced that the secret ceremonies carried on outside the walls of Athens, on the banks of the Ilissos, constituted a necessary preparation for their own rites. It has also come down to us that these mysteries—and this is never said expressly of the Eleusinian Mysteries—served the purpose of *instruction,* which would imply preparation for what was to occur later at Eleusis.[5] The progression from Agrai to Eleusis developed into a strict religious law. In the year 302 B.C., in the month of Mounichion, corresponding roughly to our April, the Macedonian general Demetrios, known as Poliorketes, "capturer of cities," on whom the Athenians were very dependent, presented himself for initiation into the Lesser and the Great Mysteries.[6] The Lesser Mysteries were held at Agrai in the month of Anthesterion, our February, and by then it was not permitted to hold them elsewhere. The initiates were not even admitted to the *epopteia* in the same year, but only in September of the following year. Demetrios wished to receive both initiations in the month of April. The representative of the Eleusinian priesthood, the Dadouchos Pythodoros objected, since it was not the right month. Thereupon the Athenians decided to rename the month of April Anthesterion and, after Demetrios had been initiated at Agrai, to name the same month Boëdromion. Thus the Macedonian partook of the Great Mysteries without infringing the holy law—we see how *literally* it was taken. After 215 B.C., the Lesser Mysteries were celebrated twice in years when large numbers of foreigners came to attend the Eleusinian games.[7]

A relationship maintained so insistently cannot have been acciden-
tal. The sacred precinct of Agrai was situated on the banks of the Ilissos.
Even today that name recalls the *lygos* blossoms and the shade of plane
trees immortalized by Plato in his dialogue between Sokrates and
Phaidros. In this form, the name Agrai means the hunting reserve of
Artemis the Huntress, of Artemis Agrotera. Here the goddess, in keeping with the epithet, was revered in her usual form, bearing a bow.[8] The
older name of the place and its goddess was somewhat different and
meant the opposite. The traditional, official, more sacred name was *en
Agras,* signifying "on the territory of the goddess named *Agra,* 'Spoils
of the Chase.'" A different name with the same meaning was given
also to her from whom the island of *Thera* had received its name.
"Thera," too, signifies "Agra." A persecuted Artemis-like goddess with
the foreign name Britomartis, "the sweet virgin," or Aphaia, was
common to the Cretans and to the inhabitants of the island of Aegina:

8. *Small Ionic temple on the Ilissos near the mystery sanctuary of
Agrai during the Turkish period (about 1760)*

9. *Scene in relief from the frieze of the Ionic temple on the Ilissos:
the abduction of the Hyakinthidai. Berlin, Staatliche Museen*

she was hunted and in the end fell into a net.[9] One story was that as
she was being pursued, her dress caught on a myrtle.[10] This Cretan
myth had reached Attica as well as Aegina by way of the Aegean Sea.
It is probable that the other goddess of the Ilissos, who was originally
called only Meter, "the mother," her temple being named Metroion,
"temple of the mother," [11] also came from Crete. In the classical period
the cult at Agrai was regarded as the "Lesser Mysteries of Demeter"
and as the "Mysteries of Persephone." These are Eleusinian names.
The frieze of a small Ionic temple, which was still standing by the
Ilissos in the Turkish period [8], disclosed scenes connected with the
ravishing of maidens and with their sacrifice [9]: the sacrifice of
the Hyakinthidai. This tragic incident was said to have occurred when
Athens was besieged by Minos, king of Crete.[12]

Apart from the fact that the mysteries of the Ilissos were dedicated
to Persephone, the ravished daughter of Demeter, and to Demeter

herself, one more tradition concerning them has come down to us: that they were connected with Dionysos.[13] This is also indicated by the name of the Athenian king's daughter Oreithyia, who according to a widely known story was ravished by Boreas, the North Wind.[14] Oreithyia means "she who rages in the mountains." And that is what the women did at their Dionysos festivals. Oreithyia was also numbered among the Hyakinthidai.[15] Her story suggests both the festival of Dionysos and the ravishing of a virgin. The close connection of the Lesser Mysteries and the Dionysian festival cycle in February, the Anthesteria, and particularly with the "Day of the Pitchers," the Choës, is attested by a monument that was found in the bed of the Ilissos [10]. It represents Herakles, accompanied by Hermes—both bearing the characteristic

10. *The arrival of Herakles at the Ilissos. Relief found in the bed of the Ilissos. Athens, National Museum*

pitchers—coming to be initiated. He is received by the gods of the
countryside. The male god sitting on the mask of the river-god is a
Plouton figure. But here he lets his barely visible companion carry the
cornucopia, and he, too, bears a pitcher. In the night before the Choës,
the mysterious marriage between Dionysos and the bearer of the title
of queen was celebrated in the city. The tradition does not tell us on
what day the mysteries of Agrai were celebrated, but only that it was
in the same month.[16] Otherwise, as I have said, we know only that the
rites by the Ilissos were an imitation of the events revolving round
Dionysos.[17] What the priests of Eleusis in the classical period, from the
middle of the fifth century on, regarded as a necessary preparation for
their own Mysteries was committed to the mystai at Agrai in connection with the marriage feast of Dionysos. The initiates at Agrai learned
of Persephone's marriage, though in what form we do not know with
certainty. We do know that the mysteries consisted of things that were
shown and actions that were performed—*deiknymena* and *dromena*[18]
—and probably also of things that were said, *legomena*.[18a] These were
subject to the law of silence. The story of Herakles coming to be initiated was no secret. The rites in which he took part were represented
in art. This proves that they were not the content of the *myesis* itself.
We learn, however, what preceded them in that exemplary case.

The Purification of Herakles

ONE OF the labors of Herakles—those tales so often told as to become almost canonical—was his journey to the underworld[19] whence
he was to bring Kerberos, Hades' dog. The monster took refuge under
his master's throne. Pursuing him, the hero came into the presence of

the king and queen of the underworld, for Hades did not rule alone but in conjunction with the queen he had abducted. Thus Herakles stood before Persephone. This scene called forth a very special explanation at Eleusis, where it was said that Herakles was able to stand before the queen of the underworld only because he had previously been initiated. The pious gave a good deal of thought to this point. How could Herakles be initiated if in those days no non-Eleusinian or non-Athenian was admitted to the Mysteries? [20] For there seems to have been a precise tradition in regard to the date when outsiders were first received. Here is how the problem was solved: An Eleusinian was invented with the transparent name of Pylios—"of the Gate," that is, the "gate of the underworld"—and this Pylios was said to have adopted Herakles. Another version made its appearance when the initiations came to be performed at Agrai and non-Athenians were admitted. The new usage was justified by the story that Herakles had been the first initiate of Agrai and that the Lesser Mysteries had been established for his benefit.[21] Euripides seems already to have been familiar with this version; this is shown when his Herakles refers to his own initiation.[22]

However, there were obstacles in the way of Herakles' *myesis,* as no doubt in the case of other foreigners, particularly soldiers. He, too, was tainted with the blood of many enemies and defeated monsters. The initiation had to be preceded by acts of purification. These could be spoken of quite openly, although there was a certain reluctance to reveal all the details. The rites of purification may have varied considerably. It was only such late philosophical authors as Theon of Smyrna who counted the *katharmos,* the purification in general, as part of the *myesis.*[23] Particularly those who had committed murder or homicide, even involuntarily, were in need of purification. For others some lesser type of purification sufficed. How the impure speech characteristic of

11. *The purification of Herakles, on the sarcophagus from Torre Nova. Rome, Palazzo Spagna*

many foreigners was dealt with and whether those who could not speak Greek were at all times excluded from the rites we do not know. We hear that the initiands bathed in the Ilissos, which had ample, though very cold, water in February.[24]

The preparation of Herakles for the *myesis* is represented in a relief which probably stood outside the sanctuary by the Ilissos. The work of a Hellenistic artist, it was much imitated later. A rather fantastic version of the preparatory rites may be seen on a sarcophagus of Ephesian origin, found at Torre Nova near Rome [11]. Here we see the purifying flames of torches borne by a priestess, and two additional divine persons, a goddess on one side, Iakchos on the other. A simpler representation appears on a marble cinerarium found in Rome [12a–12d] and known as the Urna Lovatelli after Princess Ersilia Caetani Lovatelli, who published the discovery. Every phase of the long ceremony could not, of course, be represented in a single work of art. A youthful Herakles, moving from right to left, enters upon the lustral rites that will prepare him for initiation. The hero—prototype of the man in need of purification—can be recognized at once by his lion's skin.

Those undergoing the rite brought along their own animal, which first of all had to be sacrificed: here it is a pig [12a]. Herakles holds it over the low altar. In his left hand he holds the pelanoi, the round cakes which the priest will offer up after the bloody sacrifice. The Hierophant is seen dressed as Dionysos, a costume which the Eleusinian priests were said to have taken over from the actors in the tragedies of Aischylos.[25] Indeed, the Hierophant at Eleusis appears as a second Dionysos. It was incumbent on him to undertake the first act of purification at Agrai with Herakles. According to one tradition, this was done by Eumolpos, the first high priest, appointed by Demeter.[26] In both Mysteries the Eleusinian priesthood received a part of the sacrifice.[27] Here the Hierophant is engaged in pouring some sort of liquid over the pig. In his left hand he holds a dish in which we can distinguish poppies, a flower sacred to Demeter.

What was probably to happen next is described elsewhere: in the purification of the blood-stained Iason and Medeia by the sorceress Kirke.[28] Hands dripping with the pig's blood, the sacrificant prayed to Zeus and then cleansed himself (or herself) with a bloodless sacrifice. In this particular connection, the pig was something more than Demeter's favorite animal; even the poorest mystai had to sacrifice pigs to her before they could be initiated.[29] The slaughtering of the "mystical pigs"[30] was a true expiatory sacrifice. The animals died in place of the initiand. The victim, Sokrates explains in Plato's *Republic* (378 A), was sacrificed in order that one *might* hear what it was otherwise forbidden to hear. The order of sequence—first expiatory sacrifice, then the "hearing" at Agrai—certainly accords with the historical facts.

12A–12D. *The purification of Herakles, on the Lovatelli urn. Rome,*
Museo Nazionale Romano

Sokrates' words also give us an intimation of what the mystai were destined to hear: something which reminded the philosopher of myths that it was inappropriate to tell the young people. The initiands washed the animal before it was slaughtered, if possible in the sea [31]— herein the identification of the sacrificer with the sacrifice is clearly expressed—and ate it in honor of the goddess. The whole region surrounding the initiation site smelled of roast pork.[32]

In connection with Herakles the second priest, the Dadouchos, also had to appear and slaughter the ram [33] on whose skin the greatest sinners sat during the remaining rites of purification. This, too, is to be seen on the urn [12b]. Herakles sits there swathed in a great cloth which falls over his head and face. The ram's head at his feet shows that the skins beneath him are not his lion's skin alone. A priestess

56

C   D

now undertakes a more detailed purification. (There were two
priestesses at Eleusis.[34]) Over his head the priestess holds a plaited
winnowing fan, an instrument with which the grain was ordinarily
cleansed and in which the accessories of the Dionysian rites were kept
and carried about: the phallus or the mask.[35] Infants, divine as well as
human, were placed in such baskets.[36] They were looked upon as the
grain, as the seeds of what was to come. In viewing the liknon, the
winnowing fan, one thought of both: purification and the state of
infancy to which the initiand was restored.

All this was not the *myesis*. The veiled Herakles had no doubt
withdrawn into himself. He was shrouded in darkness, very much in the
manner of brides and of those dedicated to the underworld gods. But
even after he was cleansed, nothing was shown him. In the better

13. *Herakles prepared for the Lesser Mysteries. Terra-cotta relief. Rome, Museo Nazionale Romano*

representations [e.g., 13] we see Herakles, grown much more beautiful, in a fringed white garment over which the Dionysian deerskin is thrown, leaning on a bundles of myrtle branches and standing before Demeter. This scene is the last of the series on the urn [12c]. At Agrai as at Eleusis, the goddess, turned outward, is seated in front of the secrets. She is sitting on a great round basket, the *cista mystica*, in which the paraphernalia of the *myesis* are hidden. Now that the initiand is cleansed and ready, they may be shown him. Now he may receive instruction and learn what he has to learn. Behind her mother's back she, too, stands there, the well-known figure of the Kore [12d]. And also visible is a great snake twined round the Mystery basket. It offers itself to the initiand. Herakles holds out his right hand: a sign of complete readiness for the *myesis,* but not the *myesis* itself [12c; also 13]. The snake was probably an accessory of other mysteries. At

Agrai it merely foreshadowed the secret: otherwise we should not see it. To make friends with the snake was Dionysian: the bacchantes did so too, though with less reserve than Herakles on the Lovatelli urn.[37]

The Cost of Initiation

THUS FAR we have been able to follow Herakles' preparation for *myesis.* Not only the purification but the initiation as well involved the sacrifice of animals and was consequently an expensive affair, even though large animals such as bulls were offered up only by the state. We have learned by chance, from a speech attributed to Demosthenes,[38] that Lysias, the famous stylist who provides the starting point for the dialogue between Sokrates and Phaidros on the banks of the Ilissos, was in love with a slave girl. She was named Metaneira, like the queen in the Homeric Hymn to Demeter, and was owned by a Corinthian woman. Lysias wished to make her an impressive present, but he knew that her mistress appropriated all his presents to the girl. Thus he decided to have her initiated: here was a present that was expensive enough and could not be taken away from her.

A few details are supplied by inscriptions recording the accounts of the Eleusinian officials, the Epimeletai and Tamiai, who attended to the practical affairs of the sanctuary. The necessary work was done by slaves belonging to the state. But since no one who had not been initiated was permitted to enter the sanctuary, they, too, had to receive the *myesis.* The accounts for the year 329/328 B.C. show the considerable costs of initiating two state slaves—thirty drachmas—in the first days of the month of Anthesterion, hence certainly at Agrai.[39] It is previously noted that the offerings, the pitchers, and the wine for the day of the Choës were paid for the slaves.[40] According to the accounts of 327/326 B.C., five men had to be initiated in order that they might put the interior of the Telesterion in order.[41] For a group of slaves a sheep was sacrificed as a preliminary offering, another sheep was sacrificed to Demeter, and a ram to Persephone.

Demeter herself, in her mourning for her daughter, sat on a white sheepskin; [42] her face was veiled, but the *white* sheepskin showed that she was not, like Herakles, in need of purification. There is no doubt that the initiates desirous of witnessing the *epopteia* at Eleusis had to make an appropriate sacrifice in order to be worthy to take the goddess' grief upon themselves. Demeter's mourning also included fasting. The Homeric hymn emphasizes a nine-day period (47), although the goddess went on fasting still longer (200). The mixed beverage, the *kykeon*, also had to be prepared; its readiness announced the beginning of the great Mystery Feast in September, just as the finished wine announced the beginning of the festivals of Dionysos in the winter: in January the Lenaia in which the Dadouchos took part [43] and the Epimeletai sacrificed.[44]

The Procession to Eleusis

I T W A S in mid-September, or more exactly on the 16th day of Boëdromion, that the cry rang out: "Initiates into the sea!" [45] As they had bathed in the Ilissos before the *myesis*, now they bathed in the sea between which and the goddesses of Eleusis there were certain secret bonds, described perhaps in very ancient sacred legends, which may have explained, for example, why the mystai were forbidden to eat certain fishes. The common purification in the sea seems, however, to have

14. *Goddess sprinkling an Eleusinian hero (probably with water). Fragment of a relief from Eleusis. Athens, National Museum*

been a relatively late institution. An inscription of the year 215/ 214 B.C. praises the Epimeletai [46] who had organized it. Perhaps the Hydranos [47] of Eleusis, the priest who attended to the purification by water, was beginning to have too much to do, and possibly that is why the bath was introduced in its place. At the Rheitoi, the place favored by the Eleusinians, salt water flowed into the sea. In the early period— as we can see in an Eleusinian relief [14]—one of the goddesses herself sprinkled the man whom she chose for initiation: Triptolemos or another Eleusinian hero.[48] All this was no secret.

On the following day, the 17th, a sow was offered up to Demeter and Persephone by the peasants; [49] previously the mystai probably sacrificed the animal on whose fleece they were to sit in silence. The mystai are said to have stayed at home on the 18th,[50] while outside a procession was held in honor of Asklepios according to the Epidaurian rite.[51] On this day the ruler of the underworld, assuming the form of the god of healing, showed a gently radiant, kindly face. But it was also the day on which—according to the Attic calendar, which prescribed that Demeter and Persephone should receive their sow on the day before—a libation was offered to Dionysos and to the other gods.[52] Though this libation bore the name of *trygetos,* "vintage," it was a vintage offering that could be scheduled on any day whatever, not merely at the time of vintage.[53] However, it was a feast having to do with wine, from which Demeter abstained during her period of mourning. Herein the mystai imitated her when they did not leave their homes. It was probably on this day that the *kykeon* was made ready. A writer of comedies tells us how an inexperienced foreigner who was preparing for the Mysteries ran out in the street—he was an Epidaurian and wanted to see the procession of Asklepios—with barley from the *kykeon* in his beard.[54] This he should not have done, and he should not yet have partaken of the beverage.

Then came the 19th of Boëdromion,[55] the first day of the festival which was called Mysteria, The Mysteries, for everything else was mere preparation, and other mysteries were not the true Mysteries, which were now about to begin. This day had the special name of *agyrmos,*[56] "gathering." In the morning the procession of mystai assembled, began to move, left the city by way of the potters' quarter and the Sacred Gate, and marched along the Sacred Road to Eleusis, where it arrived in the evening. By the Greek reckoning the next day, the 20th of Boëdromion, began with the evening and the holy night.[57] But the rule of secrecy was in force from the moment of gathering. We do not know precisely what sort of sacred objects had been brought from Eleusis to Athens five days before[58] but only that after crossing the Athenian border those bearing them had stopped by the *hiera syke,* the sacred fig tree.[59] But as we shall soon see, the choice of this site probably had to do with these objects. They were kept for a time in the Eleusinion of Athens, and finally carried back to Eleusis in the procession. The priestesses bore them [60] on their heads in baskets. Statues of these basket bearers later flanked the inside of the gate leading into the sacred precinct [23]. We should know still less but for the discovery of a painting, the gift of a certain Niinnion, representing the procession and more than that: the idea of the procession [15].

It was impossible to keep secret certain of the elements characteristic of the procession: the myrtle boughs in the hair and in the hands of the mystai, the cry of "Iakchos," the presence in the procession of a statue of the young god thus invoked, and the torchlight by which the

15. *Votive painting of Niinnion, found at Eleusis. Athens, National Museum*

procession reached its destination. Why so much myrtle? That is the most striking feature. Herakles leaned on a bundle of myrtle branches before his *myesis* at Agrai [13]. Bundles of myrtle were carried to the initiation. This as well as the participation of Iakchos is explained by a story that was related to the profane and could even be heard on the tragic stage.[61] Iakchos was an alter ego of Dionysos, going to Eleusis as though in quest of his mother, Semele. Originally—so the story ran— Dionysos had three sacred plants: the vine, ivy, and myrtle. In exchange for the myrtle, Hades gave his mother, Semele, back to him. The mystai may still have known that myrtle played a part in the abduction of the queen of the underworld: it has been associated with marriage ever since.

In Niinnion's painting [15], Iakchos and the goddess Hekate, both bearing torches, lead the initiates—men and women—toward the Great Goddesses of Eleusis. In dark clothing and bearing pilgrims' staffs like the simplest wanderers, the mystai follow in the traces of the grieving goddesses. White garments were first introduced into the festival in A.D. 168.[62] Probably this was due to the influence of the Egyptian mysteries, the cult of Isis, of which such white linen garments were characteristic.[63] But already in the classical period the garments worn on the occasion of the *myesis* were held in high esteem. They were dedicated to the goddesses or kept as swaddling clothes for the new generation,[64] although they were the simplest sort of dress, that worn by beggars and wayfarers.[65] Apart from the myrtle, the mystai are identified as such by two other signs: the women bear *kykeon* vessels carefully bound to their heads,[66] and in the hands of the men we recognize the little pitchers which Herakles, Hermes, and the gods of Agrai held in their hands in token of the Dionysos festival [10], of which the Lesser Mysteries were a continuation. What had begun in the month of Anthesterion was now to be continued. It is certain that in the procession to Eleusis the pitchers were not used for drinking wine.

It was a kind of procession of spirits, cloaked in a veil of secrecy, which became more and more dense as the mystai approached Eleusis. If not for the rule of secrecy, we should surely have explicit descriptions of what happened when the river Kephisos in Athens was crossed. In modern times the broad river bed has disappeared from view, though in antiquity a powerful bridge was needed to cross it.[67] On the bridge the procession was awaited by mockery and strange games, the *gephyrismoi*, or "bridge jests." According to one report, they were performed by a woman, a hetaira; according to another, by a man masked as a woman.[68] In Aristophanes a comic old woman boasts of having figured at the bridge, in a cart.[69] She was playing the role of Iambe, or rather of Baubo, who with her jokes and obscene gestures moved Demeter to laughter. This episode served also to relieve the mourning of the mystai. It was the moment to drink of the *kykeon* which the women had brought along on their heads, and it was probably from that moment that the joyous cries of "Iakchos" resounded.

A second watercourse, which is today still in evidence, the salty Rheitoi, was also crossed by a bridge. This bridge was so narrow that in the classical period no vehicles could take part in the procession.[70] Here, on the property of the Krokonidai, an Eleusinian priest family, the initiates were visibly designated as such. The place was called "Krokon's Royal Palace." [71] Supposedly it was the descendants of a king of this name who attached a thread (*kroke*) to the right hand and to the left foot of the mystai.[72] Here, in all probability, the mystai had to identify themselves with the words that have come down to us as their password and sign of recognition, or *synthema*.[73] They are a summary of everything the initiates had to do before being admitted to the *epopteia*. In the form that has come down to us, only what was no secret is stated clearly: "I have fasted, drunk the *kykeon,* taken things out of the big basket and, after performing a rite, put them in the little basket, whence I put them back in the big basket."

The word I have translated as "little basket" is *kalathos,* while the "big basket" is *kiste,* the *cista mystica.* The "rite" refers to the *myesis.* This may well have happened at Agrai or in the Eleusinion of Athens, but not in Alexandria in a temple without any actual mysteries, of which we shall speak in the hermeneutical essay (pp. 115 ff.). The order of the *synthema* is a relic of the days when the *myesis* was not yet performed in the Lesser Mysteries of Agrai, but after the fasting and the drinking of the *kykeon,* before the *epopteia.* For the Eleusinians themselves these ceremonies may have taken place in the courtyard of the sanctuary. The kalathos may have belonged to the Kore: for the flowers she was picking when ravished or for the wool on which she was working when seduced by her father, the subterranean Zeus, Hades or Dionysos, who had taken the form of a snake—a version to which an Orphic hymn alludes and which was perserved chiefly by Orphic poems.[74] The snake twines round the *cista mystica* on which Demeter is sitting and from which the unnamed, mysterious something is taken to be put into the little basket and to which it is returned. It is very likely that in the *cista mystica,* among the plants that can be seen on representations of the basket [23b, 23c] (see also p. 75), one or more phalluses were hidden. Thus it was appropriate,[75] when the *cistae mysticae* were carried into the city, to halt at the fig tree (see above, pp. 62 f.). It is also probable that a rite involving the phallus was performed in the course of the initiation [76]—this, however, can only have been a preparatory rite. Luckily for the historian, it was not possible to keep the great vision of Eleusis wholly secret.

IV. THE SECRET OF ELEUSIS

Outside the Gates of the Sanctuary

T O D A Y   W E enter the sacred precinct of Eleusis from the Sacred Road [16, 17], just as the Athenians did. The plan of the little city into which the few houses of the Albanian village of Lefsina developed is later than the excavations which began early in the last century [18]. When the new town was built, the ancient *hiera hodos* was taken into account, and the new road of access also bears this name. But even today Eleusis is not very large, and we need not draw many breaths of the dusty air before we suddenly find ourselves standing on the smooth rectangular stone slabs with which the outer court of the sanctuary was paved under the Roman emperors [2]. We have designated the area outside the Great Propylaia as the "outer court" in order to distinguish it from the inner court, hidden beneath many layers of ruins, where the first initiation, the *myesis*, was conferred upon the Eleusinians and in still earlier times, before the mysteries of Agrai were recognized and associated with those of Eleusis, upon the Athenians as well.

In the Roman period, chariots, which in the classical period were not allowed to cross the Rheitoi bridge, were permitted to come as far as the steps of the Great Propylaia [19], which formed the northeastern entrance to the sanctuary. To right and left, the area was bounded by Roman triumphal arches. One bore the dedication: "To the Two Goddesses and to the Emperor [by] all the Hellenes." [1] Three wise emperors, related by adoption, were responsible for this elegant arrangement of the entrance: Hadrian, Antoninus Pius, and Marcus Aurelius Antoninus (A.D. 117–80). We find the bust of Antoninus Pius on the medal-

67

16. *Air view of the sanctuary of Demeter: the Telesterion in the process of excavation. For key to numbers, see 17*

ELEUSIS
SANCTUARY OF
DEMETER AND KORE

1. Sacred Road
2. Holy Well
3. Temple of Artemis Propylaia
4. Great Propylaia
5. Lesser Propylaia
6. Ploutonion
7. "Thesauros"
8. "Megaron B"
9. Peisistratean Telesterion
10. Telesterion
11. Anaktoron
12. "Sacred House"

J TRAVLOS
1966

50

100

M

17.   General plan of the sanctuary

lion of the restored pediment of the Propylaia [see 2], erected in the reign or condominium of his adoptive son, the philosopher-emperor. The small temple whose ground plan has come to light in the outer court, outside the Great Propylaia, also was erected in the Roman period, perhaps replacing a simpler Hekataion, a sanctuary of Hekate, guardian of the gate. Dedicated to Artemis Propylaia, Artemis guardian of the gate, and to Father Poseidon, the little temple served the same goddess under another name and at the same time represented for the initiates a bond with the mysteries of Lykosoura. For there, in Arcadia, Artemis was the sister and Poseidon the father of Persephone. In addition to the two altars, a large sacrificial hearth stood beside the temple, intended for gifts to the gods of the underworld: in Lykosoura to the Despoina, the Mistress, and here, too, in all probability to none other than the goddess of the underworld, whose name in both places was Persephone.

In the archaic period the great dancing ground extended thus far and still further to the inner walls that were cut through by the Great Propylaia. On it the initiates danced round the Well of the Beautiful

18. *General view of Eleusis during the war of liberation (1821–29)*

19. *The Great Propylaia: steps and other remains*

Dances [6], the *kallichoron phrear* of the Homeric Hymn to Demeter.
The division and disuse of the dance ground—and with it the passing of
the archaic features of the Mystery rites outside the sanctuary—can be
read from the archaeological findings in the outer court. The traveler
who arrived here in the days of the Antonines found a basin with
flowing water beside the eastern triumphal arch. Like us today, he could
also see the sacred well, where the goddess Demeter once sat down to
rest, in its archaic form with its sixth-century margin. A special room
had been set aside for it by the wall of the sacred precinct beside the
Great Propylaia, with two entrances for visitors. The initiates were
forbidden to sit down here as the Goddess had once done: [2] this prohibi-

tion presumably had its source in the fact that in archaic times the mystai danced round the well and did not sit down at this point. In every other respect they imitated the mourning of the Great Goddess.

The Roman wall was built on an older wall, erected in the fifth century B.C., which already cut across the dance ground. When the Persians withdrew from the Greek mainland after the battle of Salamis, they set fire to the sanctuary of Eleusis.[3] Thus the new wall, which also enclosed grain magazines but ruined the dance ground, was built in the classical period. The magazines were protected, but the grain that was brought in for the priests had no bearing whatever on the secret of Eleusis. It formed a considerable part of the temple treasure without which no temple could be maintained. The walls had the thickness of fortifications, and the gate, which the Great Propylaia replaced after the example of the Propylaia of the Akropolis in Athens, resembled the gate of a castle.

Through the Gateways and the Courtyard

THE PERIEGETE Pausanias, a contemporary of Marcus Aurelius, was warned in a dream not to describe anything he saw inside this wall. An extremely pious man, he found this prohibition quite natural,[4] but the mere mention of his dream proves that between the threshold of the Great Propylaia and the threshold of the sanctuary, the Telesterion, different degrees and conceptions of secrecy were possible. A few steps behind the Great Propylaia arose a narrower and more severe entrance, called the Lesser or Inner Propylaia [20–23], which also replaced an older castle gate: it should have been called the Inner Gate,[5] although the word *propylum* occurs in the builder's inscription. It was built in

A

20. *The Lesser Propylaia.* A. *The floor, showing marks of the door opening inward and ruts worn by vehicles.* B. *General view of the remains*

B

fulfillment of a vow made about 40 B.C. by the Consul Appius Claudius Pulcher, a contemporary of Cicero; the latter twice mentions this project in his letters.[6] The remains of the building enable us to reconstruct it both in its smaller and simpler original form and as expanded with two secondary passages in addition to the main one. Vehicles proceeded as far as this gate until the Great Propylaia was built; their tracks are still to be seen [20a]. The number of people seeking admittance to the Telesterion seems to have grown considerably from the first century B.C. to the end of the second century after Christ.

The inside of this festive gate has been more revealing than the simpler outside, where nothing unusual seems to have met the traveler's eye except for the capitals of the two Corinthian columns on either side of the Sacred Road, with the heads of fantastic winged animals in the corners [22]. The architraves that rested upon them bore, upon the usual triglyphs and metopes, representations of sheaves of grain, tied

A

B

21. *Triglyphs and metopes decorated with Eleusinian objects*
A. *Examples showing bundles of myrtle, poppies, cup, metal receptacle for the* kykeon, *skull of a steer. Perhaps from the Athens Eleusinion. Built into the church of Aios Elevtherios, Athens*
B. *Examples showing wheat sheaves, deeply carved rosettes, round pyxides, skull of a sacrificed steer. Excavated and exhibited in the Lesser Propylaia at Eleusis, which they once adorned*

together with woolen string, and replicas of the skulls of sacrificed bulls or cows, of rosettes and familiar ritual utensils, hence of things that were worn, displayed, and used in public [21]. The standard number of petals in the Eleusinian rosette is not five, as it is in the rose, but four. This number corresponds to the poppy. Reduplicated, it provides the eight-petal motif. It would be hard to decide whether these motifs occurred only on the inside or also on the outside. But it was only on the inside that two caryatids [23a], great female figures bearing baskets, replaced the two pillars to right and left of the main entrance. One of these great *kistophoroi*—for what each is carrying is a *cista mystica*, a basket concealing the sacred utensils—is now in the museum of Eleusis [23b, 23c], the other is in Cambridge, England. They represented two priestesses, who strode through the festive gate to the great ceremony, bearing sacred objects on their heads.[7] Since the statues were on the inside, they probably represented the priestesses as they actually appeared in the festive procession. The baskets, however, were adorned only with objects that were no secret but were characteristic of the Mysteries of Eleusis: for example, the metal vessel for the *kykeon*, similar to that which Demeter had used,[8] rosettes which served also to adorn the ears of the *kistophoroi*, cakes, sprouts and ears of grain, bundles of myrtle, and innumerable poppy capsules laid out on leaves. Beneath such covering the baskets probably contained the things which were kept strictly secret.

We seem to be able to follow the procession through this passageway.[9] Holding a torch in each hand, the Dadouchos [24], the second priest of the impending great rite, must at nightfall have lighted the way for the procession on its ascending path. The *mystagogos*, "leader of the *mystai*," was not a high official of the Eleusinian priesthood.[10] But in a vase painting of the fifth century B.C. we see the Dadouchos striding

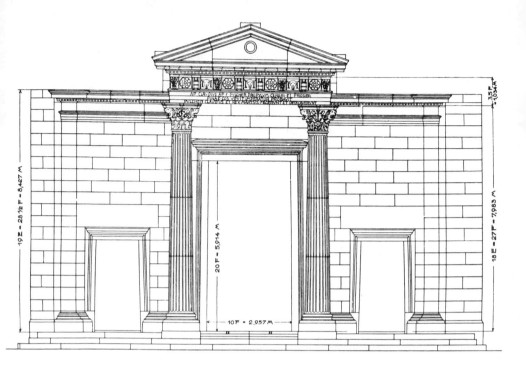

22A. *The Lesser Propylaia, exterior: reconstruction (by Hans Hörmann)*

22B. *Capital from the exterior of the Lesser Propylaia. Eleusis Museum*

OPPOSITE: 23A. *The Lesser Propylaia, interior: reconstruction (by Hans Hörmann)*

23B/ 23C. *Priestess with the* cista mystica. *Caryatid from the interior of the Lesser Propylaia. Eleusis Museum*

B

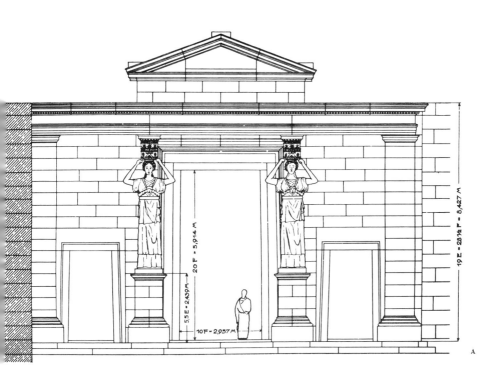

A

C

24. The Dadouchos between Herakles and a young man. Skyphos
decorated by the Painter of the
Yale Lekythos. Brussels, Musées
royaux d'art et d'histoire

25. The Dadouchos leads
young mystai. Amphora in
the Eleusis Museum

ahead of young men on their way to the *epopteia* [25]. We also learn that
in the gathering of the mystai at the Stoa Poikile in Athens he officiated
along with the first priest, the Hierophant.[11] Though part of the procession is depicted on the remains of a pedestal which probably stood
in the sacred precinct [26], we possess no representations of the whole
procession that might have shown us all the priestly dignitaries at its
head: the Hierophant, the Dadouchos, the priestesses, and the Hiero-
kerykes, or Mystery heralds, who preceded the rest. But it is certain
that they all took part in the procession and that the holy night had
already begun when they reached the dancing ground outside the walls
of the sacred precinct. Thus within the walls we may safely assign the
leading role to the torch-bearing Dadouchos.

The painter of Niinnion's votive tablet (about 400 B.C.) put two
torches in the hands not only of Hekate, the leader of the women
initiates, for whom this is nothing surprising, but also the youthful god
Iakchos, who on this occasion appears in the role of Dadouchos [15]. In
the present ruins, however, we search in vain for the place of arrival of
the mystai in this idealized representation. It must have been the *aule*,
the courtyard, across which the procession moves on its way to the
Telesterion. In the rock to the right, beyond the entrance to the grotto of
Pluto, traces of steps are discernible [27]. On Niinnion's tablet Demeter

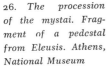

26. *The procession*
of the mystai. Frag-
ment of a pedestal
from Eleusis. Athens,
National Museum

receives the arriving mystai near the omphalos [15]. In radiant color, she is sitting on the rock, the *agelastos petra*, which is suggested by a line on the ground; this rock also actually was on the right. Beside her a soft seat is prepared for her daughter, who, painted in dark colors, sits enthroned in the background: the true queen of the underworld. On the ground in front of the white hemisphere lie two bundles of myrtle, which have been laid down by the mystai, and some sacrificial cakes such as those depicted on the baskets of the *kistophoroi*. There can be no doubt that Eleusis, like Delphi, possessed its omphalos and that it played a part in the cult. It can have been situated only in the Plouto-nion, the grotto which indicated the entrance to the underworld [27]. Foundations have just been discovered there, though the archaeologists have not realized that they may be the foundations of an omphalos.[12] The use of the term "navel" for a place of worship derived from the an-cient Orient, where it signified a "bond between heaven and earth."[13] This is just what the omphalos was at Delphi[14] or at Eleusis, though in the latter case in the sense of a bond between the underworld, on the one hand, and heaven and earth, on the other.

It was probably here, near the Ploutonion, that the procession and chorus of dancers transformed itself into a festive community. A boy celebrant took up his function under priestly guidance. In an archaic vase painting we see him in the procession, walking behind a priestess who bears no basket [28]. Nor is a boy lacking in the representation of the Mystery procession in Niinnion's tablet [15]. We hear of him as the *pais aph' hestias*, the "boy of the hearth," who was chosen by lot from among the most distinguished families of Athens and initiated at the expense of the state.[15] The term "of the hearth" did not refer to the state character of his initiation, which is especially mentioned and for which this term is never used, but to the fact that this boy, who was taken from

27.   The sacred precinct of Plouton, seen
from the Lesser Propylaia

28.   A boy celebrant in the procession. Detail from the neck of a large amphora in
the Eleusis Museum

the family hearth, required no further purification ceremonies as did adults who had once more to achieve this state of innocence. His mythological prototype was Demophoön, the king's son, whom Demeter wished to make immortal in the fire and in the end left lying on the ground beside the hearth.[16] The noble boy chosen by lot took his place in the ceremony: it was he who now precisely enacted the prescribed sacred actions in behalf of the entire festive community, so moving the Goddess to grant the great vision of which the mystai were to partake in the Telesterion.

On the Threshold of the Telesterion

THE MYSTAI streamed toward the Telesterion, which did not resemble other Greek temples. In the Periklean age, Iktinos, architect of the Parthenon, drew up the plans for the imposing rectangular edifice, with entrances on three sides, which was to replace at least three more or less similar structures [29, 31–33]. It was to have a decorative colonnade in front of it. The building bore a roof with a peak which could be opened to serve as a kind of chimney.[17] In the holy night of the 19th of Boëdromion great fire and smoke burst forth from it, breaking, as it were, the secrecy of the Mysteries.

In addition to the archaeological discoveries in the sanctuary, literary evidence also was needed before we could come close to the content of the *epopteia*. How strictly the secret was kept and of what nature it was we learn from a late teacher of Greek rhetoric by the name of Sopatros. Sopatros simulated a strange case of Mystery betrayal. The known cases of this sacrilege—apart from a book by Diagoras of Melos, known as "the godless"—were in general designated by the word *exor-*

cheisthai, "to dance out," rather than "to speak out": [18] as imitations of the ceremonies by similar movements and presumably also in song. The liturgy of the Orthodox and of the Roman Church has also been subject to such profanations, but these are not, as at Eleusis, a betrayal of secret rites. The punishments imposed for that betrayal were death or banishment. Sopatros invented the story of a man who dreamed the *epopteia* with its entire secret ceremony. Since he was not sure whether his dream represented the Mysteries of Eleusis, he related it to a man who had received the supreme initiation. The latter nodded. He was indicted for sacrilege, and the death penalty was demanded. He was to be defended. Sopatros gives an outline of the speech for the defense, including the argument that for the dreamer the gods performed the office of the Dadouchos and imitated the voice of the Hierophant.[19] They had celebrated the highest initiation, which made the dreamer a true *epoptes,* to whom nothing more could be betrayed.

The content of the *epopteia* is named in a papyrus fragment [20] with a few lines from an oration of Hadrian's time. The words are put into the mouth of Herakles, in a situation that the author had no need to invent. He drew on the Eleusinian tradition to the effect that the hero caused himself to be initiated into the Mysteries before descending to the underworld to bring back Kerberos, merely changing the order of events. According to the author's fiction, Herakles wished to be initiated after he had returned from the underworld and slain his children in a fit of madness. The orator had in mind the well-known rites of purification which introduced the initiation of the bloodstained hero. An example of a similar scene was provided him by the story that Herakles had gone to Delphi for advice as to how to purify himself and was rebuffed by the Pythia.[21] At Eleusis, too, initiation was at first refused him. I translate only as much as can be translated with some degree of certainty: "Speech of Herakles whom they do not wish to initiate into the Eleusinian Mysteries: 'I was initiated long ago [or: elsewhere]. Lock up Eleusis, [Hierophant,] and put the fire out, Dadouchos. Deny me the holy night! I have already been initiated into more authentic mysteries.' " And the last words of the fragment: " '[I have beheld] the fire, whence [. . . and] I have seen the Kore.' "

In his anger Herakles says what it is that makes the supreme vision of Eleusis superfluous for him; having seen Persephone, he is in need of purification only. This text, quite explicit in itself, is confirmed by another relating to the Eleusinian ceremonies. An instrument named *echeion* and used in celebrating the *epopteia* is mentioned. The word probably found its way first into the historical literature and hence into the commentaries of the grammarians who had to explain such words. Thus we learn that, at the moment when the Kore was called, the Hierophant beat the *echeion*,[22] and with the help of these same grammarians we can say that this instrument was a kind of gong, not an oriental one but an enormous contrivance with a nerve-shattering effect, which the Greek theater employed to imitate thunder [23] and had probably borrowed from an archaic cult of the dead.[24] According to the Greek belief, shared by the Etruscans and Romans,[25] thunder also came from the underworld. Such thunder resounded in Sophokles' tragedy *Oedipus at Colonus* when the underworld opened and Persephone appeared only to the blind king (1456 ff.). The scene is conceived with great art and restraint—restraint to avoid the sin of betraying the Mysteries.

The aged poet—this tragedy was his last work—succeeds here in representing a very sacred event, the approach of death, in a setting full of the aura of the underworld gods. The scene is enacted on the soil of the deme of Kolonos, Sophokles' native place, near the rocky hill that was regarded as an entrance to the underworld. Here the Erinyes, avengers of mothers, possessed their sacrosanct grove which no one might enter, for it belonged to the realm of the underworld gods, the goal of Oedipus' wanderings. The blind king arrives in this place and calmly enters the forbidden precinct. He knows that he must here await the announcement of his impending end and predicts the signs: earthquakes, or a kind of thunder, or the lightning of Zeus (95). To Theseus, king of Athens, he entrusts himself and the secret of his tomb, which will be no common tomb but a source of safety to the Athenians. After perceiving the first sign, he has Theseus summoned in haste. It is thunder (1456). Oedipus interprets the sign: This winged thunder of Zeus will lead me straight to Hades (1460). Thereupon lightning upon lightning, thunder upon thunder, like a storm that will never cease.

Now it is the blind man who guides Theseus, and his own two daughters accompany them. With a sure step he follows the guide of souls, whom he seems to see, for he utters the name of Hermes: he also follows the goddess of the underworld, whom he fears to mention by name. An epiphany of Persephone is presupposed, but not as a vision for common eyes; she is visible only to the blind man in the hour of his death. I cite the last words of Oedipus (1547–55):

> This way. O come! The angel of the dead,
> Hermes, and . . . Persephone lead me on!
> O sunlight of no light! Once you were mine!
> This is the last my flesh will feel of you;
> For now I go to shade my ending day
> In the dark underworld. Most cherished friend!
> I pray that you and this your land and all
> Your people may be blessed: remember me,
> Be mindful of my death, and be
> Fortunate in all the time to come! [26]

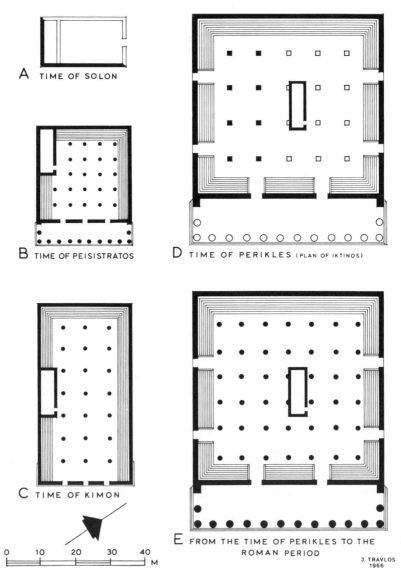

A TIME OF SOLON

B TIME OF PEISISTRATOS

C TIME OF KIMON

D TIME OF PERIKLES (PLAN OF IKTINOS)

E FROM THE TIME OF PERIKLES TO THE ROMAN PERIOD

J. TRAVLOS
1966

0   10   20   30   40
M

29. *Ground plan of the Telesterion in various periods*

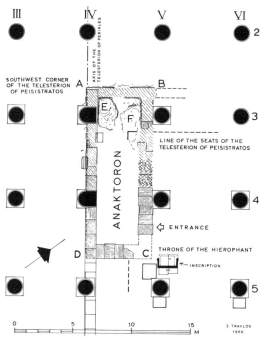

30A. *Ground plan of the Anaktoron in the Telesterion*

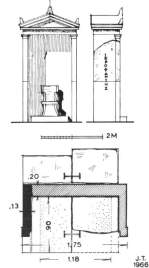

30B. *The Hierophant's throne: reconstruction*

The rest we learn from the messenger's report. Near a steep preci-
pice the blind man stops. Brass steps lead down it, forming an entrance
to the roots of the cliff. Here the innumerable paths leading to the
underworld meet. Between a hollow pear tree and a stone tomb Oedipus sits down. He casts off his soiled clothes and lets his daughters
bathe and dress him as befits a dead man. His daughters bring water
from the grove of Demeter. When they have finished, the thunder of
the subterranean Zeus (1606)—expressly named—rings out: it is the
thunder of the underworld. The daughters are transfixed. They begin to
chant the dirge of parting and Oedipus with them. When it is finished,
all fall silent. With a shudder of horror they suddenly hear a voice calling. From all sides "God" is calling Oedipus (1626).[27] "God" calls and
asks (1626 f.): "Hear, hear, Oedipus! Why are we waiting?"[28] Only
Theseus was privileged to see Oedipus disappear.

In the Telesterion

THE ENTIRE procession did not enter the Telesterion *in order
to see*. For it consisted of mystai of the Lesser Mysteries and possibly
of *epoptai*, who had already "seen" Eleusis. It was not forbidden to
participate several times in the *epopteia*. But the Telesterion was not
large enough to hold the whole procession. Only those entered who had
prepared themselves by special sacrifices and fasting. They had fasted
for nine days; on the tenth they marched, and drank the *kykeon* on the
way. Starting in the early morning, they reached the threshold of the
sanctuary in the darkness. But they were not yet at their goal. "Until
thou has reached the Anaktoron," says the orator Maximos of Tyre
(XXXIX 3), "thou hast not been initiated." The word *anaktoron*,

"palace," also applied, but only in an extended sense, to the whole building which received the mystai. Within it was a small edifice which originally bore this name [30a] and which is the important archaeological discovery with which we must concern ourselves if we are to form a picture of Kore's epiphany in the Mysteries.

The large building, the Telesterion, had finally acquired the ground plan we see now [29E, 31–33]. Built into the rock of the mountainside, it occupied an area of 58 by 58 yards. Lest anyone be pressed against the wall, it had steps on three sides, which served more for standing than for sitting. In the age of Perikles, the roof was supported by pillars, later on by six times seven columns which divided the whole interior into equal sections: a forest of columns with no clearing in the middle. Not exactly at the center, in the interval between two rows of columns, stood the small edifice, an elongated rectangle with a single entrance close to the end of one side [30a]. This was the ancient nucleus of the building, which was never moved from its original location, while the large building round it was extended more and more. Like the little

31. *The Telesterion in its present state, seen from the vestibule side*

32. *The Telesterion: lateral view*

chapel of the Santa Casa within the great sanctuary at Loreto, or the original Franciscan church, the chapel of the Porziuncula, in Santa Maria degli Angeli near Assisi, the Anaktoron proper was situated within the Telesterion.

It has been possible to determine precisely the situation and orientation of the throne [30b] [29] on which the Hierophant sat or in front of which he stood when, like the bishop in the Christian liturgy, he officiated at the ceremony. The nature of his office is expressed in his title: strictly speaking, *hierophantes* means not he who "*shows* the holy things"—that would have had to be called *hierodeiktes* in Greek [30] —but "he who makes them *appear*," *phainei*. His throne, to the right of the single door of the little Anaktoron, was turned toward it. There can

33. *The Telesterion: the floor, with (center) the emplacement of the Anaktoron*

be no doubt that what he "made to appear" came from there. On the other three sides the throne was screened off: no other impression must distract the Hierophant in his concentration on the awaited epiphany.

An account of what now happened is provided by a passage in which Plutarch likens philosophical illumination to the experience of the mystai.[31] In the beginning the throng, pressing toward the supreme initiation, had pushed noisily ahead, until the sacred action began. The dark night and the forest of columns necessitated light. This the Dadouchos with his two torches provided, displaying inside the great edifice which received the mystai (*mystodokos domos anadeiknytai* are the words employed by Aristophanes [32]) the little building within the big one. "But he who is already *within* it," the passage continues, and here Plutarch is referring to the larger edifice, "and has beheld a great light, as when the Anaktoron opens, changes his behavior and falls silent and wonders."

The smaller edifice with its secrets must have been opened at a word from the Hierophant. A great light burst forth, a fire blazed up; [33] but it is certain that this was not yet the ineffable, holy thing that was to appear. Many authors speak of this fire. The chimneylike opening at the top of the Telesterion served to let out the fire and smoke. We hear from the Christian scholar known to us under the name of Hippolytos [34] that the Hierophant officiated at night "under the great fire." His throne was quite close to the erupting fire and was protected by a roof of its own. "Celebrating the great and ineffable secrets," Hippolytos writes, "he proclaims in a loud voice: 'The Mistress has given birth to a holy boy, Brimo has given birth to Brimos! that is, the Strong One to the Strong One.'" The Hierophant sang in a characteristic high voice. It was believed in late antiquity that he had done what other singers did for this purpose, namely, diminish his manhood.[35] This is the most implausible assertion made by a Christian source. The words *brimo* and *brimos* in the Hierophant's song are no invention. They occurred in northern Greece and were foreign names in Attica.[36] The Thracian forerunners of the priests of Eleusis may have brought these names with them (see above, p. 25). The words, which served to translate the foreign names for the Mother and Son, were taken by the Christian scholar from one well versed in the subject, who probably had been led by purely linguistic considerations to cite the cry, with a view to explaining it. Brimo is primarily a designation for the queen of the realm of the dead, for Demeter, Kore, and Hekate in their quality of goddesses of the underworld. So Medeia invokes the queen of the underworld in Apollonios of Rhodes,[37] meaning principally Hekate, her most spectral manifestation:

"Brimo, the wanderer by night, the subterranean, goddess of the underworld!" *She* then gave birth in fire: the goddess of death gave birth.
What a message! In the flame of the funeral pyres which blazed round
the cities of Greece, the dead—one would have thought—were turned
to ashes or at most to shades.

The Hierophant's words divulged something else. The burial prac-
tices found in the tombs of Eleusis [38] show that cremation was sometimes the prevailing method of disposing of the dead, but never
universal. The way of the cremated led through the earth, with Demeter's help, to Persephone. The Athenians called the dead Demetreioi,
"the folk of Demeter." [39] The most important fact is, however, that fire
marks from the Protogeometric and Geometric periods (about 1100–
700 B.C.) have been found on the terrace where the temple of the
Mysteries was at that time already situated. [40] These can hardly have
been made by burnt offerings, for there is no sign of an altar. [41] Thus it
seems that people already had themselves cremated there, in order to
be near the sanctuary of the Mystery goddess who ruled over the dead
and who would take them from the funeral pyre to her abode.

And now, it was proclaimed—in the loud, chanting voice of the
Hierophant—that the queen of the dead herself had given birth in fire to
a mighty son. Of this mythology offered examples. Dionysos had been
born amid the lightnings that consumed Semele, though his birth had
been premature and Zeus, his father, had had to deliver him. [42] According to another variant of the myth, the mother of Dionysos was not
Semele but Persephone, who gave birth to him under the earth. [43] Ariadne, wife of Dionysos, it was related, had met her death as she bore a
child, [44] who could only have been a second, a little Dionysos. [45] Asklepios had been born on the funeral pyre of Koronis, a double of the
unfaithful Ariadne, [46] and Apollo had delivered the child from his

dead mother.[47] A birth in death *was* possible! And it was possible also for human beings if they had faith in the Goddesses; that is the message which Demeter herself proclaimed at Eleusis, when she laid Demophoön in the fire to make him immortal.

This truth was impressed on the mystai with all the power of a nocturnal ceremony. And that was not all. The queen of the underworld would be called. We know that three months later, at the Lenaia, the Dadouchos summoned the Athenians to call Iakchos, son of Semele, and they called him.[48] At Eleusis, however, it must have been the Hierophant who intoned the call for Kore. He beat the *echeion,* the instrument with the voice of thunder. The *epopteia* began; ineffable things were seen. A vision of the underworld goddess may be derived from the papyrus fragment.[48a] If an unintelligible passage in Sopatros' text has been properly corrected, a figure—*schema ti*—rose above the ground.[49] In a second phase—how much later we do not know—the Hierophant, silent amid profound silence, displayed a mown ear of grain, as the Buddha showed a flower in his silent "Flower Sermon." [50] All who had "seen" turned, at the sight of this *concrete thing,* as though turning back from the hereafter into this world, back to the world of tangible things, which include grain. The grain *was* grain and not more, but it may well have summed up for the *epoptai* everything that Demeter and Persephone had given to mankind: Demeter food and wealth, Persephone birth under the earth. To those who had seen Kore at Eleusis this was no mere metaphor proving nothing, but the memento of an encounter in which the goddess of the underworld showed herself in a beatific vision.

The Eleusinian Version of the *Visio Beatifica*

THE TERM *visio beatifica* (beatific vision) was coined to designate
the supreme goal, the *telos,* of Christian existence. In medieval usage it
signifies the immediate sight of God, *videre Deum;* those who obtain this
vision are transported into a state of eternal beatitude. In this case the
word vision, *visio,* must be taken as a real seeing, not as a subjective
illusion. But the subjective element cannot be entirely excluded. The
vision requires a subject who "sees." And of course *beatitude,* happiness,
presupposes a subject who is happy.

Thus *visio beatifica* embraces a subjective element and implies no
linguistic distinction between reality and illusion. From the standpoint
of the history of religions, we are also justified in speaking of a *visio
beatifica* in connection with the pagan mysteries.[51] The medieval
concept of the *visio beatifica* forms the highest conceivable stage in a
series of historical religious experiences: the ideal limit toward which
each particular experience tends. The historical examples, such as the
Eleusinian mode of religious experience, may be interpreted as approxi-
mations to this limit and appraised, as it were, by its standard.

This can first be attempted from the standpoint of the function,
namely, beatification. There is undeniable evidence (see above, p. 14)
that the *epopteia* conferred happiness. Unquestionably *beatitudo,* the
telos attained in the Telesterion, was engendered at once, *hic et nunc.*
But it left room for *elpis,* hope and anticipation. Thus the degree of
beatitude which the Christians expected of their *visio beatifica* cannot
be said to have been attained. Nevertheless, this well-attested function
permits us to consider the Mysteries as a link in the series culminating
in the Christian *visio beatifica.* It provides a basis for an approximate

characterization. The beatific effect was one of the characteristic properties of the Eleusinian phenomenon.

The nature of a vision is determined not only by its function but also by the actual quality of the seeing. A vision may be seen with closed or with open eyes. Seeing and "having seen" are sufficiently stressed by the words employed to designate the source of the beatitude obtained at Eleusis (see above, p. 15). The tone of these words in Greek does not suggest a "seeing" in the figurative sense, with closed eyes. But it does not necessarily exclude it. However, a seeing with open eyes may be inferred from the explicit references to closing the eyes, or to letting them close, to *myein* and *myeîn,* in the *first* phase of initiation, the *myesis.* A "showing" is mentioned just as explicitly on the occasion of the *myesis.* The term *deiknymena,* "things shown," has gained acceptance in the scientific literature on the Eleusinian Mysteries along with two others, the *legomena* and the *dromena:* it has come to designate a *part* of the secrets.

This is a mistake in so far as in certain locutions the "showing" refers to the Mystery ceremonies as a *whole.*[52] But when the "Mysteries" were "shown"—regardless of what was shown, the ceremonies or certain objects or both—the initiates had to keep their eyes open. There is nothing whatsoever in the tradition to indicate that the mystai had to close their eyes again for the *epopteia.* This word for the highest stage of initiation, the "having seen," seems indeed to have been chosen in contrast to *myesis.* After the eyes had already been opened for the "things shown," they were truly opened by the *epopteia.*

This opening of the eyes was taken so literally as to form the basis of the assertion that on at least one occasion Demeter had given sight to a blind man at Eleusis. Demeter is not one of the deities to whom cures were ordinarily ascribed, as they were to Apollo, Asklepios, and Athena

34. *Votive relief of Eukrates, found at Eleusis. Athens, National Museum*

Hygieia.[53] If it was related that sight was given to a blind man in the *epopteia* at Eleusis, Demeter must nevertheless have done the giving, for it was she who had brought men the Mysteries. Persephone was the object of vision and herself a gift.

The cure of a blind man seems to be attested by a painted marble votive relief of the fifth century B.C., found in the excavation of the Telesterion [34]. It was dedicated to Demeter by Eukrates. The inscription runs: "To Demeter Eukrates." Over the inscription are two eyes which, along with the nose, have been cut out of the face.[54] Above, separated from the nose and eyes by a cornice, is the head of a goddess surrounded by red rays. The rays suggest the light in which the goddess appeared. In no event was it permissible to name Persephone in her quality as the Mystery goddess who appeared, the *arrhetos koura*. When an initiate contemplated the head, he was probably reminded of the epiphany of Persephone, even if the inscription under it expresses gratitude to Demeter. The other testimony to the cure of a blind man, perhaps to the same case, which had become famous, an epigram of Antiphilos from the Augustan age, is put into the mouth of the cured man. He is referring to the "Mysteries of Demeter" but gives thanks to the "Goddesses." [55]

These testimonies show indirectly that the great vision, the *visio beatifica* of Eleusis, was seen with open, corporeal eyes: no distinction was made between the light of the Mysteries and the light of the sun. For the devout such a seeing was important.[56] It was a different matter in the philosophical myth of the soul, which spoke of a *visio beatifica* in a bodiless state, before birth. But such a vision was also described in the terminology of the Eleusinian Mysteries. Sokrates does so in Plato's *Phaedrus*, in such a way as to disparage the Eleusinian vision but at the same time to attest its existence.[57] At the end of the classical period the philosophical imagination set a higher *visio beatifica* above the Eleusinian vision, building on this religious experience, known to almost every Athenian, as on an existing, self-evident foundation, which is indirectly characterized as a phenomenon of lesser radiance.

"But then," we read in the *Phaedrus* (250 BC),[58] "there was beauty to be seen, brightly shining, when with the blessed choir . . . the souls beheld the beatific spectacle and vision [59] and were perfected in that mystery of mysteries which it is meet to call the most blessed.[60] This did we celebrate [61] in our true and perfect selves, when we were yet untouched by all the evils in time to come; [62] when as initiates we were allowed to see perfect and simple, still and happy Phantoms.[63] Purer was the light that shone around us, and pure were we." By speaking of *telete, myesis, epopteia,* and "happy *phasmata*" in his account of this higher *visio beatifica* beheld by the disembodied souls, Sokrates confirms that visions were seen in the Telesterion of Eleusis, even if they were not "perfect" and "simple" and "still" enough.

They did not satisfy the philosopher, and in this way he indicated their spectral, fluttering character. But once the word *phasma*, "phantom," had been spoken by Plato and the "Phantoms" he had in mind were recognized as the content of the *epopteia*, writers ventured to employ the same word when speaking directly of the Eleusinian visions. They were praised as "ineffable" [64] and "holy" [65] *phasmata*.[66] In the classical period the godless treatise of Diagoras of Melos, which was later carefully destroyed, had undermined many men's faith in these visions.[67] It would certainly not have done so if they had been the same sort of thing as the vision of Ideas described in the *Phaedrus!*

If the fact that Aischylos remained aloof from the Mysteries and declined to be initiated does not imply a negative characterization of the Eleusinian *visio beatifica*, it surely suggests that he thought it inferior to the mythical vision which a tragic poet was able to offer his audience. The case became famous, because Aischylos was born in Eleusis. Aristophanes puts into his mouth a prayer in which he names the goddess and the Mysteries of his native place with veneration, saying that Demeter had reared him.[68] Probably Aristophanes had him say this in order to bring out, in every possible way, the contrast between him and Euripides, who had been educated by the Sophists.[69] Nevertheless, something similar to the *phasmata* of Eleusis was discovered in one of Aischylos' tragedies. Perhaps it was at the end of his *Oedipus*,[70] a scene in the construction of which he had not exerted the same restraint as Sophokles. He was put on trial [71] but acquitted, for he was able to prove that he had not been initiated—as every Athenian must have known—and could consequently not be guilty of an intentional imitation.

A negative appraisal of the Eleusinian *visio beatifica* and an opinion of it from a foreign, non-Greek point of view are provided by a historical episode which took place at the time of Augustus. It offers an odd confirmation of the conception of the Eleusinian secret here presented. Like many subsequent Roman emperors, Augustus was initiated at Eleusis.[72] Immediately after his victory at Actium he participated in the Mysteries,[73] so showing the religion of the Greeks the same respect as at home he conferred on the religion of Rome. In the year 20 B.C. he returned to Greece and spent the winter on Samos.[74] Here news reached him that King Poros [75] of India wished to establish friendly relations with him and that an embassy was on its way. One of the ambassadors was a celebrated Brahman named Zarmaros [76] or Zarmanochegas,[77] who, it transpired, was eager to learn the secret of Eleusis. Augustus gave orders that the Mysteries should be celebrated out of season, and he himself hastened to attend. After witnessing the secret, the Brahman, evidently in the intention of going the *epopteia* one better, offered a display of his own, surpassing the *visio beatifica* by a *sacrificium beatificum:* he walked into the fire, so showing that he did not think very highly of the greatest Mystery of the Greeks.

Voluntary death by fire was for the Indians a *sacrificium beatificum,* whereby they believed they could enter immediately into the world of the gods.[78] But there was something terrifyingly violent about this action, which could also be attributed to an ascetic pride, directed against other men. Even Indian legislators did not all take the same view of it; most had forbidden it.[79] The Greeks witnessed this terrible act for the first time when the Brahman Kalanos, who had joined Alexander the Great and followed him as far as Persia, there mounted the funeral pyre.[80] In this case as well, ascetic pride seems to have gone hand in hand with an oriental arrogance toward Westerners. The emulative

character of the Brahman was pointed out by Onesikritos, the helms-
man and cynic philosopher in Alexander's retinue.[81] When in the period
of Hadrian this act was imitated at Olympia by an oriental Greek calling
himself Proteus and Peregrinus, who wished to show that "he was in no
wise inferior to the Brahmans in steadfastness," Lucian remarked:
"Why should India not have its notoriety-seeking fools just as well as our
country?"[82]

We are told that Zarmaros or Zarmanochegas wished to provide an
epideixis, or public demonstration, and that he took his life in the
traditional Indian manner.[83] This was even to be read on his funeral
monument, which was erected at Eleusis.[84] It is impossible to say exactly
where he had his funeral pyre erected after witnessing the *epopteia.* The
festive assembly—Augustus and the Athenians [85]—must still have been
present to witness the great feat of Indian asceticism. The times that
had left fire marks near the Telesterion [86] were long past. But a tragedy
of Euripides, *Hiketides,* or *The Suppliants* (1 ff., 1001–3), proves that
the burning of corpses and even voluntary death by fire—the suicide of
a heroine—were held to be permissible at the altar of Demeter.[87]

It is attested that Persephone was looked upon as the goddess of fire.
She was evoked along with Hephaistos, the god of fire.[88] The reason for
this was evident at Eleusis: through her power the evil element was
transformed into a kindly one. The Indian had his body anointed with
oil in the manner of Greek athletes. Thus he, a champion of the Orient,
leapt into the fire laughing, in accordance with the rules of Western
athletic contests.[89] This was *his* beatific act, which he wished people to
compare with the *epopteia.* In the Telesterion the Hierophant had
celebrated only "under the fire," that is, *beside* it. The Brahman celebrated immortality *in* the fire.

The fire of Persephone in the Telesterion was only a curtain of fire and outwardly, for the world, an announcement of the beatific event that had taken place within. In this form it was inherited by Christianity. Let me quote a present-day account of Easter Sunday morning in Jerusalem. "Then at last the church rings with cries of jubilation. Cries from men's mouths and cries of light. From the Holy Sepulcher leaps the fire; flames are passed out of the sepulchral chapel. From them hearts and candles are kindled. There is a unique, overpowering explosion of joy, a chain reaction of light: each person present passes the flame he has received on to two or three neighbors; in a matter of seconds the fire spreads through the church and is carried out to the parvis. All are infected with joy, while amid a tumult of hymns and banners priests, monks, and faithful circle indefatigably around the tabernacle enclosing the tomb of Christ. 'Christ is risen. . . . Verily, Christ is risen. . . !' This is the 'Divine Service of Fire' in the Eastern Church." [90]

Part Two

V. A HERMENEUTICAL ESSAY
ON THE MYSTERIES

Introductory Observations

I T I S nothing so very unusual that a vision, quite regardless of its type and origin, should confer happiness. Yet because it was repeated each year, because it *could* be repeated over a period of more than a thousand years, and because a whole festive assembly participated in it, the *visio beatifica* of Eleusis does seem to stand in a class by itself. Its unique position in the world known to the Greeks and Romans is confirmed by our sources (see pp. 115 f.). As a *religious* phenomenon of such uniqueness it differs—and I believe this to be worth stating—from the objects in connection with which the competence of classical scholars and archaeologists can be recognized. This is demonstrated by the many contradictory judgments and interpretations, all of which there is no need to cite. These judgments seem all the more astonishing when we consider that most of those who emitted them accepted the commonplace that the secret of Eleusis was so well preserved that we can never learn it.

One extreme judgment—referring to the classical period of Athens—runs: "The sacred actions, which were performed in the Mystery temple before the eyes of the initiate, were crude and meaningless in the extreme, and all those who had received the new kind of education regarded them as nothing but priestly deception and childish nonsense." [1] According to another opinion, on the contrary, "the sublimity of the Eleusinian worship" was so unquestioned in that same period that Aischylos "felt it strongly." [2] The author of this judgment could not very well admit that the great tragic poet was not an initiate (see above, p. 99). In any case, those who felt in this way [3] did not believe that the Eleusinian secret was very well preserved. "By touching a reproduction of a womb, the initiate evidently gained certainty of being reborn from the womb of the Earth Mother and so becoming her very own child." [4] The assumption which—if justified—would in one opinion give the Mysteries a sublime and in another a rather crude content is as follows: A replica of a womb was contained in the *cista mystica*, and with it the action mentioned in the *synthema* was undertaken (see p. 66). We cannot say that this is excluded since we do not know what actually was in the big basket.[5] Whatever its contents may have been,[6] we have no testimony on the matter; much less have we any evidence to support the suggested symbolic interpretation of the womb.[7] Moreover, the first proponents of this view did not have the object and content of the *epopteia* in mind. After all, it would seem rather exaggerated to call those blessed who had seen *that*.

This hermeneutics extended only to a part of the content of the Mysteries and was based on a mere hypothesis. Another attempt at hermeneutics rested on a somewhat more solid foundation. Nothing about the Eleusinian Mysteries was so striking as the initiates' awe of Demeter's gift, the grain, and their hope of life after death. In one Christian source the ear of grain is designated mockingly but also precisely as "the great, admired, and most perfect epoptic Mysterion" at Eleusis.[8] Thus it was quite natural to recall the words from the Gospel of St. John (12: 24): "Except a corn of wheat fall into the ground and die, it abideth alone: but if it die, it bringeth forth much fruit." [9]

There is still another passage in the New Testament and a similar passage in the Talmud which make it easier for those raised in the Christian or Jewish faith to gain access to the Eleusinian Mysteries. In St. Paul we read (I Cor. 15: 35–37): "But some man will say, How are the dead raised up? and with what body do they come? Thou fool, that which thou sowest is not quickened, except it die: And that which thou sowest, thou sowest not that body that shall be, but bare grain, it may chance of wheat, or of some other grain: But God giveth it a body as it hath pleased him." Here Paul combines the word of Christ with rabbinic wisdom. "I know," said Queen Cleopatra to Rabbi Meir (Sanhedrin 90 b), "that the dead will revive, for it is written (Psalm 72: 16): 'And they [that is, the righteous] shall . . . blossom forth out of the city like the grass of the earth.' But when they arise, shall they arise nude or in their garments?" By "garments" the body was meant. The rabbi replied: "Thou mayest deduce by an *a fortiori* argument [the answer] from a wheat grain; if a grain of wheat, which is buried naked, sprouteth forth in many robes, how much more so the righteous, who are buried in their raiment!" [10]

These are parables drawn from other religions. But mere parables can never explain the vital force of a religious institution: neither the longevity of the Eleusinian Mysteries nor that of Judaism or Christianity. Religions and cults that live a thousand years are not based on parables alone. A *religious experience* is a very different matter, and we must assume that such an experience was present at Eleusis, for this alone could have given the parable content and validity. Hermeneutics must recognize the existence of an experience deserving of the name as a fact and take this fact as its foundation. The step from the notion of a universally intelligible parable to the idea of an authentic religious experience is bound to be a step *forward* for hermeneutics, provided this second assumption proves compatible with a reconstruction effected without hermeneutics, and this I believe is here the case. To forgo such an assumption—of a parable and in still greater degree of an authentic religious experience—is, on the contrary, a regression.

This is what was done in the most significant archaeological work on the Mysteries.[11] Important as are the findings set forth in that book for the reconstruction of the settlement and sanctuary, everything it has to say about the content of the Mysteries is based on false or insufficient arguments. It was a mistake, for example, to reject all Christian sources on the ground that their authors were not initiates (p. 287). They could perfectly well have had pagan sources, who spoke to them of particulars without any intention of revealing or betraying secrets. Thus, for example, the ear of grain was certainly not the "great epoptic Mysterion," as Hippolytos supposed. But he would not have reached any such conclusion if he had not come across a report to the effect that the ear of grain played a role in the *epopteia*. The Christian adversaries of the Mysteries were assuredly careful to invent nothing which any initiated pagan reader would know to be a lie. Their literary technique was to quote from several sources, including, to be sure, some which did not in fact refer to the Eleusinian Mysteries. Some referred to the happenings in the Eleusis of Alexandria.[12] Thus confusion arose. The confusion is to be rejected, not the sources.

In Mylonas' book, otherwise our most useful archaeological source work, the word *megaron* has made for confusion. The smaller building in the large Telesterion, in the center of it from the age of Perikles on, was properly called "the Anaktoron" [29, 30a] (see also our pp. 88 f.). Mylonas also is of this opinion. But he believes that the "primary function" of the Anaktoron was "to serve as the repository for the *hiera*"—the sacred objects—"of the cult. Its doors were opened at the close of the initiation when the Hierophant stood in front of them to exhibit the *hiera*, or some of them, to the attending initiates" (his p. 84). According to Mylonas, this is the correct reconstruction of the *epopteia*. There is no text to confirm it, but Mylonas cites the authority of

Ailianos, a Greek author of the second century after Christ. "Aelian," he maintains, "states definitely that only the Hierophant had the right to enter the Anaktoron and this in accordance with the law of the telete" (p. 86).

Mylonas' contention is based on a misunderstanding. Ailianos does not speak of an Anaktoron, but of a place called "the Megaron." [13] In quoting him Mylonas uses the word *anaktoron* for *megaron.* The reason for this change in the text was presumably that he, along with other archaeologists, believes a predecessor of the Anaktoron at Eleusis to have had the shape of a megaron. This is probably correct. What is not correct is to equate the form of building which the archaeologists call by a name borrowed from Homer, namely, *megaron,* with the historical designation of a building at Eleusis which was called "the Megaron." We should ask: What was the building to which the Eleusinians themselves gave this name? The pious story which Ailianos tells us about a godless Epicurean may well refer to this building and not necessarily to the "Anaktoron." This Epicurean, the story goes, entered the forbidden Megaron in defiance of the Mystery law and was punished by the gods with sickness. In almost two thousand years many buildings were erected at Eleusis which because of their shape archaeologists are obliged to call "megara." These include the oldest templelike struc-ture, which was excavated in a deeper stratum than the later Telesterion and Anaktoron. But there is no evidence to indicate that the Eleusinians called the Anaktoron "the Megaron" down to the time of the story about the punished Epicurean.

There is, however, a likelihood that the Eleusinians called some *other* building "the Megaron." The pious tale of Ailianos is a typical miracle tale, which merits no credence except for the assertion con-tained in it that there was a room which only the Hierophant was allowed to enter. There is an inscription attesting the existence of a room which was officially termed "the Megaron" at Eleusis.[14] The *apometra*, or emoluments,[15] for "the Priestess" were to be brought "to the Megaron." It is unlikely that produce serving for the sustenance of the priestesses would have been brought to the Anaktoron, which, as Mylonas agrees, was the "holy of holies." The Megaron must have been a place to which the priestesses had a special relationship. Ailianos tells us that the godless Epicurean was an effeminate man who might have passed for a woman.[16] He rushed into the Megaron, was overcome with terror, and came down with a protracted illness. Probably the law was that the Hierophant was the only *man* permitted to enter this room. The priestesses had the same right as a matter of course, because the Megaron was in a sense *their* precinct. Three such rooms can be identified among the buildings excavated at Eleusis.

Mylonas did not take the inscription into account.[17] However, he cites the case of the Emperor Marcus Aurelius: "he was allowed to enter the Anaktoron, the only lay person ever admitted to that sanctum in the long history of Eleusis" (p. 162). In the Latin text of the source, the word used is *sacrarium*,[18] a word which primarily denotes a place where sacred objects are not worshiped but stored.[19] At Eleusis it is the so-called "Sacred House" that best answers this description.[20] Since there were two priestesses who carried the secret sacred objects back to Athens and thence again to Eleusis on their heads in the Mystery baskets, it is quite possible that these objects were stored in the place where the priestesses lived while in office, and that no man except for the Hierophant was permitted to enter this house. Another possibility, apart from the "Sacred House," is the temple of Plouton. The inscription mentioning "the Megaron" speaks of "the Priestess" and "the Priestess of Plouton." In this case, the word *megaron*, as so frequently,[21] is chosen to designate a "chthonian" sanctuary. The function of the temple of Plouton at Eleusis and its situation in a large grotto [27] may reasonably be called "chthonian." A third possibility is the treasure house or sacrarium near the Telesterion (see p. xviii).

Mylonas is able to indicate no appropriate place for the *epopteia* which he constructed: a place where the Hierophant, standing in front of the Anaktoron, the small building in the large Telesterion [29, 30a], could, in a dazzling light, have shown the initiates the objects Mylonas had in mind. According to Mylonas' reconstruction, the Anaktoron would have stood between the Hierophant and a large part of the assembly, whose view would have been further impaired by the inner columns. And what objects does he have in mind? ". . . we have to confess that we do not know what those sacred objects were. We have suggested in an early part of our study that they may have been small relics from the Mycenaean age handed down from generation to generation; such relics must have seemed strange and consequently awe-inspiring to the Greeks of the Historic era. Their age and the unfamiliarity of their appearance would have lent the impression of objects used by the Goddess herself during her stay in the temple within which they found themselves" (pp. 273 f.). A decisive argument to the contrary is that in 415 B.C. Alkibiades attempted to show the Mysteries to his friends in Athens.[22] In his oration *On the Mysteries* (12, 16, 17) Andokides tells us that this attempt was made in at least three houses. Such attempts would have been impossible if particular sacred objects from Eleusis had been required.

Finally Mylonas admits: ". . . I cannot help feeling that there is much more to the cult of Eleusis that has remained a secret; that there is meaning and significance that escapes us" (p. 284). And: ". . . we cannot help but believe that the Mysteries of Eleusis were not an empty, childish affair devised by shrewd priests to fool the peasant and the ignorant, but a philosophy of life that possessed substance and meaning and imparted a modicum of truth to the yearning human soul" (p. 285). But this is a regression to the eighteenth century when, far from thinking of a religious experience, let alone a *visio beatifica,* at Eleusis, it was assumed that the Mysteries embodied a *secret philosophical doctrine.* I hardly need to say that this assumption was unfounded and is still unfounded.

The Uniqueness of the Eleusinian Mysteries

T H E   E V O C A T I O N of a beatific vision at Eleusis was an annual venture, repeated over a period of more than a thousand years. It cannot, like a tragedy, for example,[23] be traced back to its birth, to the time when it was first successfully attempted. The phenomenon is more readily comparable to that of Delphi,[24] the functioning of the Pythia. Under conditions which were kept strictly secret, after preparations which proved their worth for many centuries, in sacrosanct forms whose efficacy it would have been godlessness to deny, the venture succeeded time and time again. This success was in the nature of a psychic reality. Tragedy also produced a psychic effect, but of a different kind. The continuity of the Mystery cult was an important element in the religious experience it conferred. But this continuity was broken off forever fifteen hundred years ago. To us the total experience, the *empeiria,* is unavailable, and not even a *peira,* a "testing," [24a] can be attempted; the most we can achieve in this direction—and it is not very much—is an understanding of what distinguished this vision from a stage spectacle, even of a religious nature.

Aristotle investigated both what happened in the minds of the audience at a tragedy and the experience offered by the annually recurring venture of Eleusis. The spectator at the tragedy had no need to build up a state of concentration by ritual preparations; he had no need to fast, to drink the *kykeon*, and to march in a procession. He did not attain a state of *epopteia*, of "having seen," by his own inner resources. The poet, the chorus, and the actors created a vision, the *theama*, for him at the place designed for it, the *theatron*. Without effort on his part, the spectator was transported into what he saw. What he saw and heard was made easy for him and became irresistibly his. He came to believe in it, but this belief was very different from that aroused by the *epopteia*. He entered into other people's sufferings, forgot himself, and—as Aristotle stressed—was purified. In the Mysteries a purification—*katharmos*—had to take effect long before the *epopteia*. The theater audience achieved *katharsis* only at the end. "Through pity and terror," wrote Aristotle in his *Poetics* VI 2 (1449 b), "tragedy brought purification from all those passions."

This cannot be regarded as a purely "aesthetic" doctrine; we must view it, rather, as an empirical contribution to the phenomenology of the Greek tragedy's effect on its original public. Aristotle's contribution to the phenomenology of what the initiates, in addition to purification, had to achieve before the *epopteia* was to be found in his treatise *On Philosophy*. This work was much read in antiquity; one of its latest readers was the bishop Synesios, and it was probably read also by the Byzantine scholar Psellos. Even if Psellos did not expressly tell us that Aristotle was referring to Eleusis, it would be quite obvious. When Aristotle compares the progress of instruction in philosophy with the progress of initiation in the mysteries, he could, as an Athenian, have had only the Eleusinian Mysteries in mind. In these Mysteries—so his words are cited [25]—the initiate has not to learn but *pathein kai diateth-enai*, "to be passive" and "to be put into a state." This passage is not, as had been mistakenly supposed,[26] a description of Aristotle's own religious feeling or even of the religious experience of his day. Its significance lies in its emphasis on the preparations without which the *epopteia* was impossible. A state of particular passivity had to be attained if the venture was to succeed. Epiktetos—or Arrian, who committed his *Discourses* to writing—calls the initiate who has thus been prepared *prodiakeimenos* (III xxi 13). Obviously alluding to Aristotle's dialogue, he also indicates the next stage after the preparation. The term he employs for it, *eis phantasian,* cannot for Epiktetos have meant an experience of *phasmata,* apparitions, but for Aristotle it very likely did. Psellos, who was well versed in all the writings about the Mysteries that were still available to the Byzantines, calls the phenomenon to which the passive state leads *ellampsis,* "flaring up," and *autopsia,*[27] a term for divine apparitions which could, it was thought, be induced by magical ceremonies.[28]

The Eleusinian venture could be imitated and misused for purposes of magic and fraud, which in Greek religion were looked upon as ungodly and were strictly dissociated from the Mysteries—particularly from these most holy mysteries of Greece. This, however, and especially in late antiquity, does not exclude phenomenological similarity or mutual influence. Herein lies the significance of a report of Pausanias about an Egyptian sanctuary in Greece (X 32 17). He tells of a temple of Isis in the region of Mount Parnassos. A curious person, who had not been initiated, so Pausanias relates, once entered the abaton, the forbidden room, and saw it filled with spirits. He divulged what he had seen and died on the spot. The passage is a testimonial to faith in such happenings. Within Greek religion the Eleusinian Mysteries were unique of their kind, and this uniqueness was their characteristic trait, which was indeed stressed. Whereas in the history of religion doctrines and cults have laid claim to the one and only truth, Eleusis was held to be the one and only *place* where what happened before the eyes of the initiates in the Telesterion was permitted and true.

The Ptolemies, the successors of Alexander the Great in Egypt, considered it extremely important that their Greek subjects in Alexandria should, like the Athenians, have an Eleusis in their immediate vicinity: a suburb of Alexandria was given this name. At the court of Ptolemy Lagos officiated a theologian named Timotheos, of the family of the Eumolpidai, whom the king had sent for from the Athenian Eleusis. His mission was to guide the religious life and satisfy the religious needs of the Graeco-Egyptian kingdom.[29] His regulatory and organizational activity was probably responsible for the positive as well as the negative features that can be derived from the information we have about the Koreion, the temple of Persephone, in the Alexandrian Eleusis. The negative element clearly bears witness to the uniqueness of the Mysteries that were celebrated in Attica.

This fact is preserved indirectly in a scrap of papyrus found at Oxyrhynchos.[30] The sentences formed part of a speech which was probably delivered in Alexandria during the Roman imperial age. The orator waxes indignant over the mysterylike ceremonies of an emperor cult that had just been introduced in Asia Minor. He dislikes the rite and objects to its implantation in the place where he is speaking—probably Alexandria. But because the cult is a variety of emperor worship, the speaker cannot cast doubt on its justification. He merely says: "Let them celebrate there and among those people in such a way, for example, as the Athenians celebrate the Eleusinian Mysteries. Or do we wish to commit sacrilege against the emperor? Just as it would be a sacrilege against Demeter, whom we worship here, were we to celebrate the Mysteries of that place [he means Eleusis] here." These words are complemented by a passage in Epiktetos (III XXI 13): Someone might say: "There is an edifice at Eleusis: behold, here, too, there is one. There is a Hierophant: I, too, shall appoint a hierophant. There is a herald: I, too, shall name a herald. There is a Dadouchos; I, too, shall take a dadouchos. There are torches: here, too. The tones are the same: wherein differs what happens here from what happens there?" "Thou godless man," the philosopher continues. "Does it differ in no way? What avails it if it happens at the *wrong place* and the wrong time? Only after the sacrifice, after the prayers, and after one has been made aware that one is approaching sacred rites, rites that have been sacred since time immemorial, can the Mysteries serve their purpose!"

In the Alexandrian Koreion the Eleusinian rite had been replaced by other ceremonies, namely, the dramatic performances which the Church Fathers, who had not been initiated, hand down as the elements of the Eleusinian Mysteries. A *drama mystikon*—that is the term used by Clement of Alexandria [31]—in several acts was performed on different levels: below the earth and upon it. Such a drama was possible in the Koreion of Alexandria, but not in the Attic Telesterion. Epiphanios [32] describes a nocturnal rite in the Koreion; not that which in Alexandria corresponded to, without being identical with, the Eleusinian rites, but a later phase of the holy history, the pagan feast of Epiphany in the night of January 5. The people spent this night in the temple, singing to the accompaniment of flutes. A troop of torchbearers entered and went down into the underground cult chamber—*sekos hypogaios*—whence they brought up a statue: "A wooden idol, its forehead, hands, and knees adorned with golden cruciform seals, otherwise naked, was placed in a litter and carried seven times round the inner temple." When someone (a profane stranger who had been admitted to these nocturnal ceremonies) asked: "What is this Mysterion?" the answer was: "Today, at this hour, the Kore, that is, the virgin, gave birth to the Aion." That night, we are told, the virgin's divine child bore the name of a god, whose birth signified the beginning of a new era, although only of a new year. The golden cruciform seals on the hands and knees were not Greek but oriental. And, as we have seen, the temple was so built that in it the drama which the ecclesiastical authors falsely impute to the Eleusinian Mysteries could be enacted underground and round an "inner temple."

In his contemptuous account of the Mysteries Asterios, Bishop of Amaseia, at the turn of the fifth century, goes into still greater detail than Clement of Alexandria on one point. He speaks of two "women's temples," *gynaioi naoi,* where Demeter and Kore are worshiped.[33] This was the case at Alexandria, which, in addition to the Koreion, possessed a Thesmophorion, a temple of Demeter especially devoted to a women's cult.[34] This entire religion, Asterios insists, had its source in the Eleusinian Mysteries, and he goes on to transpose the "insane cult," which was obviously known to him in Alexandria, to Attica: "Is there not there"—he asks—"the dark subterranean passage (*katabasion to skoteinon*), and is it not there that occur the sacrosanct encounters of the Hierophant with the Priestess, of a man with a woman alone? Are the lights not extinguished? And does the multitude not believe that they achieve salvation through what the two of them do in the darkness?" Tertullian asks: "Why is the priestess of Demeter ravished if this is not what happened to Demeter?"[35] Clement relates a whole sequence of scenes.[36] It begins with the "mysteries of Deo." These consisted in the amorous embraces of Zeus and his mother, Demeter. Thereupon followed the Goddess's anger—"as mother or as wife?" the Church Father asks scornfully—and Zeus' penance. Psellos, drawing on another source, speaks also of an embrace between Persephone and her father; however, it was not enacted;[37] instead, Aphrodite appears from an artificial womb as though rising from the sea. "Persephone is sought in the night by torchlight," writes Lactantius,[38] "and after she is found, the entire ceremony ends in rejoicing; the torches are thrown up in the air."

These are the echoes of the Eleusinian nights of Alexandria which Christian authors mistook for scenes from the Attic Mysteries. The Alexandrian celebration took place on the 28th of the month of Epiphi, in our July.[39] In Alexandria the rites were not even protected by a rule of secrecy—that is why the Christians knew so much about them. Anyone who wished to could attend and ask questions concerning what happened in the darkness and what happened in the light. Christian scholars supposed that similar things were done behind the high walls and imposing gates of the original Eleusinian sanctuary or even in the narrow interior passages of the crowded temple. But there the secrecy was so rigorous that two innocent young men from distant Akarnania, who had unwittingly attended a Mystery festival and given themselves away by asking questions, were executed in 200 B.C.[40] A different atmosphere prevailed in the Eleusis of Alexandria, where the poet Kallimachos was schoolmaster for a time.[41] The temple was situated between the quarter inhabited by the hetairai[42] and—probably—the tombs of Hadra, where religious emissaries from Greece, who had stayed on and died in Alexandria, were buried.[43]

This Egyptian, Hellenistic Eleusis differed in every way from the austere Attic Eleusis, although the seeds of the Alexandrian development were already present in Greece, perhaps at Agrai still more than at Eleusis. The Goddesses, Mother and Daughter, were looked upon as the protectors of young women—such as the mistress of Lysias the rhetorician and the celebrated Glykera, to whom Menander allegedly swore

fidelity at the Mysteries of Eleusis [44]—whose loves were not sanctioned
by the patriarchal bond of marriage. The experiences conferred were
radically different: on the one hand, to witness the epiphany of a divine
Phantom; on the other, to be enraptured by an erotic drama. Goethe
speaks in one of his Maxims [45] of an "erotomorphism" which springs, as
it were, from anthropomorphism and "transforms all happening into
ethical-sensuous feeling." In the Attic Eleusis anthropomorphism remained predominant; in Alexandria the emphasis was designedly erotomorphic. No attempt whatever was made to conceal it, and it was far
from being the Mystery secret.

There was so little secrecy about these nocturnal rites that a false
prophet was able to devise "mysteries" on the basis of the artistic device
on which they were mainly formed. This device consisted in successive
genealogical scenes leading up to the beatific event round which the
"mysteries" centered. The charlatan in question hailed from Abonouteichos, a small town on the shore of the Black Sea. His portrait, like that
of Peregrinus, who imitated the Indian ascetic and was burned alive,
was penned by his contemporary Lucian in the second century after
Christ.[46] Alexander of Abonouteichos represented himself as an Askle-
piad, a son of the hero Podaleirios, son of the Divine Physician. This
was the foundation of his "mysteries." They lasted for three days. On
the first day the spectators saw how Leto gave birth to Apollo, how the
god mated with Koronis and Asklepios was born. The second day was
devoted to the epiphany of Glykon, the artificial giant snake through
the mouth of which Alexander emitted his oracles. On the third day
occurred the marriage of Podaleirios and Alexander's mother. It assuredly took place at night: the mother's name was Dadis, "torch maiden,"
and torches shone at the ceremony. The final scene represented the
love of Selene and Alexander. The new Endymion officiated as dadou-

chos and hierophant. He lay on the central level as though asleep. To him descended from the ceiling, as though from heaven, not the moon goddess but the fair Rutilia, the wife of an imperial manager, who loved the pseudo prophet and was loved by him in return. Before the eyes of all, they embraced and kissed one another: "If not for the many torches, something secret might easily have happened" (*Alexander* 39).

The development that made it possible for the player of this scene to appear before and afterward in the costume of the Hierophant and, like a Hierophant, to raise his voice in solemn proclamation began in the true Eleusis but was continued in the new, Alexandrian Eleusis. In an attempted hermeneutics of the Eleusinian experience, we cannot fail to note the anthropomorphism which also embraced an erotomorphic element, but did not—assuredly not in the *epopteia*—display it as in Alexandria.

The Relation of the Mysteries to the Grain

U N I Q U E N E S S   I S an important characteristic of the Eleusinian Mysteries. Their extraordinary religious significance resided in the belief that here alone did a pious encounter between the living and the queen of the underworld become possible. An equally important characteristic seems to be their link with Demeter's gift, the grain. But if, as has hitherto been the case, only this connection and not its *special nature* is considered, a false picture arises. For this connection implies a careful disjunction. The ornamental sheaves of grain are not necessary to the inner ritual or psychological cohesion of the Mystery action. On the contrary, the public nature of everything connected with Demeter—from her mourning to her gift of the grain—has convinced us that the grain cannot have been part of the *aporrheta,* and was certainly not the *arrheton*. On the other hand, the connection between the "two gifts," *dittai doreai*, the Eleusinian Mysteries and the grain, is historical: in the Homeric Hymn to Demeter, one follows the other; the gift of the Mysteries follows the gift of the grain. This succession is deserving of closer attention.

The formula of the *dittai doreai*, considered as two inseparable and equivalent gifts of Demeter and the city of Athens to mankind, occurs in the *Panegyrikos*, the festive discourse of Isokrates, about 380 B.C. (see p. 15), and it is by no means certain that it possessed universal validity for the Athenians themselves. A funeral oration for those who fell in the year 386, which Sokrates puts into the mouth of Aspasia, Perikles' mistress (in it the spirit of the philosopher merges with that of the wise woman), is handed down to us among the Platonic writings. It cannot have been written by Plato, for he surely had no wish to obscure the fact that his master had then been dead for thirteen years. But this oration was held in high esteem by the Athenians; we are told that it was delivered each year at the annual feast of the dead.[47] It does not seem to have been composed much earlier than the Panegyric of Isokrates. The oration tells us [48] that the Attic earth had *spontaneously* brought forth the wheat and barley—just as it had given birth to man. The infant's nourishment flows from its mother, and herein women imitate the earth. But if this was so, there was no need for Demeter to bring forth the grain in Attica when she found her daughter.

And even if it was believed that Demeter brought forth the grain—and this was quite possible in view of the contradictions in the mythological tradition—the Athenians performed ritual plowings in three different places where agriculture was supposed to have begun.[49] Two of these, Skiron and Bouzygion, are not on Eleusinian soil; only Rharia, the third site, was a part of Eleusis. Ultimately the Eleusinian tradition of the origin of agriculture—we shall soon see that the gift of agriculture was sharply differentiated from the initiation of the Mysteries—came to be accepted by the Athenians, but only from the fourth century on. According to this tradition, the hero Triptolemos, who had first sown grain in the Rharian Field, conferred a great benefit on the whole of mankind. In the speech which, according to Xenophon,[50] was delivered by the Dadouchos Kallias when he was sent to Sparta as a peace emissary in 371 B.C., Triptolemos is mentioned in a manner compatible with the formula of the "two gifts." According to the oration, it was he who initiated Herakles and the Dioskouroi—who had close ties with Sparta—into the Mysteries: these three heroes were the first strangers upon whom this gift was bestowed. We are reminded of a vase painting [45], as if the oration were a text to it.

The vase paintings of the fourth century B.C., particularly the Kerch vases—so called after the place in southern Russia where most of the vases of this type were found—bear witness to the wide influence which the Eleusinian Mysteries were just then beginning to exert. In a period when death was so omnipresent, a period of wars and plagues, the Eleusinian secret took on a new power, particularly among the Eleusinians and Athenians themselves. It would be too much to speak of a religious mission, and though such a term as "propaganda" may appeal to modern thinking, such activity is hardly demonstrable. But we are perfectly entitled to speak of an expansion demonstrable in the nonliterary sphere, attested by the vases sent from Athens, which in all likelihood are furnishings for tombs. One of these is the vase referred to above [45]. Triptolemos is prepared for a journey. Toward him come the great initiands, Herakles and the Dioskouroi, bearing their bundles of myrtle. The purpose of Triptolemos' journey was to distribute Demeter's other gift, and this is also stressed by Kallias: according to him, the

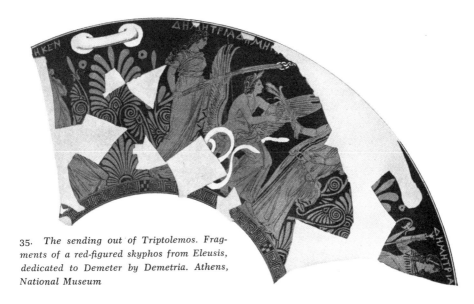

35. *The sending out of Triptolemos. Fragments of a red-figured skyphos from Eleusis, dedicated to Demeter by Demetria. Athens, National Museum*

Peloponnese was the first foreign land to receive this gift. From this time on, Triptolemos is indeed represented as having always been identified with the two missions, the dissemination of agriculture and the bestowal of religious hope, which had originally been confined to the locality of Eleusis.

The place of the hero Triptolemos at Eleusis was exactly defined. He was among the first initiates,[51] but as Demeter's pupil, who had brought agriculture to mankind, he had a cult of his own, apart from the Mysteries. One entered his temple on the way to the closed-off sacred precinct, before coming to the former Hekataion, the temple of Artemis outside the Great Propylaia. Most of the many vases representing Triptolemos and his mission are wine vessels [cf. 35]. It was only outside of the Mystery season, when the drinking of wine was permitted, that such vessels could have been used as votive offerings to him and the Two Goddesses. The great relief in the Athens National

36. *Triptolemos between the Two Goddesses. Demeter is handing him a golden ear of grain (now lost). Marble relief of the second half of the v century B.C., found at Eleusis. It was probably situated in the temple of Triptolemos. Athens, National Museum*

Museum [36], which was found at Eleusis, dates from the second half of the fifth century B.C. It shows him standing between the Two Goddesses: Demeter is holding a golden ear of grain out to him. In the vase paintings he appears, from the sixth century on, on a fantastic throne equipped with winged wheels and adorned with snakes [38, 45, 52]. Sophokles presented him thus on the stage, probably in 468 B.C. But whence had he come in such a vehicle? According to the myth concerning his mission, Triptolemos made his way with ease among all the peoples of the earth, even the most remote. On a sixth-century vase [37] Triptolemos in his chariot, preceded by Hermes, has a pendant in Dionysos, riding in a winged chariot and bearing a goblet and clusters of grapes; a Silenos accompanies him with wine jar and *kantharos*. To judge by such testimonies, the wine, like the grain, was sent forth from Eleusis after the conclusion of the Mysteries, the gift of the subterranean Dionysos, like the gift of Demeter.

Triptolemos is only *one* name for the primordial man who played a part in a certain myth of the Goddess. At Eleusis he was associated with the Rharian Plain, where he possessed his altar and his cult.[52] But the myth was known far beyond the confines of Attica. Two other names have come down to us for the bearer of this role at Eleusis. Demeter—so

37A. *Triptolemos in his miraculous chariot, with Hermes. Obverse of a black-figured vase. Compiègne, Musée Antoine Vivenel*
37B. *Dionysos in his miraculous chariot, with a Silenos. Reverse of the same vase*

the myth goes—came to a primordial man who was very much in need of her. In every version available to us, Demeter was a potential Mystery goddess, but she was *needed* in her quality of grain goddess. She appeared everywhere as bestower of the grain. The names of the primordial men to whom she repairs express the need for the grain in different ways. The two others (we have already spoken of them) were called in Eleusis Keleos and Dysaules. Keleos, the "woodpecker," is the name of a forest dweller, Dysaules that of a peasant, to whom the soil gives nothing and who is therefore constrained to "dwell poorly." That Triptolemos could also be a name for the primordial man is shown by a genealogy which represents him as the son of Okeanos and of Ge, the Earth.[53] The authors who looked upon Keleos or Dysaules as the Eleusinian first man have assigned him to the family of one or the other. The name of the king's son Demophoön, "slayer of the people," whom Demeter put into the fire, is merely a variant of Triptolemos, and there was a tradition to the effect that the Goddess was *his* nurse.[54] According to another tradition,[55] he was Demeter's lover under the name of Iasion.

A hero named Triptolemos, "threefold warrior," must have been a wild man comparable to Ares, the war god. The name of the woman, Deiope, who is mentioned in connection with him, and concerning whom Pausanias (I 14 1), in religious awe, declines to say more, also implies hostility and the love of killing. This couple was in need of taming and conversion to peaceful agriculture. The name of the future apostle of Demeter seems to have been invented with a view to such conversion. In the light of the civilizing influence of agriculture, one may even speak of a religion of Demeter, but it is not permissible to identify this religion with that of the Eleusinian Mysteries. Triptolemos was always connected with Demeter, hence with the outward aspect of the Mysteries and not with the *arrheton*. From a purely linguistic angle it is also possible to interpret his name by associating it with the *neios tripolos,* the "thrice-plowed field," and with a verb that can be formed from it, *tripolein.*[56] An acclamation has come down to us which was allegedly uttered at the Eleusinian Mysteries, in all probability after the festival, when the initiates crossed the bridge on their way home: "Cross the bridge, O Kore, before it is time to begin the threefold plowing."[57]

Thus the time of Triptolemos came *after* the Mysteries, in any case. But in the sacred legend of the Mysteries his conversion from "threefold warrior" to "threefold plowman," his plowing and sowing of the Rharian Plain, were necessary before Demeter could perform the Mysteries and inaugurate them with her example: Triptolemos played his part both *after* and *before* the Mysteries. In the introductory act a characteristic and always prominent position is occupied by the drinking of the *kykeon,* the barley mixture. In the prelude to the Mysteries, Demeter shows the mixing of the beverage, but it is not at this time that she makes the barley grow. Grain grew plentifully on the Rharian Field until the Goddess in her anger caused it to stop growing. The story in the Chronicle of Paros[58] is well conceived: in the first sentence it relates Demeter's coming to Triptolemos during the reign of Erechtheus; in the second, it tells of the first Rharian harvest; and only in the fifth does it speak of the first Mystery festival at Eleusis. The Homeric hymn—which reflects the prevailing archaic conception—tells the same story (450–74): the grain grows *again* after the Two Goddesses are reunited; it was not on this occasion shown and given to man by Demeter for the first time.

Triptolemos and, in the early times no less pronouncedly, Dionysos spread their gifts—on the one hand, the grain; on the other, the wine—over the whole earth, after the initiates, among them the Eleusinian [8] hero of agriculture, had received the blessing of the Mysteries. Here begins another story, that of the spread of "civilized life"—*hemeros bios* [59]—among men. The cultural significance of Triptolemos is stressed by the three commandments pertaining to a simple, pious mode of life that were ascribed to him—to Triptolemos and not to the Eleusinian Mysteries, whose import was far broader, relating to the whole of human existence. The commandments were: "Honor your parents." "Honor the gods with fruits." (For the Greeks fruits included grain.) And: "Spare the animals." [60] These commandments, which seem to be more Pythagorean than Eleusinian in origin, could never have supplied the meaning and content of the Eleusinian religion. The unique position of the Eleusinian Mysteries in the Greek world would have been perfectly conceivable without them and, for that matter, without the part played by Triptolemos. Our oldest document, the Homeric Hymn to Demeter, mentions him but by no means prominently: he is just one of the kings of Eleusis to whom Demeter showed the sacred rites.

Though the unique religious significance of the Eleusinian Mysteries would be conceivable without their link with Demeter's gift and *without Triptolemos,* the "two gifts" were a part of the historical form of the Eleusinian religion. The Mysteries themselves conferred but *one* gift: initiation. It alone was essential to all who visited Eleusis for religious purposes. On the other hand, the grain appears as a gift of Demeter even in the deepest stratum of Eleusinian mythology to which we can penetrate, and there is no doubt that the myth of Triptolemos leads us back to early archaic times, preceding the existence of the Homeric hymn. However, it was not only at Eleusis that Demeter was revered as the bestower of grain and the giver of agriculture, and it was not everywhere that she performed these functions in the forms of a

secret cult and in the frame of a myth recalling the Eleusinian Mysteries. Even at Eleusis she bestowed the grain through Triptolemos *outside*
the Great Mysteries (in respect of both place and time). If the Daughter
is mentioned in connection with the mission of Triptolemos and represented beside the Mother as she entrusts him with it [38], it was no doubt
in order that the Daughter might adorn this festival—which was not a

38. *Fragments of votive
reliefs representing Eleusinian scenes and deities,
the largest scene pre-
served probably depict-
ing Demeter, Persephone,
Plouton, and Triptolemos.
Found at Eleusis along
with the votive painting
of Niinnion [15]. Athens,
National Museum*

Mystery festival—by her presence and give it greater sanctity: in the Mysteries themselves the first to receive a gift was Demeter, who only handed on Persephone's gift of initiation to mankind.

Until Demeter became reconciled with the realm of Hades or of Plouton (the Homeric and official name for Persephone's husband) she withdrew into her quality as grain goddess and ordered the barley beverage. But she consumed the *kykeon* in another quality as well, the quality by virtue of which she herself in grief and mourning entered upon the path of initiation and turned toward the ineffable core of the Mysteries, namely, her quality as *her daughter's mother*. One characteristic trait of the Eleusinian Mysteries was their bond—bond and disjunction in one—with grain and with agriculture as well. This bond did not necessarily reach to the innermost core. We may simply describe it as the bond of the Mysteries with their economic foundation, with a civilization which in the historical era was based predominantly on the raising of grain. It received religious expression at Eleusis through the myth and cult of Triptolemos. But once the bond existed, it was possible for grain to become the symbol of the ineffable core of the Mysteries.

Pomegranate and Vine

DEMETER SEARCHED for her vanished daughter as though she were the lost half of herself and found her at last in the underworld. This myth can be recognized in the story that is enacted in the heavens in the second half of every month, when the moon is robbed of itself and goes wandering in search of the ravished portion until at last it reaches total darkness—but then this phenomenon must be seen in terms of the destiny of Mother and Daughter. Taken together, the heavenly and the earthly happenings constitute the *circulus mythologicus,* the indivisible circle in which this myth, though not all of it, appeared. The Eleusinian Mysteries were celebrated in the last third of the month, in accordance with the lunar calendar. A second element had to do with vegetation, and a third was such that it could take the form of a *phasma,* the beatific vision of the Mystery Night. Other myths of the searching Goddess who was first to attain the *telos,* the goal, of the Mysteries, and even the names belonging to her myths, are of secondary importance beside these central happenings in heaven and on earth.

Since the Mother was the grain mother, the Daughter must have been the grain maiden. The ear of grain in the Hierophant's hand at the end of the Mystery rite evinced this aspect of the great underworld Goddess. This aspect assumed special importance in the remote grain-growing regions to which the Greeks brought the Eleusinian myth, though not the Eleusinian Mysteries: in Sicily, for example, where to the historian Diodorus, in the first century B.C., wild wheat was a familiar plant (V 2 4), or in southern Italy. In an Apulian vase painting [39], five ears of grain are displayed in a small chapel in place of the

39. *Aedicula with ears of grain displayed on a tomb. Painting on an Apulian vase. Leningrad, Hermitage Museum*

plant shoots (Greek, *korai* [61]) ordinarily represented. According to Athenian law, burial sites were sown with grain, expressly in order to purify them and give them back to the living.[62] But Attic authors of comedies, burlesquing the obscure language of the tragedies, refer to flour as the daughter of Demeter.[63] And Cicero speaks of her as the seed grain,[64] an explanation that has no greater validity than other "physical" explanations of the gods in Stoic theology.

For the Mother was not always the grain mother. The older goddess who originally no doubt played the part of the mother was not entirely forgotten, even after Demeter had taken her place. According to the Homeric hymn, it did not occur to Demeter, even after her reunion with her daughter, to make grain grow again on the Rharian Plain, where before the rape she had caused it to grow abundantly and after the rape had made it die out. Rhea, mother of the gods, in relation to whom Kore's mother was herself a daughter, was sent to her by Zeus to lead her back to the gods. On her own initiative, Rhea persuaded Demeter to bestow the "life-giving fruit" on mankind (469). Thus, according to the Homeric hymn, this gift was also a gift of Rhea. Whether or not Euripides in his *Helen* also calls the Great Goddess "Deo" (1343; the text is not certain on this point), his chorus looks upon the "Mountain Mother" and the "Mother of the Gods," who can only be Rhea, as the mother of the *arrhetos koura* (1307)—the mother who searches for her daughter with resounding instruments characteristic of the ecstatic procession of Kybele and who, in her grief, withholds all growth and stops all springs from flowing. Here Rhea and Demeter are one person. The same is evident in an Epidaurian hymn [65] in which the rape of Persephone is not named as the cause of the Mother's anger, because its author no longer possessed the boldness that enabled Euripides to go back to the *other* tradition.

In the Hesiodic genealogy of the gods, which is applicable also to the Homeric hymn, Demeter, as daughter and mother, stands in the middle between Rhea and Persephone. But she had not always occupied that position. The Orphic genealogy of the gods shows how later theologians tried to reconcile two traditions. According to one tradition, Rhea was the mother of Persephone; according to the other, Demeter. In the first tradition, moreover, Persephone bore by her own father the subterranean child Dionysos as a kind of second, subterranean Zeus. None other than she can be meant when an *arrhetos* is mentioned among the mothers of Dionysos.[66] The myth of Persephone as mother of Dionysos is ascribed by Diodorus to the Cretans (V 75 4 f.). The names of Rhea and Demeter for the same goddess alternate in the myths not only of Persephone but also of Dionysos,[67] and the names of both Demeter and Persephone are used for the mother of the child Dionysos.[68] Obviously the grain goddess was a latecomer, fitted into an older genealogy, now in one way, now in another. The later conception that Demeter and not Rhea was Persephone's mother won out and became classical. The two traditions were reconciled by the Orphic theologians. The latest version of the Orphic theogony [69] tells us that "After becoming the mother of Zeus, she who had formerly been Rhea became Demeter."

Thus the great Mother Goddess of an older, in part pre-Greek world was not forgotten behind the figure of Demeter the grain mother, who could not wholly conceal Rhea at Eleusis! And still less was the primordial connection of the Persephone myth with a certain plant and with an entire characteristic vegetation forgotten. This relationship may well be regarded as primordial, for in the myth no other plant is so explicitly and exclusively decisive for Persephone's fate as the pomegranate. The god of the underworld gave Persephone "only a single sweet pomegranate seed; she barely noticed"; and forever after she was in his power. So goes the story as related in the Homeric hymn (372). The *eating* of the pomegranate seed cannot have been the secret, else it would not have been told; but neither would it have been told if there had not been an intimate relationship between the queen of the underworld and the pomegranate tree. The poor folk ate their pomegranates in a manner recalling the myth of Persephone: "Wilt thou eat the sour-sweet pomegranate seed for seed?" asks someone in Aischylos,[70] and from Aristophanes we know that it was possible to make a simple meal of apples and pomegranates.[71] There seems to have been a belief that the souls nibbled at the pomegranates that were laid on their graves. The story of Persephone eating pomegranate seeds was related like a fairy tale in place of the original myth: Ovid speaks once of three,[72] once of seven, pomegranate seeds and related that the tree grew in the garden of the king of the underworld.[73]

The pomegranate was only one of many Mediterranean plants from which food and drink were derived; the thirst-quenching and intoxicating vine was another. These plants may be divided into two groups, each with its religious associations: pomegranate, apple, fig, and vine had to do with Dionysos; pomegranate, almond, and date palm were connected with Rhea, mother of the gods, in her Phrygian form, that is, with Kybele and her lover Attis. In the "Ark of Kypselos," an archaic work of art shown at Olympia, a bearded, long-robed Dionysos was represented lying in a cave, holding in his hand a golden cup; around him grow the vine and the apple and the pomegranate tree.[74] For the Greeks these three fruits and the fig belonged to the same family. The island of Melos was so called after the apple tree, but the coins of the Melians always show a pomegranate, never an apple.[75] The black fig was called "the sister of the vine." This figure employed by the poet Hipponax might seem to be purely poetic,[76] but there is a genealogy that supports it. Oxylos was said to be a son of Oreios. (In another myth it was a hero, probably a hunter, with a similar name, Orestheus, whose bitch gave birth to the vine.[77]) Oxylos, the son of Oreios, "man of the mountain," begot by his own sister, Hamadryas the tree nymph, Ampelos and Syke, "vine" and "fig tree." [78] It has already been mentioned that on Naxos the mask of the subterranean Dionysos was carved from the wood of the fig tree (see p. 35); on the same island the mask of the Dionysos of the living was fashioned from the wood of the vine.[79] Cult observance and genealogy expressed the same relationship with fig tree and vine. According to a genealogy that was recognized at least on the islands of Delos and Euboia, Rhoio,[80] the divine person of the pomegranate tree, the *rhoa*, was a daughter of Staphylos, the personified grape. She became the mother of Anios of Apollo, a Delian priest whose name may very well conceal an allusion to the suffering Dionysos.[81] The three Oinotropoi, the sisters whose common name is probably a reference to their ability to turn water into wine at a certain festival of Dionysos, were regarded as the daughters of Anios. The individual names of these granddaughters of Rhoio were: Oino, Spermo, and Elaiïs, "wine maiden," "seed maiden," and "oil maiden." [82]

The question may at least be asked whether Rhea's name, which is otherwise inexplicable, might not, like Rhoio, be connected with *rhoa*. In the epic language, the goddess was called *Rheie,* the pomegranate *rhoie,* as though they formed a regular Greek vowel gradation. But the connection can be similar to that between Greek *oinos,* "wine," and the Latin *vinum,* a comparison to which the name of the Dionysian goddess *Ino* can be added: [83] these, as well as the similar Semitic words for wine, may have come from a common pre-Greek, pre-Semitic root.[84] More significant than the possible linguistic connection is the fact that the initiates in the mysteries of Kybele and Attis were forbidden to par-

take of pomegranates, a prohibition which, according to the Emperor
Julian,[85] extended also to dates. In the sacred legends of these mysteries, a kind of identity is manifest between the pomegranate tree
—or the almond tree, in a different version—and Attis. His embodi-
ments, the priests of Attis, and their statues bore pomegranates in their
hands or on their heads in the form of wreaths.[86] When Agdistis, the
bisexual primordial form of the Great Goddess, was emasculated, so ran
the sacred legend,[87] the pomegranate tree sprang from the blood that
flowed. Nana—another name for the Great Goddess—was got with
child by its fruit. She bore Attis, whose destiny was just as bloody as that
of Agdistis. But to the initiates it was a pledge of immortality, for Attis
never died wholly.

Such myths were connected with subtropical or, in the case of the
date palm, still more southern fruit-bearing plants. A migration of
myths between the Mediterranean and Indonesia by way of Arabia is
conceivable in the pre-Islamic period. And it is in the Indonesian island
of Ceram that we find the tales most closely related to the Persephone
myth,[88] the myths of Hainuwele and Rabie. The name of the maiden
Hainuwele means "branch of the coconut palm"; she was born from the
drops of her father Ameta's blood, which had fallen on a palm blossom.[89]
Before the tuberous plants sprang from the body of the slain maiden,
she herself was the fruit of the palm. The ethnological view is corrobo-
rated, above all, in relation to a "pomegranate maiden" who, supported
by the archetypal image of the Primordial Maiden, may have provided
the prototype for the "coconut maiden." In a very old stratum of Greek
mythology, which is accessible to us only in scattered fragments, sometimes only in a name, there *was* a myth of the pomegranate tree which
was not very different from that of Hainuwele or from that of Persephone.

It is believed that the pomegranate was a mere fertility symbol, though this view was already amply refuted in the middle of the nineteenth century by Karl Bötticher,[90] who wrote: "How could the pomegranate be a symbol of happy fertility when it was a fruit of bloody death, dedicated to Hades?" Among the modern Greek peasants it has indeed become an instrument of magic and an expression of the desire for fertility. In the region of Epidauros the peasants break pomegranates on their plowshares, mix a few grains with the seed, and in sowing cry out: "Let it thrive." [91] In Crete when a newly wedded bride crosses the threshold her husband hands her a pomegranate. But here we are as far as possible from the myth. None of the old tales is remembered, and the meaning of the pomegranate is found in its most obvious characteristic, abundance of seeds. This is taken as a basis of sympathetic magic. The same remoteness from the myth is to be found in those writers of late antiquity who interpreted the pomegranate in the hand of Hermes, god of the dead, as an attribute of Hermes Logios, the god rich in *logoi,* words and ideas,[92] whereas Pausanias (IX 25 1) still stressed the relation to bloody death and explained it on the basis of the dark-red color of the opened fruit.[93]

The bloodlike color and abundance of seeds may have played a part in the origins of the Persephone myth; yet it is doubtful whether we shall ever be able to trace this myth back to its remote beginning, particularly as it was a tragic myth and a secret legend underlying Mystery ceremonies. "Such are the Mysteries," says the Church Father Eusebios in this connection. "Summing up, we may say: murders and funeral rites!" [94] No Eleusinian representation of Persephone holding a pomegranate is known to us. Elsewhere, however, she appears with this attribute, identifying the goddess of the underworld.[95] Another Great Goddess, the archaic cult image of Athena Nike in her temple on the Athens Akropolis, held a pomegranate in her right hand, in her left a helmet: the simple explanation of this[96] is the somber Persephone-like aspect of the goddess, which, though not emphasized, least of all in classical Athens, was demonstrably present.[97] Polykleitos also put a pomegranate into the hand of his statue of Hera at Argos,[98] and Pausanias (II 17 4) remarks that he may not tell why the goddess bears a pomegranate: it is an *aporrhetoteros logos,* a story told under strict injunction of silence.[99] This same *logos* doubtless had currency in the great sanctuary of Hera at Paestum, where large numbers of terra-cotta pomegranates—votive offerings, no doubt—have been found near the temple, at the mouth of the Sele, dedicated to the subterranean aspect of the goddess.[100]

The prohibition against eating pomegranates or apples at certain feasts at Eleusis and in Athens was also based on a *mystikos logos,*[101] a secret holy legend. The most important of these festivals was, of course, the Mysteries themselves. Another was the Haloa, a winter festival for women, held in honor of Demeter, Kore, and Dionysos and characterized by abundant consumption of wine, obscene speeches, and the veneration of sexual symbols. At Eleusis the Haloa took on the character of a mystery rite.[102] Here the pomegranates seem to have been prohibited because of the somber memories they called to mind. At the Thesmophoria, another women's festival celebrated soon after the Great Mysteries, the pomegranate played a very different role. On this occasion merriment alternated with gloom, and it seems that the women ate nothing but pomegranate seeds, at least on one fast day.[103] They were forbidden to touch the seeds that fell to the ground. For this Clement of Alexandria offers the strange explanation that the pomegranate tree had sprung from the drops of Dionysos' blood.[104]

This tradition is to be found only in Christian authors,[105] and it is not easy to find a place for it among other statements about the death of Dionysos. The blood of the he-goat which replaced the god and was slaughtered in a somber sacrificial rite [106] was offered to the vine. But for the Greeks pomegranate and vine were so closely related—Pausanias, too, jumps straight to the vine from a description of the open pomegranate (IX 25 1)—that quite possibly the myth of the violent death of a divine being, from whose blood the first pomegranate tree sprang, was also related to Dionysos. Despite the law of silence, certain elements of the original myth are still discernible. The motif of the blood-colored fruit appears in Pausanias (ibid.), who relates that a pomegranate tree had sprouted from the grave of Menoikeus outside one of the gates of Thebes: Menoikeus had killed himself of his own free will to save the city. The tomb of the Theban brothers Eteokles and Polyneikes, who had killed each other and one of whom had likewise died for the city, was also represented with a pomegranate tree which had supposedly sprung from their blood. [107] Here we perceive the motif of a bloody death for the community as an element of the original myth. In Boeotia—and elsewhere—the pomegranate tree was called *side;* but Side was the name of the wife of Orion the hunter. For a reason that in our tradition is obscure or superficial, [108] she was dispatched to the underworld. Side was also the name of certain cities and the mythological women after whom they were named. [109] Here again we discern an element of the pomegranate myth and indeed the central meaning of this mythical tragedy. A woman had to go down to the underworld for the benefit of the community. A final element follows from the story of the virgin Side, who took her life on the grave of her mother because her father wished to seduce her: from her blood the earth caused the pomegranate tree to grow. [110] Here it is the father who replaces the subterranean god in the role of seducer.

Here we are very close to the tales of Hainuwele and Rabie, and still closer to the myth of Persephone. But do we know the sacred story of the disappearance of Persephone as it was told to the initiates at Eleusis or still earlier at Agrai? We know the epic account of the abduction by Hades or Plouton, and we know the Orphic tale of the Kore's seduction by her own father in the form of a snake. This variant is too plainly alluded to in the relief of Herakles being prepared for the Lesser Mysteries [13] to have been the secret version. Kept secret from the noninitiate was a tale in which, as in the fragments attesting the myth of the pomegranate, blood was shed—hymeneal blood—while the Kore was leaving this earth for the realm of the dead, the realm of the subterranean Dionysos, whence come all living creatures and their food. Concerning the identity of the seducer, certain hitherto little regarded details of the tradition have told us more than was formerly known. Clearly he is one with the wine god, and this would be evident even if Persephone's mysterious relation to the pomegranate had not brought us near him, into his atmosphere and upon his ground—the ground of vineyards and orchards.

The prohibition of pomegranates and apples corresponds to, and complements, the prohibition of wine at the Great Mysteries. Did the apple play a part in the seducer's courtship? Apart from five different kinds of fish, eggs and poultry are also mentioned as forbidden foods: [111] egg and rooster may also have been gifts of the Dionysian god of the underworld, who is often represented with them. Regardless of how much may still be lacking in our reconstruction of the Eleusinian holy legend of the seduction of Persephone, one thing rises above the mists of uncertainty: a divine triad which also presided over the Haloa, the merry women's mysteries held in December. Its members are Demeter, Kore, and Dionysos, who belong inseparably together. All three were present at the Dionysos festivals at Eleusis: choruses were held in their honor.[112] These are the gods who arrived in Rome together by way of Sicily and Magna Graecia and who for the Latin-speaking world formed the triad Ceres, Liber, and Libera.

The last day of the Great Mysteries at Eleusis was devoted to plenty in its liquid form. This was the day—we do not know whether it followed immediately after the Mystery Night—of the Plemochoai, the "pourings of plenty." So called, also, were the two unstable circular vases that were set up for this ceremony. The writer who is our source on this point[113] cites a line from a tragedy according to which the plemochoai were poured into a cleft in the earth, a *chthonion chasma*. Thus it seems likely that the Eleusinian rite took place in the Ploutonion. One vessel was set up on the east, the other on the west side, and both were overturned. The liquid with which they had been filled is not named. A "mystical formula" (*rhesis mystike*) was recited as the vessels were upset. A Christian author probably gives us this formula when he tells us that the "great and ineffable secret of the Eleusinian Mysteries" resided in the cry "*Hye kye!*"[114] Proklos the Neoplatonist, who lived too late to have witnessed the normal, traditional functioning of the Mysteries, also cites the cry with the remark that the officiant uttered the first word in a loud voice, looking heavenward, and the other looking toward the ground. He interprets them as invocations of the paternal and the maternal origins.[115] In any event *hye* must be translated as "Flow!" and *kye* should probably be translated as "Conceive." There was no need to name the god if the name Hyes was taken as referring to Zeus and perhaps not if it referred to Dionysos. This name was known in Attica,[116] though, very much like Brimo or Brimos, it was felt to be foreign. It probably designated the wine god as the lord of all life-giving liquids. To Zeus the Athenians cried, "*Hyson,*" the other imperative form of the same verb "to flow," bidding him at last to make the rain fall on fields and meadows.[117] This was not expected to happen before the plowing and sowing which took place immediately after the Mysteries.

The possibility that the cry *"Hye kye"* was a part of the Mysteries takes us to their periphery, and even this perhaps in a late state. We are brought close to their center and assuredly carried back to an early stratum of Eleusinian mythology by the Apulian vase paintings to which I have already twice referred (pp. 37, 131), representing plants on tombs encompassed in a small sanctuary, or *heroön*, where we usually find idealized statues of the dead. A poppy, perhaps a substitute for the mystic pomegranate, is not lacking among these epiphanies in plant form [40].[118] A male and a female worshiper approach it to perform the rites for the dead. On a higher level, figures in a transcendent, godlike state are visible. This cult at a grave, which was the scene of a divine epiphany in the form of a plant, was based on the myth to which we have been led over various paths: a mythical being dies, but though attended by pain and bloodshed, his death is only an apparent one. Ever since this mythical death, every death has been a prolongation of life in two dimensions, the one plantlike, the other divine. To achieve such immortality it was only necessary to *take* death—as this mythical being did—upon oneself. In the cult of the dead, it was supposed that all the dead had done so. It was believed that those who suffered the death of the mythical being in the form of a ceremony, a ritual imitation of the myth, and took it on themselves were sure to live on after death in the same way—a godlike and a plantlike way, between which no very sharp distinction seems to have been possible. The Dionysos religion had such a ceremony, an initiation which, like the Eleusinian Mysteries, can be reconstructed up to a certain point.[119] The imitation of a divine

40. *Aedicula with a poppy growing out of a tomb. Reverse of an Apulian vase in the Vatican*

being's suffering and death, whence benefits flow for ourselves and all men, is a feature common to more than one religion.

This is the usual tendency displayed in the stories about transformation into plants, which represent a non-Olympian and probably pre-Hellenic stratum of Greek mythology: first the human form and human suffering, then a plant form and a divine state without suffering and without death: the unindividualized form of *zoë*, of indestructible life. Dionysos and Persephone break with this tendency. They not only guarantee plant nourishment for men and the potion of plant origin with its ecstasy. Through them the plant form of *zoë* itself—and through Dionysos, the animal form also—appear endowed, as it were, with a godlike human face. An unusual terra-cotta statuette from the end of the classical period (or shortly thereafter) shows a pomegranate cut in two as the basis of an epiphany [41]. On a half of the fruit kneels a maiden in a short dress, tucked up around the waist. She holds her cloak as befits an epiphany: she discloses herself. Over her shoulder a little Eros looks out, raising the disclosure scene into the higher sphere where the disclosed ones are gods—such as Aphrodite. Or in the present case: Persephone re-appeared.

Duality

L E T   U S   S E E how the *imitatio dei vel deae,* the imitation of a deity, enacted in the *epopteia* of Eleusis, discloses the unique character of these Mysteries. Among all the direct or indirect, true or false testimonies there is not so much as a hint that anyone played the part of Persephone in the Telesterion at the climax of the Mysteries.[120] Going to the Telesterion was not like going to the theater. Those visiting the Telesterion had been specially prepared. In the theater the personae

41. *Terra-cotta statuette of a girl with Eros. She is kneeling on a half pomegranate. Amsterdam, Allard Pierson Museum*

appeared to the audience in masks, like spirits from the underworld.[121] Moreover, we have no indication that a mask was shown the initiates in the *epopteia*. They themselves were "personae" in their own drama, and if not masked, they were at the very least dressed as they had to be for the procession, hence in a sense disguised. They had entered into the role of the Goddess searching for her daughter; they were prepared in the same way as Demeter herself. The *imitatio* there enacted was an *imitatio Cereris*. Men and women alike appeared in the role of the Goddess [122] searching for her daughter, for a part of herself in her daughter.

The separation of Mother and Daughter, with all its anguish, may in itself be termed archetypal, characteristic of the destiny of women. If men take part in this destiny as though it were their own, the explanation must be sought on a level deeper than the divided existence of men and women: here only women, there only men! The separation of Mother and Daughter, the yearning of Demeter for her own girl-child, the Kore, must be characteristic of undivided human existence, of men as well as women, but in one way of men and in another of women. The assumption that the Eleusinian *epopteia* was originally—in a "matriarchal period"—exclusively a women's Mystery and that men had begun to participate in mere imitation of the women is false, because men's imitation of the questing Goddess led to the same *telos,* the same goal and fulfillment, as the women's *imitatio deae*—to the same *epopteia,* the *visio beatifica.* For men and women alike this was a true *visit,* a *visitatio,* for which the Greek word is *theoria,*[123] and the relationship of men and women to the person visited and beheld was the same.

Another difference between the *epopteia* and the *theama,* the vision obtained in the theater, was that the *epopteia* was closer to *theoria* in the original sense of the word:[124] closer to the visiting and beholding of divine images. It would indeed be almost that, a "visit of spectators," if the visitors had not specially prepared themselves and if, in this *imitatio,* they did not participate in a vision, which is something very different from looking at a statue. The objects of the original *theoriai,* which constituted one of the high points of Greek religion, were *agalmata,* statues of gods. The *theoriai* were thought to rejoice the gods represented, as well as men, and to confer a perfectly natural *visio beatifica:* the word *agalma* signifies as much.[125] The *agalmata* were created by artists, who were guided, inspired, and limited by a collective imagination along with their own: by an imagination that was characteristic of the Greeks and disciplined by a living tradition. That a statue was shown in the *epopteia* at Eleusis is no more attested, hinted at, or likely than that any person appeared in the role of Persephone. Statues played a part in the Egyptian mysteries, and this could not be kept secret.[126]

The *visio beatifica* of the *epopteia*, the epiphany of Kore, who—as the Hierophant proclaimed—had already given birth, continues the *imitatio deae* of all the mystai. It represents, in the souls of the initiates, the split which was necessary to the experience of finding-again in the *visitatio* to the Ineffable One. This was no intellectual experience of the obvious fact that every daughter is the disjoined continuation of her mother—this alone could scarcely have produced the beatific effect—but something visible which surpassed the artist's imagination in so far as hands were not needed to achieve it. A mystic, who was an artist but not a Greek, once wrote: "He who does not imagine in stronger and better lineaments, and in stronger and better light than his perishing and mortal eye can see, does not imagine at all." [127] The Eleusinian vision must have had a power which the philosophers were unwilling to recognize. It had, above all, a claim to truth, which was recognized by the souls of the *epoptai*. It did not negate the duality of the questing one and the found one. This duality—the scission of the Mother into "mother and daughter"—opened up a vision of the *feminine source of life*, of the common source of life for men and women alike, just as the ear of grain had opened up a vision into the "abyss of the seed." [128] The reason for this is probably that all human beings and not women alone bear this origin and this duality—that *is* both the Mother and the Daughter—within themselves and are therein the heirs of an endless line, not only of fathers but of mothers as well.

In all likelihood the duality of the Mystery goddess, of the inseparable Two Goddesses Demeter and Persephone who nevertheless separate and are reunited, is only seemingly at the beginning of the series of archetypal images which ring the changes on duality in the Eleusinian mythology. Before them there was probably a duality in Rhea, the Primordial Mother.[129] Even apart from the Mystery Night, these dualities surround Eleusis, the historical holy place, which we are able to reconstruct thanks to its monuments, with a strange, almost spectral atmosphere. The student of Eleusinian mythology must acquire a kind of double sight if he wishes to do justice to the entire tradition—the literary and the pictorial—with all their contradictory statements which were allowed to stand side by side.

The double vision I have in mind is not subjective: the two simultaneous visions have their Eleusinian counterpart in two mythological stages on which the same divine persons appear in different roles and sometimes even simultaneously. This is the case, above all, with Persephone, who appears as queen of the underworld and as the daughter of her mother, to whom she returns from the underworld. The author of the Hymn to Demeter is cognizant of the dual stage and dual role, although his Homeric attitude prevents him from acknowledging the simultaneity. "Go thou only," says Hades (360–66; cf. above, p. 44), "to thy mother . . . but when thou art *here* [in the underworld] thou wilt rule over all that lives and crawls on the earth! Thou wilt be honored above all the immortals. . . ." The Homeric poet uses the story of the division of time to bridge the gap between the two roles and two stages. In the cult of the queen of the dead, to whom the dying repair at all seasons, the underworld can scarcely have remained without a queen for two thirds or—according to a later version [130]—half of the year. Could the travelers to the underworld—Orpheus, Herakles, Theseus, and Peirithoös—have found the queen's throne empty? In the religion of Persephone such an idea was unthinkable. But the return of the goddess from the subterranean realm had assuredly been required, even by the older religion, according to which she—like Mother Rhea [131] or

Hekate [132]—had her share in the government of all three parts of the world, heaven, earth, and sea. Thus her person seems always to have admitted of a duplication.

An *anodos* of the goddess, a "return" from the underworld, is not mentioned in the Attic calendar in connection with any date relevant to the Eleusinian Mysteries. The return of a Kore is mentioned in connection with the Proschaireteria [133]—a feast of rejoicing as the name indicates—but this festival is probably no different from the Procharisteria.[134] The season of the festival and the name of the goddess to whom it was dedicated are known to us. The goddess was Athena, the "Kore of the Athenians," whose early form is perfectly compatible with the myth of an abduction and return.[135] The time was the end of winter, the period *preceding* (and perhaps this is the meaning of the prepositions in the names *pro-charisteria* and *pros-chaireteria*) the great "festival of flowering," the Anthesteria, held in February. To this same group of festivals belonged, finally, the Lesser Mysteries at Agrai. The god of the Anthesteria was Dionysos, who celebrated his marriage in Athens amid flowers, the opening of wine jars, and the rising up of the souls of the dead. Nothing has come down to us either of an *anodos* of Persephone at Eleusis or of a similar "festival of flowering," an Anthesteria, of the Eleusinians. We hear, however, of an *anodos* of Demeter in connection with the festival of the Stenia,[136] which was celebrated not only in Athens but also and far more magnificently, it would appear, at Eleusis. In Athens sacrifices were offered up on this occasion to Demeter and to the Kore.[137] At Eleusis the festival was preceded by a night celebration in which the Hierophant and the priestesses participated.[138] But it was chiefly a festival of women who mocked and reviled one another: [139] probably in order that the Kore's mother might return laughing. Demeter's journey *to* Hades *had to be followed by* such a *return*. In the calendar the Stenia, on the 7th of Pyanepsion, the month after Boë-dromion, was the last festival before the Thesmophoria, which in all likelihood also had to do with the mother's visit to her daughter in the underworld. At the Thesmophoria the women ate the pomegranate seeds.

The duplication of the figure of Persephone was necessary if immediately after her mother's visit, after the Eleusinians had celebrated the Mysteries for the first time, she was to be present at the sending out of Triptolemos. The *anodos* of Demeter, which according to the calendar took place the same autumn and was separately celebrated a short time later, was probably thought of as already past. In *one* of her roles, her daughter was still reigning in the underworld, in the house of Hades, where she gave birth to her son. In her other role, as the returning Kore, she was not expected before Anthesterion, or February, the "month of flowers." And yet in the pictures she is standing beside Demeter, blessing Triptolemos [35, 36, 38]. The story is told in the same simple way as in the Homeric Hymn to Demeter. But an artistic representation of the duplication was possible and permitted—though at first perhaps only within the sanctuary. On a clay tablet showing an idealized picture of the procession [15] (cf. pp. 63 f., 79),[140] the artist gives a pictorial hint of the simultaneous second stage on which Persephone is present. This votive offering dates from the turn of the fourth century B.C. At the bottom there is an inscription: "Niinnion has offered it to the Two Goddesses." The spelling of the name, meaning "little doll," shows that the donatrix was not an Athenian woman, while the name itself suggests that she was a hetaira. She is perhaps the white figure in the middle of the pediment, making a joyful gesture after the *epopteia*. Of the Two Goddesses in the main field of the tablet, only the one receives the arriving procession: Demeter, whose body is rendered in a bright color. The dark colors of Persephone, who sits enthroned in the background, suggest the invisible second stage. Who will occupy the empty throne in the foreground? The Mother, who is now sitting on her rock [15] [141] but who will cease to mourn once she has seen her daughter again? Or will Persephone sit or stand there beside her mother, in a twofold presence, in this world and the other at once?

The double presence of Persephone is represented in a marble votive relief [42]—"Lysimachides dedicated it"—of the fourth century B.C., to judge by the shapes of the letters. The two stages are indicated by two separate tables or altars, at each of which two divine figures have taken their places: neither pair is present for the other. Demeter with scepter, sitting on the great Mystery basket; beside her at the same table, Kore holding a double torch and crowning her mother with a diadem: these are the public figures as shown outside the Mysteries. They also include a nude standing boy who, with a small pitcher which he holds high, has taken wine from a large amphora—he is a Dionysian servant of the Goddesses—*after* the Mysteries. The deities at the second altar are named and yet not named: the recumbent god has the

42. *Votive relief of Lysimachides, found at Eleusis. Athens, National Museum*

features rather of the bearded Dionysos than of Plouton. In his right
hand, he raises not a cornucopia, symbol of wealth, but a wine vessel
with an animal's head, a rhyton; in his left, he bears the goblet for the
wine. Over his head stands the dedication ΘΕΩῖ, "To Theos," befitting
the mystery god (see p. 155). On his couch sits his wife, identified by
the dedication ΘΕΑΙ, "To Thea," and differing from the Kore both in her
features and in her headdress. Both female figures are assuredly Persephone, who showed her true face in the Mystery Night. Representations of this true face were not permitted, even in the sanctuary. But
the *two* faces shown side by side in the relief were also *her* faces.

In other reliefs all these figures are shown, without any differentia-
tion of stages, as present at the sending out of Triptolemos, and the
Dionysian boy or youth is even duplicated. Of great artistic value is the
multilated Attic marble of the middle of the fourth century B.C. [43]
found at Mondragone, not far from Naples. It may have stood in the
sanctuary of Eleusis [142] and been carried off to Italy by a Roman worshiper of the Mystery divinities. Here the whole Eleusinian pantheon is
present. In the left corner Triptolemos can be seen in his fantastic

43. *Eleusinian votive relief from Mondragone. Naples, Museo Nazionale*

44. *Fragments of Lakrateides' votive relief as assembled in the Eleusis Museum*

chariot. Opposite him sits Demeter on the Mystery basket; between the two stand two majestic figures, a duplicated Persephone: Kore with torches and Thea in the attitude ordinarily taken by Hera, queen of the gods.[143] The royal Theos sits enthroned between two standing youths. The one can be recognized as Iakchos by his huntsman's boots (he is thus attired as leader of the mystai in Niinnion's tablet [15]). Here, in addition, he wears an animal pelt round his loins in Dionysian fashion. The name of the second youth can be gleaned from the fragments of a third relief excavated at Eleusis and including a few lines of inscription [44]: he must be Eubouleus, who shared a priest with Theos and Thea.

In 97 B.C. this priest was Lakrateides of Ikaria,[144] son of Sostratos, who consecrated the relief in question for himself, his sons, and his daughter. He had himself represented in the background of the divine assembly; a flat feminine figure (barely discernible) at the left edge was presumably his daughter, and the boy prominently figured in front of her, holding a bundle of myrtle and pressed close to the goddess Demeter, was perhaps a son of his in the role, as it were, of the mystical Demophoön.[145] The grouping of the deities suggests two stages. One group consists of Demeter, Kore, and Triptolemos; the other of the more secret Mystery deities, including the king of the underworld duplicated as Plouton and Theos. Between the two enthroned gods stands Thea, and behind the throne of Theos a young god in a short chiton, with long curls and with a large torch in his left hand and a vine leaf near his right shoulder. Plouton is looking toward Kore. Thea, Theos, and Eubouleus, the young god, form a mystical triad whose cult was entrusted to Lakrateides—who is seen standing in the background.

It cannot be inferred from this testimony that Thea and Theos were looked upon at Eleusis as distinct from the queen of the underworld, who had always been worshiped there, and her lord and husband—as for Eubouleus, we shall have more to say at the end of this essay (pp. 169 ff.). But a significant inference can be drawn. Because, it seems, the mystical divine pair and their divine servant Eubouleus had taken on an importance to which the ancient cult of the Eumolpidai and of the other families that had held the Eleusinian priesthood was no longer adequate, a man from Ikaria, the oldest Dionysian locality in Attica, was commissioned to devote a special cult to them. In the fourth century B.C.—to which the votive relief of Lysimachides and that of Mondragone must be assigned—it was assuredly known that the mysteries of Samothrace and to a certain extent the Kabeirion near Thebes offered paths of initiation, if not to Persephone as at Eleusis, then at least to her husband. In the representations that have come down to us,[146] the mystery god of the Thracian island and of the Theban sanctuary bears features similar to those of Theos in the Lysimachides relief. To judge by the many vestiges of wine vessels, his Dionysian nature was freely expressed, even in the inner precincts of his cult. In the language of his Greek worshipers he was called Theos (see p. 152), and so also he was named in the Samothracian calendar,[147] although there was no obligation, or at least not everywhere, to conceal the more mystical name Kabeiros. With the great Kabeiros was associated a younger god who served him.[148] The Mysteries of Eleusis and Samothrace and the Theban cult of Kabeiros had certain elements in common. The most striking is the Dionysian character of the mystery god. Lakrateides officiated as priest of Theos, Thea, and Eubouleus, and perhaps of still other gods—there is a gap in the inscription at this point—whom the initiates of the Kabeirian mysteries were glad to meet again at Eleusis.

Kore and Thea are two different duplications of Persephone; Plouton and Theos are duplications of the subterranean Dionysos. Here we shall not speak of the duplication of the mystery god as subterranean father and subterranean son, as Father Zagreus and the child Zagreus,[149] husband and son of Persephone, for this duality has more to do with the mysteries of Dionysos than with the Eleusinian Mysteries. But a duplication of the chthonian, mystical Dionysos is provided even by his own youthful aspect, which became classical and which was distinguished in mythology as the son of Semele from the son of Persephone, the basis of this duplication being that Semele, though not of Eleusinian origin, is also a double of Persephone.[150] Among gods present at the Mystery festival itself it was Iakchos who came closest to the youthful figure of Dionysos. In the rite of the Athenian Lenaia, the

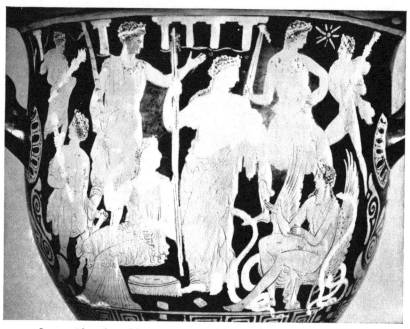

45. *Scene with gods and heroes in front of the Telesterion of Eleusis.
Obverse of an Attic vase from Santa Agata dei Goti (with transcript).
London, British Museum*

Eleusinian Dadouchos enjoined the throng: "Call the god!" Whereupon
they cried: "Semeleian Iakchos, giver of wealth!" [151] and the child
Dionysos was born up above on earth.[152] In the Mystery Night Dionysos
was present as Iakchos at his own subterranean birth—the Eleusinian
double perspective actually made this acceptable—a premature birth in
relation to his birth at the winter solstice when the Lenaia was celebrated in Athens and to the birth of Aion in the Alexandrian temple of
Kore, the new Eleusis (see p. 116). A premature birth was a familiar
element of the Dionysos religion; [153] it preceded the true birth. And, in
addition to Iakchos, Ploutos—the "bestower of wealth"—was also a
double of the child Dionysos.

156

B

This multiplicity of divine figures created by duplication of the
mystery gods was only in small part due to religious speculation. It
sprang far more from that spontaneous spiritual activity, closely related
to poetry and music, which the Greeks called *mythologia*.[154] The vase
painters made ample use of it and became great masters at it. It is a kind
of music, comparable to an opera, made with images and their variations. We perceive it, above all, in the so-called Kerch vases, whose
paintings diffused the Eleusinian religion in the Greek cities of southern
Russia and southern Italy. In one painting, which has already been
mentioned (p. 122) because it presented so striking a parallel to the
speech of the Dadouchos Kallias in Sparta (on one side of a calyx crater,
the so-called Pourtalès vase, found near Santa Agata dei Goti in southern Italy), we see Demeter, Persephone, and Triptolemos as a group
[45], the two Dioskouroi hurrying to receive initiation, and the two
youthful gods of the Eleusinian Mysteries: Iakchos, here again recog-

157

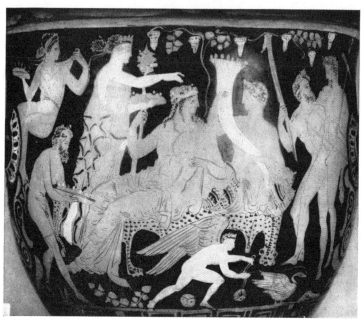

46. *Dionysos and Ploutos with other deities on the reverse of the vase in 45*

nizable by his huntsman's boots, leading by the hand one of the Dioskouroi—identified by his star—and Eubouleus. Eubouleus bears only one torch, as does Iakchos in this painting, but his dress is more like that of the Dadouchos on an Eleusinian vase [25] [155] and his sandals are more like the *kothornoi* worn by Dionysos and his servants, the actors. [156] At left, below, is Herakles. Dionysos is represented on the reverse of the crater [46]: he sits beneath hanging clusters of grapes on a couch covered with a panther skin, holding the *thyrsos* in his hand. A Silenos leads Hephaistos to his marriage with one of the Graces—we see two of them and that was their number in Athens. [157] One would think of no relation between the two paintings were it not that on this side Dionysos is shown reclining beside Ploutos—a big boy with a large cornucopia—his double, who reminds us of Eleusis. The fragments of a gilded jar cover of the Kerch type [47] show Dionysos, Demeter, little Ploutos, Kore, and a curly-haired boy clad in a long garment and bearing a scepter—one of the Eleusinian kings' sons, who were the first to be initiated. Dionysos holds his *thyrsos* and is accompanied by a panther. Herakles, hesitant and encouraged by Athena, approaches this group from one side. From the other the Dioskouroi come riding, between them the head of the torch-bearing Iakchos.

On the crater from Santa Agata dei Goti we see the pillars of the vestibule of the Telesterion in the background [45]. In the foreground Triptolemos sits enthroned, Demeter seems to hover above rather than sit on a low chair, Kore is standing, and the three heroes are seen arriving. The masters of this type of vase often placed the scene of the assemblies of Eleusinian gods at the site of the omphalos: it probably stood in the Ploutonion (see p. 80), and here Dionysos could quite

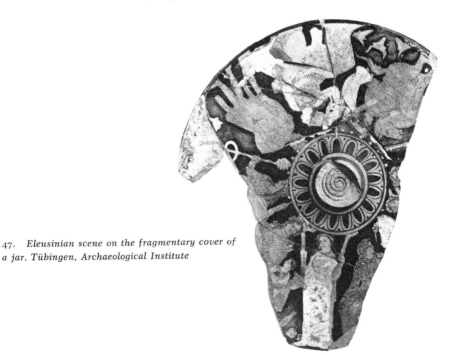

47. *Eleusinian scene on the fragmentary cover of a jar. Tübingen, Archaeological Institute*

legitimately be regarded as a double of the lord of the sanctuary. There are three hydriai—water jars—that bear such pictures. Thus we may assume that they were conceived for the Mystery season, but they may also have served as sepulchral gifts. On one [48], Dionysos himself sits swaying on the omphalos. Demeter, Kore, and a divine youth in huntsman's boots and bearing a scepter are turned toward him. The bull's skull, as elsewhere, shows that a sacrifice has been offered to the god.

48. *Gods around the omphalos of Eleusis, on an Attic hydria from Crete (with transcript). Athens, National Museum*

B

The three female figures framing the scene also have to do with Dionysos: on the one side, Ariadne, his bride; on the other, Semele, his mother, and somewhat higher Aphrodite, her presence pointing to a future divine marriage with which the sacred story will begin again. The neck of the jar is adorned with ears of grain. We find a similar picture on another jar, formerly called the Tyszkievicz vase, found in the church of Santa Maria at Capua Vetere [49].[158] Dionysos on his ompha-

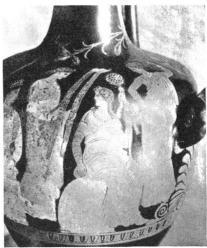

A

49. *Gods at the omphalos of Eleusis, on an Attic hydria from Santa Maria in Capua Vetere (with transcript). Lyons, Palais des Arts*

c

los, the *thyrsos* in his left hand, and Demeter, sitting opposite him, look at one another severely. The Kore moves from Demeter toward Dionysos as though to reconcile the two. Behind Demeter stands the divine youth with scepter and long garment. The frame figure beside Dionysos is probably Semele; on the other side of the frame we see a Dionysian woman with her round instrument, a *tympanon,* which reminded all the initiates of the *echeion* of the Mystery Night (see pp. 84, 94).

The most grandiose composition known to us adorns both sides of a wine vessel, a pelike from Kerch [50] [159] (we have already referred to it on page 31). On one side Demeter sits enthroned. Before her stands the boy Ploutos; to her left, Kore; to her right—somewhat more in the background—Eubouleus bearing two torches. His garment is half length, like that of the Dadouchos; his feet are shod with *kothornoi.* High overhead hovers Triptolemos in his chariot. Herakles comes in from Demeter's right, bearing his club and a bundle of myrtle; Dionysos is sitting on Demeter's left with the *thyrsos,* his left foot resting on his mother's back. For the figure crouching on the omphalos, who gives him this support, can be only Semele. Her pendant is Aphrodite, with the winged Eros at her feet: again an indication of a divine marriage. On the other side of the vase, Hermes takes possession of the divine child who is hidden and protected by Athena's shield. The great round instrument, the *tympanon,* in the hand of the seated Dionysian woman who is present, brings home to the initiates the identity of the child whose subterranean birth is proclaimed in the Mystery Night. Now it is the child Dionysos, wrapped in an animal pelt. It is thus that the goddess of the earth, Ge, wreathed with flowers, takes him from a cave and hands him to the messenger of the gods. Zeus, who is going to nurture the seven-month baby to maturity in his thigh, awaits it on his throne.

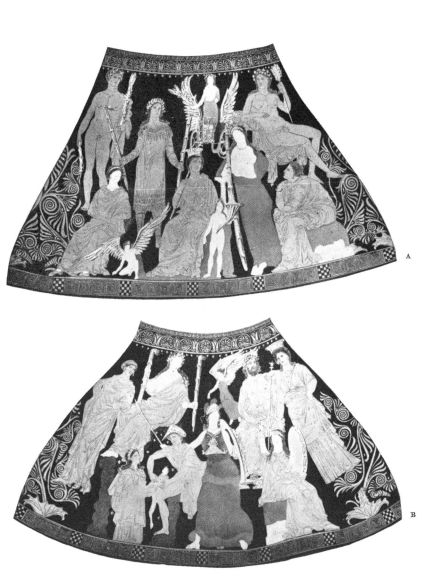

A

B

50. *Eleusinian scenes on a pelike from Kerch. Leningrad, Hermitage Museum. Transcripts by* K. Reichhold

51. *Eleusinian scene on an Attic hydria from Rhodes (with transcript). Istanbul, Archaeological Museums, Museum of Classical Antiquities*

A

Beside him stands Hera, for from this point on the great event has the consent of all the gods. The little winged Nike belongs, as usual, to Athena, who guards and to some extent also hides the taking-over of the divine child. Kore, also, with two torches, is present up here in the heavenly sphere; she sets her foot on a rock that frames the epiphany of Ge with the child. What happens below her happens in the realm over which she rules. Against her daughter's knee leans Demeter, who had consented to the marriage of the lord of the underworld with no lighter heart than Hera to the birth of Semele's son.[160]

On the vases proclaiming the Eleusinian religion, the non-Eleusinian mythology becomes a colorful, thinly woven veil through which in every case shines the holy event of the Mystery Night. The episodes shown on these vases are not dry theological allegories but

B

almost endless variations on a single theme. On a hydria from Rhodes
[51], now in Istanbul, the goddess of the earth emerges from the ground
and holds out the child Ploutos in a cornucopia to Demeter. The curly-
headed divine youth bearing two torches and clad in a half-length
garment and huntsman's boots leaps by: he is more probably Eubouleus
than Iakchos, but it is possible that the artist did not wish to distinguish
the two. From one side, Kore looks back on the event in amazement. The
other witness, more concealed by her cloak, is no doubt Semele. Higher
up, Triptolemos sits enthroned in the middle of the group; a young god
mounts the couch of love, upon which sits a divine maiden who awaits
encouragement from Aphrodite on the other side. Here again Aphrodite's presence announces the recurring divine marriage and a new
beginning of the holy story which leads each year to the Mystery rite.

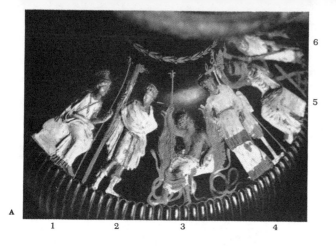

A   1   2   3   4   5   6

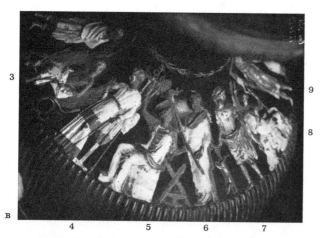

B   4   5   6   7   8   9

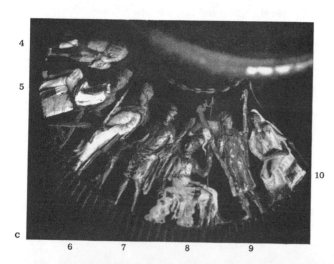

C   4   5   6   7   8   9   10

52. *The deities of Eleusis in painted relief on a hydria from Cumae (details). Leningrad, Hermitage Museum. For identifications of the numbered figures, see 53*

53. *Transcript of the scene in 52: 1, Hera; 2, Iakchos (with one torch); 3, Triptolemos; 4, Dionysos; 5, Demeter; 6, Kore; 7, Herakles; 8, Athena; 9, Eubouleus (with two torches); 10, Semele*

This erotic atmosphere is absent from two other vessels. One is re-minded of an assembly of the Olympian gods by the scene on a hydria of the fourth century B.C. from Cumae, now in Leningrad [52, 53],[161] for the vase is adorned in colored relief with figures of the ten Eleusin-ian deities. On an oil jug of the early fourth century B.C. [54], clusters of grapes surround a god, as though the *thyrsos* in his hand was not sufficient identification. On one side the presence of Athena bears witness to the great importance for the city of Athens of this divine triad—Dionysos, Demeter, Kore—and the happenings in which they were involved. The frame figures on the other side are Eleusinian, a

54. *Eleusinian deities on a lekythos from Kerch with figures in relief (with transcript). Paris, Louvre*

hovering Triptolemos, bearing ears of grain, and a nude or half-nude divine boy, apparently an Eleusinian king's son. He bears a bundle of myrtle, his eyes are closed, and he is leaning against a rock. Before him we see a candelabrum of a kind used in tombs. Behind the rock grows a laurel tree. This picture, more than any other, reveals a dimension apart from what can be seen with open eyes. Oil jugs like this one found at Kerch were used in the cult of the dead. The plant most often enclosed in the tombs of Kerch was the laurel.[162] The boy hovers, but not over the earth like Triptolemos; he is musing before his subterranean journey to Persephone.

Eubouleus

ONCE UPON a time the path to the underworld was opened. Persephone was the first who took this path into the darkness as booty and bride of the subterranean god with whom she celebrated her marriage as marriages are celebrated here on earth and to whom she bore a child as women bear children here above. Since *then* the world has been what it is for us mortals: full of plant food and full of hope—of hope because the way she first traveled has led to her ever since. This hope would not have had such great religious value for those who cherished it if they had not, already here on the earth, attained certainty of the goddess's existence, certainty conferred by the beatific vision they had of her. In addition, they possessed a myth to which the experience of the Mystery Night gave a particular credibility. It was a sacred tale that has not come down to us. We do not know what part Eubouleus played in it. This figure was represented not only by the vase painters but also by the sculptor Praxiteles. For centuries there was only a headless herma, all that remained of a copy of the original, to show that this sculpture had ever existed.[163] Later the fragmentary bust of the god, the head with thick curly hair, was unearthed in the sanctuary of Plouton at Eleusis.[164]

According to the Homeric Hymn to Demeter, it was Zeus who gave his daughter to the lord of the underworld (3), and it was *dios boulesi*, "according to the counsels of Zeus," that the Great Goddess Earth helped the ravisher (9). *Boule* means "counsel" (also in the sense of taking counsel with oneself), "decision," "will." *Boule* was needed to lure Persephone into a marriage which was so like death that all dying began with it, though through it life lost none of its radiance but, on the contrary, was enriched. It was held to be the consequence of a divine plan, a *boule*, that everything had come to pass as the divine tale related. To impute the plan to Zeus was in keeping with the Homeric style of the hymn. For he, the heavenly king of the gods, was in possession of the supreme, the divine *boule* (Iliad I 5). He presided over the councils, the *boulai*, of men, and in this quality was given the epithet *boulaios*.

Different from this name and distinguished from it in the language of the cult was the epithet *bouleus*. Zeus Bouleus is mentioned in connection with Demeter and Kore.[165] On Mykonos, while a gravid sow and a boar were sacrificed to the Two Goddesses on the 10th of Lenaion, season of Dionysos' winter birthday, a young pig was offered up to Bouleus. On other islands of the Aegean Sea,[166] Zeus Eubouleus, the "well-counseled Zeus," was mentioned in the same connection, and the reference was never to the god of heaven but always to the subterranean Zeus. It is expressly stated [167] that Plouton is Eubouleus. The name Bouleus or Eubouleus relates exclusively to the *boule* by which Persephone was the first led into the underworld and the path she was first to travel was opened. It was a *boule*—a plan and decision—not of heaven but of the dark god himself, who by this marriage gave life on earth its fixed order.

Of all the gods who appear in the late book of hymns that was attributed to Orpheus, Eubouleus is the most mysterious. Indeed, it is questionable whether the author of the hymns knew exactly who he was. He calls him "polymorphous" (29 8) and equates him with the mystical child Dionysos, the son of Persephone and of her father, Zeus (30 6);

and possibly also—if a suggested emendation to the text is correct [168]—with Adonis. The hymn distinguishes Eubouleus from Euboulos, a name which, in addition to Ploutos, was given to the son of Demeter and Iasion,[169] and hence in one of the hymns to Plouton himself (18 12). In Athens there was a heroine named Euboule, one of the three daughters of Leos, who sacrificed his daughters to save the polis:[170] thus the feminine form of the name was connected with a sacrificial death similar to that of Persephone, though only for the one city of Athens and not for the whole of mankind.

According to the version of the story of the rape of Persephone in which there were no kings of Eleusis but only a crude primordial man and his uncouth wife, Dysaules and Baubo, the couple had children. In other versions these children became kings' sons.[171] Where there were three sons, one, Triptolemos, was said to have been a cowherd; the second, Eumolpos, a shepherd; and the third, Eubouleus, a swineherd. The core of the story, however, seems to have been simply—for this version is also recorded by itself [172]—that Eubouleus was guarding his pigs when the earth was cleft asunder and the path to the underworld opened. The pigs disappeared into the chasm together with the goddesses—originally no doubt with only one goddess, Persephone. That is why "the sacred son of Dysaules"—as the Orphic hymn calls him (41 6)—was later able to serve as Demeter's guide. This again is not the Eleusinian holy tale. However, there is something more of Eubouleus in the tale than his mere name: he had to do with the path leading to the underworld. Was not the hero whose name embodies "good counsel," *euboulia,* something *more* than one who showed the way after Persephone had been abducted by *another*?

These attempts at a reconstruction would remain very fragmentary were we not, in conclusion, to look attentively into the face of the god

55. *Head of Eubouleus from the Eleusis Ploutonion. Fragment of a marble statue,* IV *century* B.C., *perhaps by Praxiteles. Athens, National Museum*

Eubouleus [55]. The Lord of the Underworld bore this name in the youthful form represented in the statue, ascribed to Praxiteles, which is now in the National Museum at Athens and probably stood originally in the place where it was found, the Ploutonion. This youth is Plouton himself—radiant but disclosing a strange inner darkness—and at the same time his double and servant, comparable to the Hermes or Pais beside Kabeiros or Theos. In the vase paintings Eubouleus appeared in the role of the Dadouchos, sometimes even with his two torches [50a], wearing his garment with slight changes in order not to profane it in pictures destined for the public. Or—in religious terms—it was the Dadouchos who represented him in the procession and the entry into the Telesterion. The Dadouchoi themselves traced the family of the Kerykes, to which they belonged, back to Hermes, whom they looked upon as their ancestor.[173] But neither the attitude nor the solemnity of the likenesses recalls the classical messenger of the gods. The plentiful hair or long curls suggest rather *Hades kyanochaites*,[174] Hades of the dark hair.

   In relation to the world of living men, Demeter, Kore, and Dionysos formed a divine triad. In the *mystical* triad of the underworld deities, the third person, after Persephone and her husband, was Eubouleus. These three are mentioned not only in Eleusinian inscriptions [175] but also on gold leaves found in tombs of the fourth and third centuries B.C. near the Greek city of Sybaris in southern Italy and in one case in Rome. The texts on these leaves represented greetings addressed to the queen and king of the dead—here the king bears the name of Eukles or Euklos—and to Eubouleus.[176] In Magna Graecia no Mystery secret veiled the activity of the third figure, the second underworld god of the gold leaves. Votive offerings in the form of fine classical terra-cotta reliefs found at the temple of Persephone in another Greek city, the nearby Epizephyrian Locri, represent a scene such as we do not encounter at Eleusis: a strange and puzzling variation of the abduction of Persephone, which no mythological tradition seems to account for.[177] The bearded god of the underworld is already present, but the Divine Maiden is carried away, for his benefit, by another, younger god, who lifts her into the chariot and drives her to the marriage [56].[178]

56. *The rape of Persephone. Fragments of a terra-cotta votive tablet from Locri. Reggio Calabria, Museo Archaeologico*

This no doubt was the secret service of Eubouleus, a service of "good counsel" for the perfection of the world, performed in order that men might die more confidently after having lived better. For this he provided the first condition. But the second condition was that men should also *know* about the happy marriage of the ravished Maiden—the prototype of all marriages. This knowledge was communicated to them by the beatific vision of the Kore at Eleusis—vision of the innermost "divine maiden" of men and women.

APPENDIXES

APPENDIX I

The Preparation and Effect of the *Kykeon*

T H E σύνθημα, the password indicating that one was *prepared* to receive the initiation in the Telesterion of Eleusis, began: ἐνήστευσα, ἔπιον τὸν κυκεῶνα,[1] in the Latin translation of Arnobius: *ieiunavi atque ebibi cyceonem*[2] ("I have fasted, I have drunk the *kykeon*"). The sacred text underlying these two conditions for receiving[3] the Mysteries is to be found in the Homeric Hymn to Demeter (200–1, 208–11). This proves the relevance of the hymn for Eleusis. Concerning fasting, the first condition, which already in the hymn is closely bound up with the second, it need only be said here that we have no testimony suggesting that the fast should not be taken seriously. To judge by the Homeric hymn (47–50), it must have been a strict fast extending over a period of nine days.

The word κυκεών means only a mixed and, if necessary, stirred drink. The mixture which Demeter herself asked to have prepared, in order that the initiands should drink it according to her example before receiving the supreme gift of the Mysteries, is described in the hymn (208–9): ἄνωγε δ' ἄρ' ἄλφι καὶ ὕδωρ δοῦναι μίξασαν πιέμεν γλήχωνι τερείνηι· The Goddess requested a drink of barley groats and water, mixed with tender γλήχων· The ingredients must have been known in the household of Queen Metaneira, and at least the barley groats must have been present. If anything was not present—or not present in the state required for the potion—it could easily be obtained through the power of the Goddess. This must not be forgotten if we wish to take account of a further indication concerning the ingredients of the *kykeon:* and we must take account of it, for we have so few indications, and this completion of the recipe contained in the Homeric hymn is so natural.

Ovid mentions only one ingredient of the potion which the Goddess drinks in the course of her search for her daughter in Sicily. He does not name the potion, but says that it tasted sweet:

> dulce dedit, tosta quod texerat ante polenta
> (*she gave her a sweet potion, which she had previously mixed with roasted groats*) [4]

(the subject of the sentence is an old woman, the double of Baubo and of Demeter herself). Ovid's addition to the Homeric recipe is contained in the word *tosta*. *Tosta polenta* means *roasted* barley groats. Obviously this addition springs from a Greek source, for among the Greeks barley was roasted before being crushed into groats: *Graeci perfusum aqua hordeum siccant nocte una ac postero frigunt, deinde molis frangunt.* ("The Greeks dry for one night the barley that has been soaked in water; afterward they roast it, and then they crush it between stones.") [5] In accordance with a law of Solon, the φρύγετρον, the vessel for roasting barley, was carried by the bride in the nuptial procession as a symbol of the housewife's duties (Pollux I 246). Roasted barley in water produces malt and a drink which may taste sweet without the addition of any sweetening whatever and become alcoholic after short fermentation.[6] The Goddess had no need to wait for fermentation before *her kykeon* became alcoholic. We have testimony to the effect that the *kykeon* was—illicitly—drunk in Athens on the day before the procession to Eleusis (see p. 62), and we also know the form of the characteristic vessels in which the beverage was carried in the procession.[7] It can be inferred from Arnobius' word *ebibi* ("I drank out," "I drank the whole potion") that a definite dose had to be taken. The dose in that case would have been the exact quantity contained in the small pots carried in the hands of the men in the procession [10].

This inference is not absolutely necessary. I should like to cite the opinion of a pharmacologist: "It is well known that visionary states can be induced by hunger alone. . . . The content of the visions, as experiments on visionary states induced by chemicals, that is, drugs, have shown, is largely or perhaps entirely determined by expectations, spiritual preparation, initial psychic situation, and by the surroundings. It is conceivable that in this case fasting alone had, to use Huxley's term, opened the 'doors of perception.' The content of the vision, the images, was then determined by expectations, ritual, and symbols. In such a state even a slight dose of alcohol may have sufficed to provide the initial thrust. . . ." [8]

The pharmacological question, which cannot yet be answered, relates to the effect of the third ingredient after roasted barley water, namely, the γλήχων or βλήχων, *Mentha pulegium*. The mention of its "tender," that is, fresh, leaves [9] is surely not without importance. While awaiting a more precise identification of the species, we know that we are dealing with some variety of pennyroyal. From the dried leaves of this plant the people of Central Europe make a light soothing drink, "peppermint tea"; from the green leaves the North Africans make a tea which "is taken as a mild stimulant." [10] "The principal ingredient of the poley oil (*Oleum pulegii*), prepared as an aromatic in southern Europe and obtained by distilling the wild plant, is the aromatic substance pulegone. . . . In large doses it induces delirium, loss of consciousness, and spasms." [11] In passing we might mention a plant of the same family found in the Sierra Mazateca (Mexico), namely, *Salvia divinorum*, for which Albert Hofmann more correctly suggests the name *Salvia divinatorum* as a translation of "Salvia of the diviners," and which has the effect of a *phantasticum*.

From the name βλήχων or γλήχων, to which the adjective βληχρός is related, one more readily infers a carminative, or antispasmodic, which, however, is not far removed from a narcotic. The lingering illness of Perikles after he was infected with the plague was termed βληχρός.[12] But Pindar also uses the word in connection with the rivers of the underworld, from which flows the darkness of night: βληχροὶ δνοφερᾶς νύκτος ποταμοί ("the slow rivers of dark night"),[13] and it is also applied to the gift of sleep: ὕπνου βληχρὸν ὄνειαρ ("the sluggish gift of sleep").[14] In Aristophanes' *Pax* (712), Hermes recommends κυκεὼν βληχωνίας, *kykeon* with mint, to Trygaios, who is to take Opora, "abundance of fruits," as his wife, but fears that such a bride will make him ill. Is the mixture intended to soothe his stomach? According to a famous anecdote, which may be historical, the Ephesians were in rebellion and asked the philosopher Herakleitos for advice. He said *not a word*, took a cup of cold water, sprinkled barley into it, stirred it with a branch of *Mentha pulegium*, and drank it down.[15] This was a symbolic action. Hipponax, an unruly spirit, asks for a whole bushel (μεδίμνον) of barley, from which to make *kykeon* to combat his πονηρίη, his "disease," which is surely not to be taken in a physical sense.[16]

It is possible that the *kykeon* at Eleusis conferred not only the "initial thrust" but also the necessary *inner peace* and perhaps still other prerequisites of the vision. Dr. Hofmann's words are: "The volatile oils contained in poley oil (*Oleum pulegii*) might very well, added to the alcoholic content of the *kykeon*, have produced hallucinations in persons whose sensibility was heightened by fasting."

Poppy capsules, from which opium was extracted, are often represented on Eleusinian monuments [12a, 21a]. I shall discuss the problem of the use of opium in connection with a late Minoan cult of a Demeter-like goddess in my forthcoming book on Dionysos.

APPENDIX II

Concerning the Vessels That Were Carried on the Head in the Procession

T H E K Y K E O N had not only a mythical prototype in sacred history for its preparation but also a vessel in which this beverage was made ready and from which it was drunk for the first time. The vessel, to be sure, does not appear in the Homeric version of the foundation myth, but in that other, "Orphic" version in which not Iambe but Baubo made the goddess smile (see p. 40). It *may*, however, have originally been mentioned in the Homeric Hymn to Demeter. The Homeric hymn reveals a lacuna in the place of the line where this mention may have occurred.[1] After the goddess smiles, the "Orphic" hymn has the line:

δέξατο δ'αἰόλον ἄγγος, ἐν ὧι κυκεὼν ἐνέκειτο

("she received the glittering vessel which contained the *kykeon*").[2]

The word αἰόλον, "glittering," is Homeric, for example, as an epithet applying to a shield[3] or to a complete suit of brass armor.[4] According to the scholiasts it means something that makes a restless, "motley," and mobile (ποικίλον) impression.[5] Thus it *is* possible that "Orpheus" took it over from the Homeric hymn and that the lacuna in the Homeric hymn should be filled in as follows:

211 δεξαμένη δ' ὁσίης εἵνεκεν πολυπότνια Δηώ.

211a ἔκπιεν αἰόλον ἄγγος ἐν ὧι κυκεὼ ἐνέκειτο.

"Orpheus" in any case bears witness to the existence of a special vessel which—in view of the word αἰόλον—we must conceive as made of metal in accordance with the art of toreutics. This impression is conveyed by the representation of the vessel on the Eleusinian metopes in Athens [21a][6] and on the Mystery baskets on the caryatids of the Lesser

Propylaia [23]. In regard to the vessel for the *kykeon* these representations have the value of documents, as do Athenian coins of the type reproduced below [57], dating from the beginning of the third century B.C.[7]

How such vessels as that represented beside the owl on the coin, their lids carefully attached with string or tapes, were carried by the women on their heads is shown in Niinnion's tablet [58].

Examples used as votive offerings and found in the sanctuary of Eleusis or in the Eleusinion of Athens show at several points the holes by which they were attached [59].

They were not always made of metal. Most of those whose fragments have been preserved are of pottery. But bronze versions also have been found. An imitation in pottery of a metalwork model is shown, for example, by the specimen illustrated [60].

The only possible implication of this type of vessel is that *kykeon,* intended for drinking, was actually carried in the procession. Where there are holes in the lid [61], one might suppose that fire was carried in such vessels, that they were so-called *thymiateria,* "vessels for smoke offerings."[8] In regard to vessels of the type that I mentioned first as particularly characteristic for Eleusis [21a, 23c], this is impossible, because myrtle branches were inserted in the handles, as can be seen on Niinnion's tablet [58] and on coins [57]. Branches—or ears of grain[9] —would have gone up in flames if the vessels had contained fire. Traces of gilt have also been mentioned on the votive offerings.[10] I have seen such traces on a marble imitation of this type of vessel in

57

58

59

the museum of Eleusis. As might be expected, the votive offerings made of gold were all lost in late antiquity.

Two lists of valuable objects for which the treasure custodians of Eleusis [11] had to give a reckoning mention χρυσοῖ κέρχνοι, which were kept in the Eleusinion of Athens.[12] The term κέρχνος can be related to the type of vessel we have just been discussing: first and foremost because of the material (gold), but also probably on the basis of the way the metal was wrought. κερχνωτά [13] was the term used for decoration hammered in relief on the lips of drinking cups, which are known by various names: τετορνευμένα ἐπὶ τοῦ χείλους τῶν ποτηρίων, ὥσπερ κερχνώδη, ποικίλα, τράχεια, πολύπλαστα,[14] and κερχνώματα, and even κυκλώματα.[15] κερχνωτά is also a name for the ornament around the edges of shields and goblets, ὁ περὶ τὰς ἴτυς τῶν ἀσπίδων κόσμος, καὶ ποτηρίων ἐπιχείλων. All this points clearly to the art of toreutics, employed in the making of drinking vessels—or of shields. This technique follows from the use of metal, which—if my identification of the word is correct [16]— must have been the material from which this type of vessel was originally made.

κέρνος is a word applied to another type of vessel associated with the Mystery Night at Eleusis. This type—or, rather, a combination of the two types κέρχνος and κέρνος —as well as a further combination with ἐσχαρίδες, "small hearths," was carried by the women on their heads in the procession. We have a description of the κέρνος and its contents by Polemon, a highly learned author of the second century B.C.: "After the preliminaries [the priest] proceeds to the celebration of the mystic rites (τελετή); he takes out the contents of the shrine

60   61

(Θαλάμη) and distributes them to all who have brought round their tray (τὸ κέρνος περιενηνόχοτες). The latter is an earthenware vessel, holding within it a large number of small cups (κοτυλίσκοι) cemented together; in them are sage, white poppy-seeds, grains of wheat and barley, peas, vetches, okra-seeds, lentils, beans, rice-wheat, oats, compressed fruit, honey, oil, wine, milk, egg, and unwashed wool.[17] The man who carries it, resembling the bearer of the sacred winnowing fan, tastes these articles."[18]

That the mystic rites here described cannot be the Mysteries of Eleusis is shown by both the beginning and the end of the quotation. The goddess Rhea possessed sacred Θαλάμαι[19] and one of *her* sacred servants is expressly called κερνοφόρος:[20] κερνοφόρος ζάκορος βωμίστρια ʻΡείης.

In explaining the word κερνοφόρος, a scholiast [21] speaks of κρατῆρες, vessels for mixing wine, which would have been unthinkable at Eleusis, but also of λύχνοι, "lights," which were quite possible at Eleusis: κερνοφόρος· ἡ τοὺς μυστικοὺς κρατῆρας φέρουσα ἱέρεια· κέρνους γάρ φασι τοὺς μυστικοὺς κρατῆρας, ἐφ᾽ ὧν λύχνους τιθέασι. A dance in which such a vessel was carried on the head is also mentioned (Pollux IV 103): τὸ γὰρ κερνοφόρον ὄρχημα οἶδα ὅτι λύχνα [22] ἢ ἐσχαρίδας ἔφερον—"In regard to the dance in which *kerna* were carried, I know that they carried lights or small hearths on their heads." The name of the vessel is repeated, this time in the neuter plural: κέρνα δὲ ταῦτα ἐκαλεῖτο. In the mysteries of Rhea and her lover Attis the carrying of the κέρνα was actually so important that it was taken over into the σύμβολα, the signs of recognition employed by the devotees of this religion. The mystes identified himself as an

62   63A   63B

initiate by performing various sacred actions and by declaring that
he had carried the *kerna:* ἐκερνοφόρησα.[23]

The presence at Eleusis of vessels with κοτυλίσκοι, that is, small
bowls [62], proves the influence of a cult of Rhea—or the original
kinship between the two cults. The small bowls can be grouped around
the vessel containing the *kykeon.* Wine was not permitted to be
present, and they *could not* contain fire, because they were closed, but
at the most λύχνα, "candles," on both sides. But the κοτυλίσκοι could
also be only apparent bowls [63a, 63b], so shallow [24] that they assuredly
contained none of all the things that Polemon listed. In the Mysteries
of Eleusis these bowls were not *eaten* out of! They were vestiges from
the cult of Rhea.

Another type consists of those vessels at Eleusis which can be
recognized as ἐσχαρίδες, "small hearths," but scarcely as θυμιατήρια, "vessels for smoke offerings." They were intended to carry fire—light in the
Mystery Night—and for that reason are provided with holes all
around [64].[25]

Pseudokotyliskoi [65] also could accompany such fire containers,
which served no other purpose than to be carried on the head in the
procession or in dances.[26] For it is perfectly possible that the women
initiates at Eleusis, with vessels of this type on their heads, performed
a dance in the course of which the fire—covered over with ashes—was
fanned into flames. The traces of fire and ashes that have been found
in such vessels and on fragments of such vessels [27] can, of course, be
attributed to the big fire which destroyed the sanctuary at the end of

64

65

antiquity. But the κερνοφόρον ὄρχημα, in connection with which the ἐσχαρίδες are mentioned, can in any case be claimed for the Eleusinian Mystery festival. This dance is not attributed to the cult of Rhea. The round of dancing women with lights on their heads and their reflection in the sea while the stars seemed to dance in accompaniment must have been an amazing spectacle. The choral chant in Euripides' *Ion* may be an allusion to this dance (see p. 9).

NOTES | LIST OF WORKS CITED

ABBREVIATIONS

These are used in the notes and in the List of Works Cited. Shortened titles readily identified in the List of Works Cited are not included.

AM   *Athenische Mitteilungen* (*Mitteilungen des [Kaiserlich] Deutschen archäologischen Instituts*, Athenische Abteilung). Berlin (before 1942, chiefly Athens).

Anecd. Bekk.   *Anecdota graeca.* Edited by Immanuel Bekker. Berlin, 1814–21. 3 vols. (I.)

Anth. lyr.   *Anthologia lyrica graeca.* Edited by Ernst Diehl. (T.) 3rd edn., Leipzig, 1950–54. 3 vols.

Anth. Pal.   *Anthologia Palatina.* Both Greek and English in: *The Greek Anthology.* Translated by W. R. Paton. (LCL.) Cambridge, Mass., London, 1946–53. 5 vols. (III, IV.)

ArchEph   *Archaiologike ephemeris: ekdidomene hypo tes en Athenais Archaiologikes Hetairias* (successor to *EphArch*, q.v.). Athens.

ArchRW   *Archiv für Religionswissenschaft.* Freiburg im Breisgau.

CIL   *Corpus inscriptionum latinarum.* Consilio et auctoritate Academiae Litterarum Regiae Borussicae editum. Berlin, 1863 ff. 15 vols. (III, VI: 5.)

CSEL   Corpus scriptorum ecclesiasticorum latinorum.

DarSag   CHARLES DAREMBERG and EDMUND SAGLIO (eds.). *Dictionnaire des antiquités grecques et romaines.* Paris, 1873–1919. 5 vols. in 10 parts.

EJ   *Eranos Jahrbuch.* Zurich.

EphArch   *Ephemeris archaiologike.* . . . Athens (irregularly 1837–74, 1883–1909; followed by *ArchEph*, q.v.).

FGrHist   Felix Jacoby. *Die Fragmente der griechischen Historiker.* Berlin and Leiden, 1923–59. 3 vols. in 11 parts.

GCS   Die griechischen christlichen Schriftsteller der ersten Jahrhunderte.

Glotta *Glotta: Zeitschrift für griechische und lateinische Sprache.* Göttingen.

Hermes *Hermes: Zeitschrift für klassische Philologie.* Berlin.

IG *Inscriptiones graecae.*

JDAI *Jahrbuch des Deutschen archäologischen Instituts.* Berlin.

LCL Loeb Classical Library. London and Cambridge, Mass. (earlier New York).

MIGNE, *PL* and *PG* J. P. MIGNE (ed.). *Patrologiae cursus completus.*
   PL Latin Series. Paris, 1844–64. 221 vols.
   PG Greek Series. Paris, 1857–66. 166 vols.

Mnemosyne *Mnemosyne: Bibliotheca classica Batava.* Leiden.

NS *Notizie degli scavi di antichità comunicate alla Accademia Nazionale dei Lincei.* Rome.

Orph. fr. Orphic fragments; especially *Orphicorum fragmenta.* Edited by Otto Kern. Berlin, 1922.

Paideuma *Paideuma: Mitteilungen zur Kulturkunde.* Frankfurt am Main.

POxy *The Oxyrhynchus Papyri.* Edited with translations and notes. . . . (Egypt Exploration Fund. Graeco-Roman [Memoirs].) London, 1898–1963. 29 parts. (XI, XIII.)

RE AUGUST PAULY and GEORGE WISSOWA (eds.). *Real-Encyclopädie der classischen Altertumswissenschaft.* Stuttgart, 1894 ff.

RHR *Revue de l'histoire des religions.* Paris.

SymbO *Symbolae Osloenses.* (Societas graeco-latina; Klassisk forening.) Oslo.

T Bibliotheca Teubneriana, and Bibliotheca scriptorum graecorum et romanorum Teubneriana.

TGF *Tragicorum graecorum fragmenta.* Recension by August Nauck. Leipzig, 1856. 2nd edn., Leipzig, 1889.

Tor. Harper Torchbooks: The Bollingen Library. New York and Evanston.

Vorsokr. HERMANN DIELS. *Die Fragmente der Vorsokratiker.* 4th edn., Berlin, 1922; 5th edn., Berlin, 1934–37; 6th edn., Berlin, 1951–52. 3 vols. (For English translations of the 5th edn., see FREEMAN.)

For information on the references, see the List of Works Cited. For abbreviations, see the list on pp. 189 f.

PREFACE

1 Tὸ ἔργον τῆς 'Αρχαιολογικῆς 'Εταιρίας *1957* (1960–62).

2 See I. N. Travlos, " 'Ελευσίς," *Archaiologikon Deltion 1960*, XVI (1962), 55 ff.

3 Doro Levi, "A Magnificent Crater and Rich Pottery from the Crete of 4000 Years Ago: New and Vivid Light on the Earliest Palace of Phaistos," *The Illustrated London News*, 6 Oct. 1956, p. 548.

4 Cf. Kerényi, *The Gods of the Greeks*, p. 253 (Pelican edn., p. 222).

5 Cf. Kerényi, "Miti sul concepimento di Dioniso," *Maia*, IV (1951), 1 ff.

6 Euripides, *Helen* 1314–16; Diodorus Siculus V 3; Valerius Flaccus, *Argonautica* V 345–46; Statius, *Achilleis* II 150; Claudianus, *De raptu Proserpinae* II 35. Cf. Kerényi, "Persephone und Prometheus: Vom alter griechischer Mythen," in *Festschrift für Hans Oppermann* (*Jahrbuch der Raabe-Gesellschaft*, 1965), pp. 58 ff.

INTRODUCTION

1 "Kore," in Jung and Kerényi, *Essays on a Science of Mythology*, pp. 139–214 (Torchbook edn., pp. 101–55).

2 Samson Eitrem in a letter to the author.

3 *Eleusis: Die baugeschichtliche Entwickelung des Heiligtumes.*

4 A. E. Jensen and H. Niggemeyer (eds.), *Hainuwele: Volkserzählungen von der Molukken-Insel Ceram.*

5 See n. 2.

6 "Zum Urkind-Mythologem," *Paideuma*, I (1940), 241–78.

7 Jung and Kerényi, *Das göttliche Kind in mythologischer und psychologischer Beleuchtung* (Albae Vigiliae VI/VII).

8 This study also appeared in 1941 under the title "Kore: Zum Mythologem vom göttlichen Mädchen," *Paideuma*, I (1940), 341–80, but was submitted to Jung at the same time. The volume published in collaboration with Jung,

Einführung in das Wesen der Mythologie (Zurich, 1941), combined two studies, "Zum Urkind-Mythologem" and "Kore," and their commentaries, first issued in the volumes *Das göttliche Kind* and *Das göttliche Mädchen* (Albae Vigiliae VIII/IX), with an introduction and an epilogue by me. In New York the translation was entitled *Essays on a Science of Mythology*, in London *Introduction to a Science of Mythology*.

9 A. E. Jensen, *Das religiöse Weltbild einer frühen Kultur.*

10 Cf. *Der frühe Dionysos*, my Eitrem Lectures of 1960, p. 10.

11 Jung and Kerényi, *Essays*, p. 219 (Tor. edn., p. 157).

12 Ibid., p. 217 (Tor. edn., p. 156).

13 Ibid., p. 223 (Tor. edn., p. 160).

14 Ibid., pp. 225 f. (Tor. edn., p. 162).

15 Ibid., p. 245 (Tor. edn., p. 177).

16 Cf. A. E. Jensen, *Die drei Ströme: Züge aus dem geistigen und religiösen Leben der Wemale, einem Primitiv-Volk in den Molukken*, p. 75.

17 *The Great Mother*, pp. 305 ff.

18 *Der frühe Dionysos*, pp. 9 ff.

19 In preparation.

20 *The Great Mother*, p. 305.

21 *Eleusis and the Eleusinian Mysteries.*

22 "The Meaning of the Eleusinian Mysteries," in *The Mysteries*, pp. 14 ff. and p. 27, n. 21.

23 Ibid., pp. 14–31.

24 Cf. below, p. 98.

25 *Das antike Mysterienwesen in religionsgeschichtlicher, ethnologischer und psychologischer Beleuchtung*, p. 323.

26 "Mémoire sur les représentations qui avaient lieu dans les mystères d'Éleusis," *Mémoires de l'Académie d'inscriptions et de belles-lettres*, XXIV (1861): 1, 373.

27 This theory is opposed in my "Epilegomena" to *Essays on a Science of Mythology*, pp. 249–56 (Tor. edn., pp. 178–83).

28 See my "Über des Geheimnis der eleusinischen Mysterien," *Paideuma*, VII (1959) 69–82. Cf. below, pp. 84 f. and 99.

29 Cf. E. R. Dodds, *The Greeks and the Irrational.*

I. THE GEOGRAPHICAL AND CHRONOLOGICAL SETTING

1 Barley and wheat could be harvested in April or May after being sown in October or November (in ancient times, after the Mysteries; cf. below, p. 127). In between, as I have learned from I. M. Geroulanos, a landowner in Greece,

beans could be sown and harvested as a second crop. This was also assuredly
the case in antiquity, though such was not Demeter's intention. Beans belonged
to the gods and spirits of the underworld (cf. R. Wünsch, *Das Frühlingsfest
der Insel Malta*, pp. 31 ff.). While Persephone dwelt in the underworld and
Demeter was unable to see her, the earth was not permitted to bear fruit. That
beans, a gift of the underworld, grew nevertheless, added to her rancor. It is
probably to this that Pausanias is alluding in his description of the Sacred
Road, when he says (I 37 4): "On the way stands a small temple which is called
the temple of Kyamites ('he of the beans'). I cannot say with certainty whether
Kyamites was the first to sow beans, or whether a hero was invoked [for this
task]. For they may not attribute the invention of beans to Demeter. Anyone
who has witnessed the Mysteries of Eleusis or read the so-called poems of
Orpheus on the subject knows what I mean." Kyamites was probably a name for
Hades.

2 Aischylos, *Persae* 393.

3 *Die Sage von Tanaquil* (Gesammelte Werke, VI), p. 10.

4 Cf. Plutarch, *Alcibiades* 34.

5 Censorinus, *De die natali* IV 3; Okellos of Lukania (or Ocellus) III 1–3
(ed. Harder, p. 21); in my *Prometheus*, pp. 20 f.

6 *Erga kai Hemerai* [*Works and Days*] 109 ff.

7 CIL VI 1779 (*Inscriptiones latinae selectae* 1259), cf. CIL VI 2959;
Johanna Nistler, "Vettius Agorius Praetextatus," *Klio*, X (1910), 462.

8 *Historia nova* IV 3 3.

9 In *The Homeric Hymns* (ed. Allen, Halliday, and Sikes), 2nd edn.; an
English version by Hugh G. Evelyn-White is given in *Hesiod, the Homeric
Hymns, and Homerica* (LCL edn.).

10 481; mistakenly corrected in ὁμοίως by Ulrich von Wilamowitz-Moellendorff, *Der Glaube der Hellenen*, II, 56.

11 In Pearson (III, 52), fr. 837.

12 In Bowra, fr. 121.

13 *Anthologia Palatina* XI 42 3–6:

> ἔμπης Κεκροπίης ἐπιβήμεναι, ὄφρ' ἂν ἐκείνας
> Δήμητρος μεγάλης νύκτας ἴδηις ἱερῶν,
> τῶν ἄπο κἄν ζωοῖσιν ἀκηδέα, κεῦτ' ἂν ἵκηαι
> ἐς πλεύνων, ἕξεις θυμὸν ἐλαφρότερον.

(". . . yet set thy foot on the Attic soil, that thou mayest see those long nights
of Demeter's holy rites, whereby while thou are among the living thy mind
shall be free from care, and when thou goest to join the greater number it shall
be lighter."—Tr. Paton, IV, 91.)

14 *De legibus* II XIV 36: . . . *nihil melius illis mysteriis, quibus ex agresti
immanique vita exculti ad humanitatem et mitigati sumus, initiaque ut ap-*

pellantur, ita re vera principia vitae cognovimus. . . . "No [Athenian institution] is better that the mysteries. For by their means we have been brought out of our barbarous and savage mode of life and educated and refined to a state of civilization; and as the rites are called 'initiations,' so in very truth we have learned from them the beginnings of life. . . ."—Tr. Keyes, modified, p. 415.

15 Isokrates I 1, IV 46, VI 109, VIII 34, X 62.

16 Eunapios, *Vitae sophistarum* VII 3.

17 *IG* II ² 1934 (according to Kirchner, the end of the fourth century B.C.). The mythological background is given by Apollodoros, *Bibliotheca* III xv 4, and in my *Heroes of the Greeks,* p. 290; cf. J. Toepffer, *Attische Genealogie,* pp. 29, 52, 87.

18 *Ad Atticum* I 9.

19 Mylonas, p. 30.

20 Kerényi, *Heroes,* pp. 215 f.

21 Ibid., pp. 289 f.

22 Ibid., p. 215.

23 Pausanias I 41 8.

24 Kerényi, *Der frühe Dionysos,* p. 23.

25 Kerényi, *Heroes,* p. 289.

26 Hesychios, *Lexicon* (ed. Schmidt here and hereafter), s.v.; Pausanias I 38 2 f.

27 "Epirrhema" to "Die Metamorphose der Pflanzen," in Goethe's *Werke* (Hamburger Ausgabe), I, 358 (see also 565). Cf. Kerényi, *Die Geburt der Helena,* p. 49, and "Voraussetzungen der Einweihung in Eleusis," *Initiation* (Studies in the History of Religions . . . , X), p. 60.

28 Isokrates IV 157; Scholium on Aristophanes, *Ranae* 369.

II. THE MYTHOLOGICAL SETTING

1 Euripides, *Helen* 1307 and fr. 64, in Nauck, *TGF;* Carcinus, in Nauck, *TGF,* fr. 5, line 1.

2 *The Homeric Hymns* (ed. Allen, Halliday, and Sikes), p. 119, n. 3.

2a Cf. Kerényi, *Griechische Grundbegriffe,* pp. 59 ff.

3 Wilamowitz, *Der Glaube der Hellenen,* I, 17; on the following, my *Griechische Grundbegriffe,* p. 17.

4 I owe this information to Gerda Bruns; cf. *Griechische Grundbegriffe,* p. 22.

5 Pausanias I 38 3.

6 Ibid. VIII 37 9.

7 Ventris and Chadwick, *Documents in Mycenaean Greek,* pp. 241 f.

8 Cf. Kerényi, *The Gods of the Greeks*, pp. 232 ff. (Pelican edn., pp. 205 ff.).

9 Ibid., 109, 112, 192 (Pelican edn., 96, 99, 170); Kerényi, *The Heroes of the Greeks*, pp. 35, 38.

10 *Amores* III 10 25.

11 Kerényi, " 'Herr der Wilden Tiere' ?," *SymbO*, XXXIII (1957), 129 ff.

12 Hesiod, *Theogony* 969.

13 Athenaios 694 c.

14 R. L. Herzog, *Heilige Gesetze aus Kos*, pp. 21, line 21, and 23, IIa.

15 In dissociating "Eleusinia" from "Eleusis," Toepffer (*Attische Genealogie*, p. 221) and others have not taken into account the correct derivation of the one word from the other. They would have done better to abide by Greek grammar.

16 Kerényi, *Gods*, p. 185 (Pelican edn., p. 163).

17 P. Kretschmer, "Zur Geschichte der griechischen Dialekte," *Glotta*, I (1909), 27 f.; I regard this as the definitive etymology.

18 Pausanias VIII 25 7.

19 Ibid. VIII 25 6.

20 Ibid. VIII 37 9.

21 Ibid. VIII 37 4.

22 P. Roussel, *Les Cultes égyptiens à Délos du IIIe au Ier siècle avant Jésus-Christ*, p. 199, no. 206; *Inscriptions de Délos* 2475; the inscription is complete. If the last word referred to the wife of the dedicant, her name would have to be mentioned. Incompletely reproduced in M. P. Nilsson, *Geschichte der griechischen Religion*, II, 89, n. 6 (paperback edn. in English, p. 211).

23 Strabo XIV 1 45.

24 Pausanias III 24 4.

25 Ailianos (Aelian), *Historia animalium* VII 48; Pliny, *Naturalis historia* VIII xxi 57; the story of the lion that was associated with the surname was obviously late. The closest parallel is the epithet ῥηξίχθων, "making the ground burst" (Orphic Hymn 52 9).

26 J. D. Beazley, *Attic Black-Figure Vase-Painters*, p. 184, erroneously takes Persephone and Demeter for "Ariadne (or Semele)" and "some other goddess."

27 Cf. the vase paintings collected by K. Schauenburg, "Pluton und Dionysos," *JDAI*, LXVIII (1953), 38–72.

28 Pausanias I 38 5.

29 Athenaios 78 c.

30 Erineos by the cave of Charybdis: Odyssey XII 432; behind Theseus when he is escaping on the back of a turtle: Kerényi, *Heroes*, fig. 29. Prokroustes, a Hades figure, ibid., p. 222, lived near the Erineos of Eleusis.

31 The Homeric Hymn to Demeter 99.

32 Pausanias I 39 1.

33 Kerényi, *Gods*, p. 100 (Pelican edn., p. 88).

34 Cf. the vase paintings collected by Konrad Schauenburg, "Zur Symbolik unteritalischer Vasenmalerei," *Römische Mitteilungen*, LXIV (1957), 198, and "Die Totengötter in der unteritalischen Vasenmalerei," *JDAI*, LXXIII (1958), 75; see also below, p. 143 [40].

35 Apollodoros, *Bibliotheca* I v 1; it is thus that Demeter receives her worshipers in an Eleusinian votive relief [7].

36 Suidas, s. v. Salaminios.

37 Kerényi, *Gods*, pp. 243 f. (Pelican edn., p. 215).

38 In H. Diels (ed.), *Vorsokr.*, fr. 15 (6th edn., I, 154 f.); cf. K. Freeman, *Ancilla to the Pre-Socratic Philosophers*, p. 25.

39 Cf. Appendix I.

40 Cf. Appendix II.

41 Cf. Appendix I.

42 *IG* I² 310 132.

43 In A. Körte, "Der Demeter-Hymnos des Philikos," *Hermes*, LXVI (1931), 446, line 48. Cf. Kerényi, "Zum Verständnis von Vergilius Aeneis B. VI," *Hermes*, LXVI (1931), 420. Verses 408–9: *Ille [Charon] admirans venerabile donum Fatalis virgae, longo post tempore visum*, possibly refer to the descent of Demeter to the underworld.

III. THE LESSER MYSTERIES AND THE PREPARATIONS FOR THE GREAT MYSTERIES

1 Cf. my *The Religion of the Greeks and Romans*, p. 151.

2 In K. Horna, *Die Hymnen des Mesomedes* (Sitzungsberichte der Akademie der Wissenschaften in Wien, Phil.-hist. Klasse, CCVII: 1), p. 37, IX, line 7, or Karl von Jan (ed.), *Musici scriptores graeci* (T), p. 462, line 7.

3 Cf. Hesychios, *Lexicon:* μύστα · μυστηρίων μεταλαβών. The antiquity of the verb from which the noun can be derived is shown by the *mu-jo-me-no* from Pylos (UnO3, in Ventris and Chadwick, *Documents in Mycenaean Greek*, p. 221), which possibly deals with the initiation of the king, probably his enthronement. On the formation, cf. E. Fränkel, *Geschichte der griechischen Nomina agentis auf - τήρ etc.*, I, 223, and II, 199 ff. The derivation from *mus-*, "to steal," a root nonexistent in Greek, is worthless.

4 *IG* I² 6 125.

5 Clement of Alexandria, *Stromata* V 11 71 1 (this reference, and other citations of Clement given hereafter, in Stählin).

6 Plutarch, *Demetrius* 26.

7 *IG* II ² 847 22.

8 Pausanias I 19 6.

9 Kerényi, *The Gods of the Greeks*, p. 148 (Pelican edn., p. 131).

10 Kallimachos, Hymn to Artemis 202.

11 *IG* I ² 310 132; Bekker, *Anecdota graeca* (hereafter cited as *Anecd. Bekk.*), I, 327, line 3.

12 Kerényi, *The Heroes of the Greeks*, p. 215; cf. my notes "Zum Fries des Ilissostempels," *AM*, LXXVI (1961), 22 ff.

13 Stephen of Byzantium, s. v. ῍Αγρα καὶ ῍Αγραι.

14 Kerényi, *Gods*, p. 206 (Pelican edn., p. 182).

15 Phanodemos, fr. 4, in Jacoby, *FGrHist*, pt. III, B, pp. 79 f.

16 Plutarch, *Demetrius* 26; *IG* I ² 6 76.

17 Cf. above, n. 13.

18 But it is not always possible to distinguish these from one another. Cf. below, p. 96.

18a Concerning the *legomena* in the Christian mysteries, see Kerényi, review of Josef Kroll's "Gott und Hölle . . . ," *Gnomon*, IX (1933), 367.

19 Kerényi, *Heroes*, pp. 177 ff.

20 Apollodoros, *Bibliotheca* II v 12.

21 Scholium on Aristophanes, *Plutus* 845 and 1013.

22 *Hercules furens* 613.

23 Theon of Smyrna, *Exposition rerum mathematicarum* (ed. Hiller, p. 14). Theon also knows of a stage higher than the *epopteia*: the bearing of the priests' wreaths.

24 Polyainos, *Strategemata* V 17 1; Himerios, *Oratio* XLVII 4 (ed. Colonna).

25 Athenaios 21 e.

26 Apollodoros, *Bibliotheca* II v 12.

27 *IG* II ² 1231.

28 Apollonios Rhodios, *Argonautica* IV 702.

29 Aristophanes, *Pax* 374.

30 Aristophanes, *Acharnenses* 784 and scholium.

31 Plutarch, *Phocion* 28.

32 Aristophanes, *Ranae* 338.

33 Hesychios s. v. Διὸς κώιδιον.

34 P. F. Foucart, in *Les Mystères d'Eleusis*, p. 211, presumes the one to have been a priestess of the Mother, the other of the Daughter. But it is attested that one of the priestesses at Eleusis served Plouton. Cf. below, p. 110.

35 For the mask in the winnowing fan, see Kerényi, *Gods*, pl. XII. The phallus in the liknon is not represented only from the Hellenistic period on, as M. P. Nilsson, *The Dionysiac Mysteries of the Hellenistic and Roman Age*, pp. 37 ff., maintains; cf. E. Simon, "Zum Fries der Mysterienvilla bei Pompeji,"

JDAI, LXXVI (1961), 170 and fig. 37. The earliest mention is probably Sophokles, fr. 760, in Nauck, *TGF,* or fr. 844, in Pearson.

36 The Homeric Hymn to Hermes 21; Kallimachos, Hymn to Zeus 47 and scholium.

37 Cf. Kerényi, *Religion,* pls. 58, 61, 63.

38 *In Neaeram* LIX 21.

39 *IG* II² 1672 207.

40 Ibid. 204.

41 *IG* II² 1673 24.

42 The Homeric Hymn to Demeter 196–97. The difference between this situation of Herakles in the representations of his purification [11 and 12b] and that of Demeter is that the goddess and the mystes are not purified but consecrated (*consecrati*), while Herakles has first to be purified, in one relief with the liknon [12b], in the other with fire [11]. H. Diels, *Sibyllinische Blätter,* p. 122, correctly indicated the meaning of the veiling, and added the veiling of the Roman bride with the *flammeum,* the red cloth. Obviously this ceremony played a part both in purification and in initiation.

43 Scholium on Aristophanes, *Ranae* 479.

44 *IG* II² 1672 182.

45 *IG* II² 847 20.

46 *IG* II² 847.

47 Hesychios s. v. ὑδρανός.

48 The posture of the little hero is self-explanatory. Since the stone on which he is shown [14] is only part of a larger relief, it seems likely that other Eleusinian heroes and kings' sons were represented in the relief in the same situation.

49 *IG* II² 1367 6.

50 Aristotle, *Athenaion politeia* (*Athenian Constitution*) 56 4.

51 *IG* II² 974 11.

52 *IG* II² 1367 8.

53 Kerényi, "Parva realia," *SymbO,* XXXVI (1960), 7; still, it is not impossible that on a particular day of this season—the season of the vintage—Dionysos was remembered and grapes offered up to him.

54 Eupolis, in Edmonds (I, 352), fr. 122 BC 4–5; cf. S. Eitrem, "Les Épidauria," *Mélanges d'archéologie et d'histoire offerts à Charles Picard,* a special issue of *Revue archéologique,* ser. 6, XXIX–XXX (1948), 351–54.

55 *IG* II² 1078 11.

56 Hesychios, s. v. ἀγυρμός; Kerényi, *SymbO,* XXXVI (1960), 13.

57 L. Deubner, *Attische Feste,* p. 72, n. 7.

58 *IG* II² 1078 11.

59 Philostratos, *Vitae sophistarum* II 20 3.

60 *IG* II² 81 10.

61 Scholium on Aristophanes, *Ranae* 330.

62 *IG* II² 2090.

63 F. Cumont, *Les Religions orientales dans le paganisme romain*, 4th edn., p. 241, n. 77.

64 Aristophanes, *Plutus* 844 and scholium on 845. Garments were kept in Eleusis itself: *IG* II² 1672 229.

65 Aristophanes, *Ranae* 407.

66 Cf. Appendix II.

67 *Anth. Pal.* IX 147; Hiller von Gärtringen, "'Ανταγόρου 'Ροδίου," *Hermes*, XXVIII (1893), 469.

68 Hesychios s. v. γεφυρίς.

69 *Plutus* 1014; cf. Kerényi, *SymbO*, XXXVI (1960), 11–16.

70 *IG* I² 81 11.

71 Pausanias I 38 2.

72 *Anecd. Bekk.*, I, 273, line 25.

73 Clement of Alexandria, *Protrepticus* II 21 2.

74 Kerényi, *Gods*, pp. 252 ff. (Pelican edn., pp. 221 ff.).

75 Kerényi, *Der frühe Dionysos*, p. 48.

76 This thesis put forward by Albrecht Dieterich, *Eine Mithrasliturgie*, 3rd edn., p. 125, is indemonstrable, but I believe that it must be mentioned—at least as a possibility.

IV. THE SECRET OF ELEUSIS

1 Τοῖν Θεοῖν καὶ τῶι αὐτοκράτορι οἱ Πανέλληνες.

2 Clement of Alexandria, *Protrepticus* II 20 1.

3 Herodotos IX 65.

4 Pausanias I 38 7.

5 Ap. Claudius Ap. f. *Pulcher propylum Cereri et Proserpinae cos. vovit imperator probavit Pulcher Claudius et Rex Marcius fecerunt et dedicaverunt*. CIL III 547.

6 *Ad Att.* VI 1 26, VI 6 2.

7 *IG* II² 2090.

8 Orph. fr. 52, line 5; Kerényi, *SymbO*, XXXVI (1960), 15; the Latin translation by Arnobius in *Adversus nationes* V 25 as *poclum* is wrong. Clearly Arnobius had never seen the vessel, which appears on the basket of the *kistophoroi* [23c] and by itself in [59]. Cf. Appendix II.

9 After the end of the fourth century B.C., the period of the orator Lykourgos, who once again attempted to forbid women to ride in vehicles—cf. his *Vita*, Ps.-Plutarch 19 f.; until the building of the Great Propylaia with their stairs,

vehicles accompanied the procession as far as this point, as is attested by the ruts in the pavement [20a].

10 They are mentioned as participants in the procession; Plutarch, *Alcibiades* 34.

11 Scholium on Aristophanes, *Ranae* 369.

12 Mylonas, fig. 3, no. 20; cf. his p. 147: "Some three meters diagonally across from the east end of the north wall of the temple Philios found in the rocky floor of the court a shallow round pit, one meter in diameter. This he attributed to an abandoned effort to dig a well. Svoronos believed it to be a bothros. Of course neither the date nor the purpose of this pit can be determined now." This symbolic pit, or *bothros*, may have been covered with a stone hemisphere, the omphalos; cf. [15].

13 W. F. Otto, "Apollon," *Paideuma*, VII (1959), 21; the examples from the ancient Orient quoted by G. Widengren, "Aspetti simbolici dei templi e luoghi di culto del vicino oriente," *Numen*, VII (1960), 2 and 14.

14 Allegedly the oracle at Delphi was connected with an oracle in the moon. Opposed by Plutarch, *De sera numinis vindicta* 566 C.

15 *Anecd. Bekk.*, I, 204, line 19.

16 The Homeric Hymn to Demeter 248–253.

17 Plutarch, *Pericles* 13.

18 Both in Lucian, *Piscator* 33; "to dance out" stressed in *De saltatione* 15; cf. Arrian, *Epicteti dissertationes* III xxi 16.

19 In Christian Walz, *Rhetores gracci*, VIII, 123.

20 Milan Papyrus No. 20, line 31, in *Papiri della R. Università di Milano*, I, 177, the significance of which was recognized by W. F. Otto, *Paideuma*, VII (1959), 19 ff. I am indebted to S. Eitrem for help in completing and interpreting the text.

21 Kerényi, *The Heroes of the Greeks*, p. 191.

22 Scholium on Theokritos II 35–36 (ed. Wendel, p. 279); cf. Velleius Paterculus I 4 1: *classis cursum esse directum . . . nocturno aeris sono, qualis Cerealibus sacris cieri solet* ("the voyage of this fleet was guided by . . . the sound at night of a bronze instrument like that which is beaten at the rites of Ceres"—tr. Shipley, p. 11). Pindar, Isthmian Ode VII 3: χαλκοκρότου πάρεδρον Δαμάτερος, probably refers to Eleusis, and Michael Psellos, *Graecorum opiniones de daemonibus*, in *De operatione daemonum* (ed. Boissonade, p. 39, or in Migne, *PG*, CXXII, col. 880): καί τις ἠχῶν λέβης Θεσπρώτειος, to the conjuring of the dead.

23 Scholium on Aristophanes, *Nubes* 242; Vitruvius V 5 1–2.

24 Scholium on Theokritos II 35–36 [Sparta] (ed. Wendel, p. 279); Psellos, as cited in n. 22 above.

25 Pliny, *Naturalis historia* II LIII 138; Seneca, *Quaestiones naturales* II 49 3.

26 Tr. Fitzgerald, Harvest edn., p. 159.

27 Cf. my *Griechische Grundbegriffe*, p. 18.

28 Tr. Fitzgerald, Harvest edn., p. 162 (modified).

29 Thanks to I. N. Travlos, "Τὸ ᾽Ανάκτορον τῆς ᾽Ελευσῖνος," *ArchEph*, 1950–51, pp. 1 ff.

30 Cf., if the reading is correct, *Corpus inscriptionum graecarum* 2932 (II, 589) from Tralles: δείκτης ἱερῶν ἀγώνων.

31 *De profectu in virtute* 81 DE: ὡς γὰρ οἱ τελούμενοι κατ᾽ ἀρχὰς ἐν θορύβωι καὶ βοῆι πρὸς ἀλλήλους ὠθούμενοι συνίασι, δρωμένων δὲ καὶ δεικνυμένων τῶν ἱερῶν προσέχουσιν ἤδη μετὰ φόβου καὶ σιωπῆς, οὕτω καὶ φιλοσοφίας ἐν ἀρχῆι καὶ περὶ θύρας πολὺν θόρυβον ὄψει καὶ θρασύτητα καὶ λαλιάν, ὠθουμένων πρὸς τὴν δόξαν ἐνίων ἀγροίκως τε καὶ βιαίως· ὁ δ᾽ ἐντὸς γενόμενος καὶ μέγα φῶς ἰδών, οἷον ἀνακτόρων ἀνοιγομένων, ἕτερον λαβὼν σχῆμα καὶ σιωπὴν καὶ θάμβος ὥσπερ θεῶι τῶι λόγωι ταπεινὸς συνέπεται . . . "Just as persons who are being initiated into the Mysteries throng together at the outset amid tumult and shouting, and jostle against one another, but when the holy rites are being performed and disclosed the people are immediately attentive in awe and silence, so too at the beginning of philosophy: about its portals also you will see great tumult and talking and boldness, as some boorishly and violently try to jostle their way towards the repute it bestows; but he who has succeeded in getting inside, and has seen a great light, as though a shrine were opened, adopts another bearing of silence and amazement, and 'humble and orderly attends upon' reason as upon a god."
—Tr. Babbitt, I, 435.

32 *Nubes* 304.

33 The fire, as O. Rubensohn notes in "Das Weihehaus von Eleusis und sein Allerheiligstes," *JDAI*, LXX (1955), 44, can have been of pine wood or of vine branches.

34 *Refutation omnium haeresium* V 8 40 (for an English version, cf. Francis Legge, *Philosophumena, or The Refutation of All Heresies;* here, I, 138); the locative meaning of ὑπὸ accords with the situation of the throne in the Telesterion. Hence the preposition should probably not be interpreted metaphorically as in Plutarch, *Galba* 14, or Heliodoros, *Aethiopica* X 41.

35 According to Hippolytos, who mentions this curiosity in the same context as the loud cry of the Hierophant, the emasculation was brought about by means of hemlock.

36 If the names were native to Attica, one would expect φρι- as the initial syllable.

37 *Argonautica* III 861.

38 Cf. Mylonas, Index, s. v. "burials."

39 Plutarch, *De facie in orbe lunae* 943 B.

40 Mylonas, p. 57.

41 Ibid., p. 58.

42 Kerényi, *The Gods of the Greeks*, p. 257 (Pelican edn., p. 226).

43 Ibid., pp. 252 f. (Pelican edn., pp. 222 f.).

44 Ibid., pp. 270 f. (Pelican edn., p. 238).

45 Sons of Ariadne by Dionysos are said to be Oinopion, Euanthes, Staphylos;
cf. Kerényi, *Gods*, p. 272 (Pelican edn., p. 240).
46 Cf. W. F. Otto, *Dionysos: Mythos und Kultus*, p. 55.
47 Kerényi, *Gods*, p. 144 (Pelican edn., p. 127).
48 Scholium on Aristophanes, *Ranae* 479.
48a I.e., the Milan papyrus cited in n. 20.
49 Sopatros' unintelligible text runs: ἂν δαιδουχίαν θεάσωμαι καὶ σχῆμα τι περὶ τοῦ
ἀδελφοῦ γιγνόμενον (in Walz, *Rhetores graeci*, VII, 123). On p. 372 of his posthu-
mous treatise, cited above in n. 26 of the Introduction, Charles Lenormant suggests replacing the here meaningless words περὶ τοῦ ἀδελφοῦ by ὑπὲρ τοῦ ἐδάφους:
"une figure qui s'élève au-dessus du plancher." It seems most likely that this
emendation is correct. According to Plutarch (cf. n. 31, above), the initiates
undergo a complete transformation: they act as it is fitting to act in the presence
of a deity. If we now reread the last words of the quotation, it becomes evident
that Plutarch also had in mind the epiphany of a deity.
50 Hippolytos, *Refutatio* V 8 39 (cf. tr. Legge, I, 138). The Buddha's "Flower
Sermon" is mentioned in Jung and Kerényi, *Essays on a Science of Mythology*,
pp. 209 ff. (Tor. edn., pp. 151 ff.). Hippolytos said: Ἀθηναῖοι μυοῦντες Ἐλευσίνια καὶ
ἐπιδείκνυντες τοῖς ἐποπτεύουσι τὸ μέγα καὶ θαυμαστὸν καὶ τελειότατον ἐποπτικὸν ἐκεῖ μυστήριον
ἐν σιωπῆι τεθερισμένον στάχυν. "The Athenians when initiating (people) into the
Eleusinian (Mysteries) show to those who have been made epopts the mighty
and wonderful and most perfect mystery for an epopt there—a mown ear of
corn—in silence" (tr. Legge, I, 138, modified). His words are surely to be taken
not in the sense that an ear of wheat was cut "in silence" at some time during
the Mystery ceremonies—cut ears of grain can be preserved for a long time—
but in the sense that the liturgical act of *showing* was performed "in silence."
The two interpretations of the sentence—in the first case a comma before
ἐν σιωπῆι, in the second case after it—are equally justified from the standpoint of grammar. The context argues for "showing in silence," for immediately
afterward Hippolytos tells about the loud voice of the Hierophant who, "scream-
ing," proclaims the divine birth: βοᾶι καὶ κέκραγε λέγων.
51 Cf. F. Cumont, *Le Culte égyptien et le mysticisme de Plotin*, p. 78.
52 Cf. Lobeck, *Aglaophamus*, p. 49, and especially Plutarch, *Alcibiades* 22.
53 The second example that has been cited of the cure of a blind man by
Demeter was—first by O. Kern, "Δημήτηρ-Σελήνη," *EphArch*, 1893, col. 113, after
him by O. Rubensohn, "Demeter als Heilgottheit," *AM*, XX (1895), 362, both
after L. Bruzza, "Bassorilievo con epigrafe greca provenienti da Filippopoli,"
Annali dell'Istituto di correspondenza archeologica, XXXIII (1861), 380—a votive relief from Thrace; it is from late Roman times and may have originated in
the Eleusinian religion of a private person. Worshipers of the Eleusinian deities may anywhere have thanked Demeter "for recovered eyesight," ὑπὲρ τῆς ὁράσεως.
As we shall see, the number of cases probably reduces itself to two.

54 Probably the paint was worn away from one eye.

55 *Anth. Pal.* IX 298:

Σκίπων με πρὸς νηὸν ἀνήγαγεν ὄντα βέβηλον
οὐ μοῦνον τελετῆς ἀλλὰ καὶ ἠελίου·
μύστην δ᾽ ἀμφοτέρων με θεαὶ θέσαν· οἶδα δ᾽ ἐκείνηι
νυκτὶ καὶ ὀφθαλμῶν νύκτα καθηράμενος·
ἀσκίπων δ᾽ εἰς ἄστυ κατέστιχον ὄργια Δηοῦς
κηρύσσων γλώσσης ὄμμασι τρανότερον.

56 A text for pious readers, dating from the second century after Christ, in praise of Imouthes, the Egyptian Asklepios (Oxyrhynchus Papyrus 1381, in *POxy*, XI, 227, line 107; an English version on pp. 230 f.), stresses that the god was not seen in a dream and tells with what eyes he was seen: οὔτ᾽ ὄναρ, οὔθ᾽ ὕπνος, ὀφθαλμοὶ γὰρ ἦσαν ἀκείνητοι διηνυγμένοι βλέποντες μὲν οὐκ ἀκριβῶς, θεία γὰρ αὐτὴν [the seeress] μετὰ δέους εἰσήιει φαντασία, καὶ ἀκόπως κατοπτεύειν κωλύουσα εἴτε αὐτὸν τὸν θεὸν εἴτε αὐτοῦ θεράποντας. The vision occurred in a waking state, with open eyes, but was not clear (οὐκ ἀκριβῶς). On the basis of the following quotation from the *Phaedrus* (250 BC), we must form a similar conception of the Eleusinian vision: seen with the eyes, but not clearly.

57 Lobeck, p. 57, had already cited Plato's *Phaedrus* 250 BC in order to give a general idea of the content of the Eleusinian Mysteries. But he confused them with the Egyptian mysteries described by Iamblichos in *De mysteriis II* 10 (ed. Parthey, p. 91; cf. II 4, p. 76) and believed that illumined statues of the gods were shown the mystai. K. H. E. de Jong, p. 323, followed C. Lenormant (cf. above, n. 26 of the Introduction) in citing the words of Plato and was first to take them as indirect evidence of ghostly phenomena at Eleusis.

58 English translation by Lane Cooper, *Plato: Phaedrus, Ion, Gorgias and Symposium, with passages from the Republic and Laws*, p. 33 (slightly modified); last sentence from Reginald Hackforth, *Plato's Phaedrus*, p. 83.

59 μακαρίαν ὄψιν τε καὶ θέαν . . . εἶδον. Here is meant the vision of the Ideas in the supercelestial place, the ὑπερουράνιος τόπος.

60 ἐτελοῦντο τῶν τελετῶν ἣν θέμις λέγειν μακαριωτάτην.

61 ὠργιάζομεν : another word for the celebration of the Mysteries, in the same sense as ἐτελοῦντο τὴν τελετήν.

62 After birth.

63 ὁλόκληρα καὶ ἁπλᾶ καὶ ἀτρεμῆ καὶ εὐδαίμονα φάσματα μυούμενοι τε καὶ ἐποπτεύοντες. Ὁλόκληρα should be translated rather as "whole" than as "perfect," ἀτρεμῆ rather as "firm" than as "still." The three adjectives refer to the ἀκρίβεια, the clarity of the φάσματα, the figures that appear (rendered by the English translator as "Phantoms"). This clarity was lacking in the vision cited in n. 56, above, although it was seen with open eyes.

64 ἄρρητα: Aelius Aristides, *Oratio* XXII (alias 19) 257 (ed. Keil, II, 28).

65 ἅγια: Stobaeus, *Anthologia* (ed. Hense, V, 1089, line 16), from an account of the "Great Mysteries" in a dialogue probably of Plutarch, excerpted by Themistios. The account is not so realistic as the unquestionably authentic account in Plutarch, *De profectu in virtute* 81 DE (see n. 31, above); rather, it presents a pattern applicable both to the way of initiation and to the way of the soul after death: πλάναι τὰ πρῶτα καὶ περιδρομαὶ κοπώδεις καὶ διὰ σκότους τινὲς ὕποπτοι πορεῖαι καὶ ἀτέλεστοι, εἶτα πρὸ τοῦ τέλους αὐτοῦ τὰ δεινὰ πάντα, φρίκη καὶ τρόμος καὶ ἱδρὼς καὶ θάμβος· ἐκ δὲ τούτου φῶς τι θαυμάσιον ἀπήντησεν καὶ τόποι καθαροὶ καὶ λειμῶνες ἐδέξαντο, φωνὰς καὶ χορείας καὶ σεμνότητας ἀκουσμάτων ἱερῶν καὶ φασμάτων ἁγίων ἔχοντες· ἐν αἷς ὁ παντελὴς ἤδη καὶ μεμυημένος ἐλεύθερος γεγονὼς καὶ ἄφετος περιιὼν ἐστεφανωμένος ὀργιάζει. . . . It is not a true description, as becomes even more evident further on, but an idealization of the event. The *epopteia* is touched upon in the reference to the *phasmata*, but not otherwise mentioned.

66 φαντάσματα occurs as a secondary *varians lectio* beside φάσματα; cf. F. Lenormant, "Eleusinia," in DarSag, II, 576.

67 Scholium on Aristophanes, *Aves* 1073.

68 *Ranae* 886–87:

Δήμητερ ἡ θρέψασα τὴν ἐμὴν φρένα,
εἶναι με τῶν σῶν ἄξιον μυστηρίων.

Cf. in contrast the prayer of Euripides (ibid. 892–94).

69 Cf. Ulrich von Wilamowitz-Moellendorff, "Lesefrüchte," *Hermes*, LXIII (1928), 383, who refers to the scholium on *Ranae* 886 without expressly citing it. The explanation here given of Aischylos' prayer is that he was an Eleusinian, not that he was an initiate.

70 Nauck, *TGF*, fr. 386 (an English version, in a translation by Herbert Weir Smyth, is published in the LCL edition of Aischylos, II, 499, fr. 214).

71 In the Areopagos, according to Clement of Alexandria, *Stromata* II 14 60 3, who probably made use of an amplified text of Aristotle's *Ethica Nicomachea* III 1 (1111 a), our chief source in the matter. Cf. J. Bernays, *Gesammelte Abhandlungen*, I, 161 and 163. Wilamowitz, *Der Glaube der Hellenen*, II, 221, n. 1, finds it necessary to correct the statement that the accusation of Aischylos was made in the Areopagos. It was probably in the presence of the whole people. O. Kern, *Die griechischen Mysterien der klassischen Zeit*, pp. 75 f., and "Mysterien," *RE*, XVI, col. 1249, denies the clearly attested fact. Cf. also below, p. 105.

72 Cf. P. F. Foucart, "Les Empereurs romains initiés aux mystères d'Eleusis," *Revue de philologie*, XVII (1893), 197 ff.; G. Giannelli, "I Romani ad Eleusi," *Atti della Reale Accademia delle scienze di Torino*, L (1915), 319 ff., 369 ff.; P. Graindor, *Athènes de Tibère à Trajan*, pp. 101 ff.; C. Picard, "L'Eleusinisme à Rome au temps de la dynastie julio-claudienne," *Revue des études latine*, XXVIII (1950), 77 ff., and his "La Patère d'Aquileia et l'éleusinisme à Rome aux

débuts de l'époque imperiale," *L'Antiquité classique,* XX (1951), 351 ff. Concerning Gallienus, see below, ch. v, n. 122.

73 Dio Cassius LI 4 1.

74 Ibid. LIV 9 7.

75 He is not otherwise known, and it is quite possible that the name was invented, that is, borrowed from the Poros in the story of Alexander the Great. He may, however, have belonged to the same family as the Paurava, which would seem to have been the Indian form of the name. Cf. H. Schäfer, *RE,* XXII, col. 1226.

76 Dio Cassius LIV 9 10.

77 Strabo XV 1 73.

78 Cf. A. Hillebrandt, *Der freiwillige Feuertod in Indien und die Somaweihe* (Sitzungsberichte der Bayerischen Academie der Wissenschaften, Phil.-hist. Klasse, 1917, 8), pp. 5 ff.

79 Hillebrandt, p. 5.

80 Arrian, *Anabasis* VII 3; Strabo XV 1 63; Plutarch, *Alexander* 69.

81 Plutarch, *Alex.* 65.

82 Lucian, *De morte Peregrini* 25.

83 Dio Cassius LIV 9 10.

84 Strabo XV 1 73; for the "Indian's Tomb," Plutarch, *Alex.* 69.

85 Dio Cassius LIV 9 10.

86 Cf. above, p. 93. I hold it possible that the fire marks from 700 to 600 B.C., mentioned by Mylonas (pp. 66 f.), were also brought about by the cremation of bodies in the vicinity of the Telesterion.

87 Cf. C. Picard, "Les Bûchers sacrés d'Eleusis," *RHR,* CVII (1933), 137 ff. He assumes with Conrad Kuiper, "De Euripidis Supplicibus," *Mnemosyne,* n.s. LI (1923), 126, that the vicinity of the Ploutonion was indicated on the stage. The steep cliff was visible: Euripides, *Suppl.* 987.

88 Euripides, *Phaëthon,* in Hans von Arnim (ed.), *Supplementum Euripideum,* p. 77, lines 59–60:

σὺ δ' ὦ πυρὸς δέσποινα Δήμητρος κόρη.
Ἥφαιστέ τ' ἔστε πρευμενεῖς δόμοις ἐμοῖς.

89 Strabo XVI 73.

90 G. Gerster, "Ostern in Jerusalem," *Neue Zürcher Zeitung,* 31 Mar. 1961, p. 5.

V. A HERMENEUTICAL ESSAY ON THE MYSTERIES

1 Eduard Meyer, *Geschichte des Altertums,* 4th edn., IV, 215 (1st edn., p. 504).

2 O. Kern, *RE*, XVI, col. 1249.

3 Cf. the corresponding account in Kern, *Die Religion der Griechen*, II, 182 ff.

4 Kern, *RE*, XVI, col. 1249; after A. Körte, "Zu den eleusinischen Mysterien," *ArchRW*, XVIII (1915), 122.

5 Most probably phalli. Cf. above, ch. iii, n. 76.

6 Wool, according to A. R. van der Loeff, "De formula quadam Eleusinia," *Mnemosyne*, XLV (1917), 364; earth, according to E. Maass, "Segnen Weihen Taufen," *ArchRW*, XXI (1922), 260 ff.; a phallus in the big basket, a womb in the small one, according to C. Picard, "L'Episode de Baubô dans les mystères d'Eleusis," *RHR*, XCV (1927), 237 ff.; a snake, a pomegranate, and cakes in the forms of phallus and womb, according to S. Eitrem, "Eleusinia—les mystères et l'agriculture," *SymbO*, XX (1940), 140 f.

7 The supposed testimony as to the womb—Theodoretos, *Graecarum affectionum curatio* VII 11 (ed. Raeder, p. 183): τὸν κτένα μὲν ἡ Ἐλευσίς, ἡ φαλλαγωγία δὲ τὸν φάλλον (εἶχεν αἰνίγματα)—is couched in very general terms (the Phallagogia were not mysteries) and refers most likely to an Eleusinian women's festival from which men were excluded; cf. below, p. 138.

8 Hippolytos, *Refutation* V 8 39 (cf. Legge, I, 138).

9 See G. Méautis, *Les Mystères d'Eleusis*, p. 63. M. P. Nilsson, "Die eleusinischen Gottheiten," *Opuscula selecta*, took the parallels from him (II, 594, n. 129). He stressed some verses from Prudentius' Hymn for the Dead (121–24):

> Sic semina sicca virescunt
> iam mortua iamque sepulta,
> quae reddita caespite ab imo
> veteres meditantur aristas.

(An English version by John Mason Neale in his *Collected Hymns*, p. 172:

> Thus arid and lifeless and buried
> Those seeds shall arise in their beauty,
> Restored from the turf where we laid them,
> Taking thought of a new growth for ever.)

"This is an immemorial image borrowed from agriculture: the sprouting of the new seed from the grains of old seed that have been cast upon the earth" (Nilsson, ibid., II, 591). It denoted "the change of the generations, the survival of the race" (p. 594). The words of the Gospel of St. John "are closely connected with this idea."

10 Tr. Schachter and Freedman, II, 607.

11 G. E. Mylonas, *Eleusis and the Eleusinian Mysteries*.

12 Cf. below, pp. 116–20. Following H. G. Pringsheim, *Archäologische Beiträge zur Geschichte des eleusinischen Kults*, p. 49, n. 1, Mylonas wishes to

relegate precisely the *synthema* to the Eleusis in Alexandria (p. 300). This is impossible, because the Eleusinian Mysteries were celebrated only in Attica. Cf. below, pp. 115 f.

13 Ailianos, fr. 10 (ed. Hercher, II, 192, lines 4 ff.); Suidas s. v. ἱεροφάντης: . . . ἐς τὸ μέγαρον · ἔνθα δήπου τῶι μὲν ἱεροφάντηι μόνωι παρελθεῖν θεμιτὸν ἦν κατὰ τὸν τῆς τελετῆς νόμον.

14 Prott and Ziehen (eds.), *Leges graecorum sacrae*, II: 1, 29, n. 6 B.

15 According to Prott and Ziehen, ibid., II: 1, 29, n. 6 A, the gifts intended for the Hierophant and the Keryx were brought to the Eleusinion. Aristeides, *Orationes* XXII (alias 19) 9 (ed. Keil, II, 30, line 24), makes it clear that from a certain time on (beginning with Iktinos, Rubensohn supposes; *JDAI*, LXX [1955], 34) the Telesterion was called the "Eleusinion." Since Eleusinion and Megaron are mentioned successively in Prott and Ziehen, II: 1, 29, n. 6 AB (IV/III centuries B.C.), it does not seem likely that the Eleusinion was situated in Athens and the Megaron at Eleusis. This wording alone makes it highly improbable that the Telesterion—or a part of it, the Anaktoron in the more exact sense—was called "Megaron" at Eleusis.

16 Ailianos, fr. 10 (ed. Hercher, II, 192): γύνανδρος ἀνήρ, θῆλυς γενόμενος, ὁ χλούνης τε καὶ γύννις.

17 It is mentioned by N. Kontoleon, Μέγαρον ("Megaron"), *Mélanges offerts à Octave et Melpo Merlier*, p. 7, but not separately interpreted. Mylonas (p. 87, n. 23) cites Kontoleon as his authority.

18 *Scriptores historiae Augustae: Marcus [Aurelius] Antoninus* XXVII 2: *sacrarium solus ingressus est.*

19 Ulpian, *Digest* I 8 9 2: *sacrarium est locus in quo sacra reponuntur, quod etiam in aedificio privato esse potest.*

20 Mylonas, pp. 59, 70, and 101 f.

21 Kontoleon, ibid.

22 Cf. above, ch. iv, n. 52.

23 Cf. my *Streifzüge eines Hellenisten*, pp. 42 ff.

24 Cf. my *Apollon: Studien über antike Religion und Humanität*, 3rd edn., pp. 280 ff. (*Werke in Einzelausgaben*, I, 357 ff.)

24a Kerényi, *Prometheus*, p. xxiii.

25 In Rose, fr. 15.

26 By Werner Jaeger, *Aristoteles*, 2nd edn., pp. 162 f.

27 Psellos, "Ad Johannem Climacum," in *Catalogue des manuscrits alchimiques grecs* (ed. Bidez et al.), VI, 171: αὐτοῦ παθόντος τοῦ νοῦ τὴν ἔλλαμψιν · · · αὐτοπτήσας τῶι νῶι . . . (cf. the English version included in *The Works of Aristotle*, translated under the supervision of W. D. Ross, XII: *Select Fragments*, p. 87).

28 Iamblichos, *De mysteriis* II 4, VII 3 (ed. Parthey, p. 76, line 14; p. 254, line 6).

29 Tacitus, *Historia* IV 83.

30 Oxyrhynchus Papyrus 1612 (*POxy*, XIII, 151–53); correct reading in L. Deubner, *Bemerkungen zu einigen literarischen Papyri aus Oxyrhynchos* (Sitzungsberichte der Akademie Heidelberg, 1919, XVII), p. 9.

31 *Protrepticus* II 12 2.

32 *Panarion* 51 22 13.

33 *Homilia X in SS. Martyres*, in Migne, *PG*, XL, col. 324 AB.

34 Polybius XV 27 2, XV 29 8, XV 33 8.

35 *Ad nationes* II 7, in Migne, *PL*, I, col. 595.

36 *Protrepticus* II 2 2 ff.

37 Psellos, *Graecorum opiniones de daemonibus*, in *De operatione daemonum* (ed. Boissonade), p. 39, or in Migne, *PG*, CXXII, col. 877.

38 *Institutionum epitome* XVIII 7.

39 Scholium on Aratus, *Phaenomena* 150, in *Commentariorum in Aratum reliquiae* (ed. E. Maass), p. 366.

40 Livy XXXI xiv 6–9.

41 Suidas s. v. Kallimachos.

42 Strabo XVII 1 16.

43 A. C. Merriam, "Inscribed Sepulchral Vases from Alexandria," *AJA*, I (1885), 18 ff.; Néroutsos Bey, *L'Ancienne Alexandrie*, pp. 110 ff.; a skeptical appreciation by Schiff in "Eleusis," *RE*, V, col. 2342.

44 Alkiphron, *Epistulae* IV 18.

45 No. 1221, in *Werke* (Hamburger Ausgabe), XII, 350.

46 *Alexander sive Pseudomantis* 39.

47 Cicero, *Orator* 151.

48 *Menexenus* 237 E.

49 Plutarch, *Praecepta coniugalia* 144 AB.

50 *Hellenica* VI iii 6.

51 The Homeric Hymn to Demeter 474.

52 Pausanias I 38 6.

53 Apollodoros, *Bibliotheca* I v 2.

54 Hyginus, *Astronomica* I 14 (ed. Bunte, p. 49).

55 Ibid. I 22 (ibid., p. 65).

56 Cf. Wilamowitz, *Der Glaube der Hellenen*, II, 52, n. 2.

57 Proklos, on Hesiod's *Erga kai Hemerai* 389, excerpting Plutarch (τὰ εἰς Ἡσιόδον ὑπομνήματα, fr. XXIII): Οἱ δὲ ἀρχαῖοι καὶ πρωϊαίτερον ἔσπειρον, καὶ δῆλον ἐκ τῶν Ἐλευσινίων τελετῶν, ἐν αἷς ἐλέγετο "πάριϑι Κόρη γέφυραν· ὅσον οὔπω τριπόλεον δέ." (On the authority of Wilamowitz; cf. n. 56, above, and his *Griechische Verskunst*, p. 286.)

58 In F. Jacoby (ed.), *Das Marmor Parium*, ep. 12–15.

59 *IG* II ² 1134.

60 Porphyry, *De abstinentia* IV 22.

61 Porphyry, quoted by Eusebios, *Praeparatio evangelica* III 11 7–9.

62 Cicero, *De legibus* II xxv 63.

63 Euboulos, in Edmonds (II, 116), fr. 75; cf. Antiphanes, in Kock, fr. 52, line 9.

64 *De natura deorum* II xxvi 66.

65 "Epidaurische Hymnen," edited by Paul Maas, *Schriften der Königsberger Gelehrten Gesellschaft*, IX: 5 (1933), 134 ff.

66 Plutarch, *Caesar* 9.

67 Orph. fr. 58 and 36; Diodorus Siculus III 62 7.

68 Diodorus Siculus III 64 1.

69 Orph. fr. 145.

70 Nauck, *TGF*, fr. 363.

71 *Vespae* 1268.

72 Ovid, *Fasti* IV 607.

73 *Metamorphoses* V 534–38.

74 Pausanias V 19 6.

75 A. B. Cook, *Zeus*, III: 1, 817.

76 *Anthologia lyrica graeca* (ed. Diehl), fr. 38.

77 Kerényi, *The Heroes of the Greeks*, p. 113.

78 Athenaios 78 b.

79 Ibid. 78 c.

80 Diodorus Siculus V 62 1–2; scholium on Lykophron 570.

81 Scholium on Lykophron 570: Anios διὰ τὸ ἀνιαθῆναι.

82 Scholium on Lykophron 570; cf. Ovid, *Metamorphoses* XII 652–54.

83 My proposal in "Dramatische Gottesgegenwart in der griechischen Religion," *EJ 1950*, XIX (1951), 36.

84 Cf. A. Meillet, *Aperçu d'une histoire de la langue grecque*, p. 62.

85 *Oratio* IV 174 B.

86 Cf. F. Cumont, *Les Religions orientales dans le paganisme romain*, pls. II: 1 and IV: 1.

87 Kerényi, *The Gods of the Greeks*, p. 89 (Pelican edn., p. 78).

88 Cf. Jung and Kerényi, *Essays*, pp. 179 ff. (Tor. edn., pp. 129 ff.); also my *Labyrinth-Studien*, 2nd. edn., pp. 21 ff. (*Werke*, I, 235 ff.); A. E. Jensen, *Das religiöse Weltbild einer frühen Kultur*, pp. 33 ff. and 66 ff.

89 *Hainuwele*, edited by A. E. Jensen and H. Niggemeyer, pp. 59 ff.

90 *Der Baumkultus der Hellenen*, p. 472, in which all important passages are cited and discussed. Bötticher lays stress upon Athenaios 680 a, according to whom the pomegranate was dedicated to Typhon (p. 474).

91 Deubner, *Attische Feste*, pp. 51 f.

92 Clement of Alexandria, *Stromata* VI 15 132 1; the large number and not the fertility is also stressed in a Persian tale told in Herodotos IV 143.

93 The color of the fruit is similarly interpreted in Artemidoros' *Onirocriticon libri* V ("Books of Dream Interpretation") I 73.

94 *Praep. evang.* II 3 28.

95 Collection of texts and monuments in A. B. Cook, *Zeus*, III: 1, 812 f.

96 Simpler than in my *Die Jungfrau und Mutter in der griechischen Religion: Eine Studie über Pallas Athene*, p. 34.

97 Ibid., pp. 35 ff.

98 On the statue, Harpokration s. v. Νίκη 'Αθηνᾶ.

99 Cf. my *Griechische Miniaturen*, pp. 195 f.

100 Cf. my *Abenteuer mit Monumenten*, pp. 59 ff.; on Persephonean attributes of Hera, see G. Säflund, *Aphrodite Kallipygos*, p. 81.

101 Scholium on Lucian, *Dialogi meretricii* VII 4: ἐν τῶι μυστικῶι with which λόγωι should be supplied. Artemidoros I 73 mentions τὸν ἐν 'Ελευσῖνι λόγον, but shows familiarity only with what was openly related; the prohibition of Lykosoura (Pausanias VIII 37 7) accords with that of Eleusis: Porphyry, *De abst.* IV 16, where the common apple is also mentioned.

102 Scholium on Lucian, *Dial. mer.* VII 4.

103 Clement of Alexandria, *Protrepticus* II 19 3; correctly understood by Deubner, *Attische Feste*, p. 58.

104 *Protrepticus* II 19 3.

105 After Clement; also in Eusebios, *Praep. evang.* II 3 28.

106 Kerényi, *Der frühe Dionysos*, pp. 33 ff.

107 Philostratus Junior, *Imagines* II 29 4.

108 Apollodoros, *Bibliotheca* I iv 3; Kerényi, *Gods*, p. 203 (Pelican edn., p. 179), on the basis of the reading ῞Ηραι. But it is certain that Hera came into the story at a late date.

109 Pausanias III 22 11, VIII 28 3.

110 Dionysius, *De aucupio [De avibus]* 7: ἀνῆκεν ἐκ τοῦ αἵματος ἡ γῆ.

111 Scholium on Lucian, *Dial. mer.* VII 4.

112 *IG* II ² 1186.

113 Athenaios 496 b.

114 Hippolytos, *Refutatio* V 7 34 (cf. tr. Legge, I, 129).

115 Proklos, *In Timaeum* 293 C.

116 Kleidemos, fr. 27, in Jacoby, *FGrHist*, pt. III, B, p. 59.

117 Marcus Aurelius V 7.

118 Cf., in the fragment in Athens, the metope to the left [21a].

119 Kerényi, *Der frühe Dionysos*, pp. 33 ff.

120 Joseph Campbell, *The Masks of God: Primitive Mythology*, p. 186, is the

victim of a misunderstanding when he writes "a young priestess representing Kore herself appeared" and cites the authority of Walter Friedrich Otto, "Der Sinn der eleusinischen Mysterien," *EJ 1939*, VII (1940), 99–106. Otto had in mind the epiphany of the goddess herself for the *epoptai* who had seen her.

121 Kerényi, *Streifzüge eines Hellenisten*, p. 45.

122 There is historical evidence indicating that the initiate regarded himself as a goddess and not as a god: the coins of the Emperor Gallienus from the years A.D. 265/66, with the inscription: GALLIENAE AUGUSTAE. The explanation found for this official designation is that Gallienus attached particular importance to his initiation at Eleusis; cf. A. Alföldi, "Zur Kenntnis der Zeit der römischen Soldatenkaiser: 2. Das Problem des 'verweiblichten' Kaisers Gallienus," *Zeitschrift für Numismatik*, XXXVIII (1928), 188. The identity of the emperor with Demeter, whose wreath of wheat ears he is wearing on the coin, was established by the *rite* of initiation: hence the name in the dative. The coin is dedicated to Gallienus as to a divinity. Further inferences drawn by Alföldi and M. Rosenbach, *Galliena Augusta*, from the importance attached by Gallienus to the Mysteries are based on a mistaken idea of what actually happened at Eleusis.

123 Kerényi, *The Religion of the Greeks and Romans*, p. 152.

124 Ibid., p. 151.

125 Cf. my *Griechische Grundbegriffe*, pp. 39 ff.

126 Cf. above, ch. iv, n. 57.

127 William Blake, "A Descriptive Catalogue . . ." (1809), in *The Writings* (ed. G. Keynes, 1925), III, 108, or *The Complete Writings* (ibid., 1957), p. 576.

128 Cf. Kerényi, *Essays*, pp. 211 ff. (Tor. edn., 153 ff.), where the translation "abyss of the nucleus" was not so correct. The phrase *Abgrund des Kerns* is from Goethe.

129 Concerning their duality as an androgynous being, cf. above, p. 136. For the Pythagoreans Rhea, as the Primordial Mother and the first feminine deity, was duality itself. Cf. Nikomachos of Gadara in Photios, *Bibliotheca* 143 b (ed. Henry, III, 43, lines 9–13), and my *Pythagoras und Orpheus*, 3rd edn., p. 44 (*Werke*, I, 50). The duality of the characteristic "Great Goddess" of the Aegean Isles is at least as old as the "Cycladic idols" of the third millennium B.C.; cf. J. Thimme, *Die religiöse Bedeutung der Kykladischen Idole*, pp. 79 f.

130 Ovid, *Metamorphoses* V 564–65; Hyginus, *Fabulae* 146 (ed. Schmidt, p. 20).

131 In the hymn of Epidauros; cf. above, n. 65.

132 Kerényi, *Gods*, p. 36 (Pelican edn., p. 31).

133 Harpokration s. v.

134 Suidas s. v. Proschaireteria; *Anecd. Bekk.*, I, 295, line 3.

135 Kerényi, *Die Jungfrau und Mutter*, pp. 35 ff.

136 Photios, *Lexikon* (ed. Naber) s. v.

137 *IG* II ² 674 7.

138 *IG* II ² 1363 14.

139 Hesychios, *Lexicon*, s. v. στήνια; Photios, s. v.

140 The procession is also represented on a pedestal which was probably likewise in the sacred precinct [26].

141 Demeter hovers rather than sits, as is also the case with other deities in Eleusinian representations. But she does not merely hover over her empty chair. Over the chair a line is discernible, a rise in the ground, and it is over this rise in the ground that the goddess hovers. A relief at Eleusis [7] shows her sitting on the ground as she receives her worshipers. In this situation she can also be Demeter Thesmophoros, for the Athenian women imitated her when they sat on the ground and fasted at the Thesmophoria: Plutarch, *De Iside et Osiride* 378 E.

142 Cf. P. Mingazzini, "Rilievo eleusinie rinvenuto in territorio de Mondragone (Sinuessa)," *NS*, 1927, pp. 309 ff., and E. Buschor, "Zum Weihrelief von Mondragone," *AM*, LIII (1938), 48 ff.

143 Buschor, ibid.

144 The relief is provided with an inscription which now presents gaps. Cf. *IG* II 1620 c.

145 An inscription concerning sacrifices to the Eleusinian heroes was found in the Agora of Athens: James H. Oliver, "Greek Inscriptions," *Hesperia*, IV (1935), 5 ff.; cf. A. Körte, "Eleusinisches," *Glotta*, XXV (1936), 134 ff. The hero Threptos, who is mentioned in the inscription, is Demophoön.

146 A relief head from Samothrace in Vienna (cf. B. Hemberg, *Die Kabiren*, p. 97) and perhaps a terra-cotta statuette in the Samothrace Museum (cf. K. Lehmann, *Samothrace: A Guide to the Excavations and the Museum*, 2nd edn., fig. 11); from the Kabeirion of Thebes in Wolters-Bruns, *Das Kabirionheiligtum bei Thebes*, I, pls. 5: 6 and 8: 1.

147 Dionysius Periegetes 513–32 in the initial letters; cf. my *Griechische Grundbegriffe*, p. 19.

148 Ibid., p .20.

149 Kerényi, *Gods*, p. 250 (Pelican edn., p. 220).

150 Cf. Kerényi, "Miti sul concepimento di Dioniso," *Maia*, IV (1951), 12 f., and *Der frühe Dionysos*, p. 47.

151 Scholium on Aristophanes, *Ranae* 479.

152 Cf. the vase painting in Deubner, *Attische Feste*, pl. 21: 2, correctly interpreted on his p. 130.

153 Lucian ridicules it in *Dialogi deorum*, Poseidon and Hermes, 228; cf. Diodorus Siculus I 23. But the number of months (seven) corresponds exactly to the period which elapsed between the Lesser Mysteries at Agrai—probably the mysteries of marriage—and the Great Mysteries at Eleusis, the Mysteries of birth in the underworld.

154 Cf. my *Religion*, pp. 18 ff.; *Prometheus*, pp. xxiii f.; and *Umgang mit Göttlichem*, 2nd edn., pp. 36 ff.

155 With regard to his clothing, cf. K. Kuruniotis, " Ἐλευσενιακὴ δᾳδουχία," *ArchEph*, 1937: 1, 233 ff.

156 Cf. Aristophanes, *Ranae* 47 and 557 (*kothornoi* are fine huntsmen's boots).

157 Pausanias IX 35 2.

158 Cf. A. Sogliano quoted in *NS*, 1883, pp. 49 f.

159 In the absence of photographs, Reichhold's well-known drawings possess scientific value, even if they do not show the atmospheric quality.

160 Hera was worshiped at Eleusis as the *daeira*, the angry sister-in-law of Persephone; cf. Servius' commentary on Virgil's *Aeneid* IV 58. She could have been Persephone's *daeira* as sister either of Hades, husband of Persephone, or of Zeus, if the latter was the abductor. The contradictory reports concerning her—scholia on Apollonios Rhodios, *Argonautica* III 847 (ed. Keil, p. 469), Lykophron 710 and scholium, and Eustathius on the Iliad VI 378—show that in this connection she was an older underworld goddess and rival of Persephone.

161 Obviously identical with the one produced by E. Gabrici, "Cuma," *Monumenti antichi*, XXII (1913), pls. CI–CII.

162 Cf. F. Cumont, *La Stèle du danseur d'Antibes et son décor végétal*, pp. 16 f.

163 G. Kaibel, "Zu den griechischen Künstlerinschriften," *Hermes*, XXII (1887), 151.

164 A. Philios, " Κεφαλὴ ἐξ Ἐλευσῖνος ," *EphArch*, 1886, cols. 257 ff.

165 Dittenberger, *Sylloge inscriptionem graecarum* [3] 1024 17 f.

166 *IG* XI 287 A 68 ff.; XII 7 76 f., 5 227.

167 Hesychios s. v. Ἐυβουλεύς.

168 According to G. Hermann, W. Quandt (ed.), *Orphei hymni*, 2nd edn.

169 Diodorus Siculus V 76 3; Pausanias II 30 3; Orphic Hymn 41 8.

170 Kerényi, *Heroes*, p. 215.

171 Orph. fr. 51–52.

172 Orph. fr. 50.

173 Pausanias I 38 3.

174 The Homeric Hymn to Demeter 347.

175 On the Lakrateides relief [44] and in A. Philios, as cited in n. 164 above, col. 262.

176 Orph. fr. 32 c–g.

177 These are shown with Paola Zancani Montuoro's essay "Il Rapitore di Kore nel mito Locrese," *Rendiconti della Accademia di archeologia . . .* , *Napoli*, XXIX (1955).

178 Cf. pl. VIII in Paola Zancani Montuoro, ibid.

APPENDIX I

1 Clement of Alexandria, *Protrepticus* II 21 2. Such a "password" does not fit the Eleusis in Alexandria; cf. above, p. 118. But even if Clement had learned of it there, it would have been a borrowing from Attica.

2 *Adversus nationes* V 26.

3 παραλαμβάνειν, *accipere*, is the term employed by the Mystery cults. Cf. my *Griechische Grundbegriffe*, p. 46.

4 Ovid, *Metamorphoses* V 450.

5 Pliny, *Naturalis historia* XVIII 72.

6 Armand Delatte, *Le Cycéon: Breuvage rituel des mystères d'Eleusis*, p. 33, thought of the addition of honey. He does not consider the possibility of fermentation, although the archaeologists have taken it into account: A. N. Skias, "'Ελευσινιακαὶ κεραμογραφίαι," *EphArch*, 1901, cols. 19 ff.; to the contrary, J. N. Svoronos, " 'Ερμηνεία τοῦ ἐξ 'Ελευσῖνος μυστηριακοῦ πίνακος τῆς Νιιννίου," Διεθνὴς ἐφημερίς, *Journal international d'archéologie numismatique*, IV (1901), 179, and R. Leonard, "Kernos," *RE*, XI, col. 323, on the ground that in the Homeric hymn there was no time for fermentation. Besides roasted grain, unroasted grain also can provide the raw material for alcoholic beverages. The fermentation was necessary, not the roasting.

7 Cf. Appendix II.

8 Letter from Albert Hofmann, Basel.

9 Thus correctly interpreted by Delatte, p. 39.

10 Hofmann letter.

11 Hofmann letter.

12 Plutarch, *Pericles* 38.

13 In Bowra, fr. 114 c.

14 Quintus Smyrnaeus II 182.

15 Plutarch, *De garrulitate* 511 C; Diels, *Vorsokr.*, A 3 b (6th edn., I, 144); cf. K. Freeman, *The Pre-Socratic Philosophers*, p. 105.

16 In *Anth. lyr.*, fr. 42.

APPENDIX II

1 211, *lacunam statuimus cuius sententia fuerit:*
> ἔκπιεν, ἡ δὲ λαβοῦσα δέπας θέτο' ἔνθ' ἀνάειρε
(ed. Allen, Halliday, Sikes).

2 Clement of Alexandria, *Protrepticus* II 21 1; Eusebios, *Praeparatio evangelica* II 3 34; Orph. fr. 52.

3 Iliad VII 222, XVI 107.

4 Iliad V 295; concerning the turtle's shield, the Homeric Hymn to Hermes 34.

5 Scholiast T and Eustathius on the Iliad VII 222; scholium on Hesiod's *Theogony* 299 (in Gaisford, II, 501).

6 Cf. P. Steiner, "Antike Skulpturen an der Panagia Gorgoepikoos zu Athen," *AM*, XXXI (1906), 339: "a two-handled, elegantly shaped vessel with lid, unmistakably copied from a metalwork prototype."

7 Cf. C. E. Beulé, *Monnaies d'Athènes*, pp. 154 and 344. A catalogue of the coins which document the vessel appears in H. G. Pringsheim, *Archäologische Beiträge zur Geschichte des eleusinischen Kults*, p. 69, n. 4, reprinted in *RE*, XI, col. 319 f.

8 This was Pringsheim's thesis, ibid., p. 77. To what extent it is tenable we shall see in connection with the other types.

9 The modern draftsman tended to interpret the branches as ears of grain. It is more likely that myrtle branches were intended.

10 Cf. D. Philios, " ᾿Αρχαιολογικὰ εὑρήματα τῶν ἐν ᾿Ελευσῖνι ἀνασκαφῶν," *EphArch*, 1885, col. 172.

11 This function was performed by the Epistatai.

12 *IG* I ² 313 and 314 23

13 Hesychios s. v.; cf. S. N. Dragumis, "Μυστικὴ προστροπὴ Δήμητρος καὶ Περσεφόνης," *AM*, XXVI (1901), 43.

14 This is my reading; πολύπαστα in the tradition. M. Schmidt gives the meaning in his edition of Hesychios: *caelaturae exstantes labris poculorum insculptae*. Arnobius, *Adversus nationes* V 25, translates αἰόλον ἄγγος by *poculum* because he had no idea what the vessel looked like and knew only that it was used for drinking.

15 Hesychios s. v. κερχνώμασι.

16 O. Rubensohn, "Kerchnos," *AM*, XXIII (1898), 271 ff., went too far when he lumped together under the term *kerchnos* all the vessels carried on the head in the procession.

17 The traditional text, διον ἔριον ἄπλυτον, "sheep's wool unwashed," was corrected by Meineke to ὠϊόν, ἔριον ἄπλυτον. Rightly so, for in Greece there is no other wool than sheep's wool (according to a Latin proverb, *lana caprina*, "goat's wool," means "nonsense"); ὄϊον ἔριον would be a pleonasm.

18 Cited by Athenaios, briefly at 476 ef, at greater length at 478 cd, from the work Περὶ τοῦ Δίου κωιδίου ("On the Sacred Fleece"). See Alois Tresp, *Die Fragmente der griechischen Kultschriftsteller*, pp. 87 f., translated into German by C. B. Gluck.

19 Nikandros, *Alexipharmaca* 7–8.

20 Ibid. 217.

21 Scholium on Nikandros' *Alexipharmaca* 217.

22 The text as it has come down to us has λίκνα; I read λύχνα, because of the following ἐσχαρίδες. The neuter λύχνον exists; cf. R. Reitzenstein (ed.), *Etymologicum Vaticanum* (Index lectionum in Academia Rostochiensi, 1891–1892), p. 14; Hipponax, in *Anth. lyr.*, fr. 22.

23 Clement of Alexandria, *Protrepticus* II 15 3; Dieterich, *Eine Mithrasliturgie*, 3rd edn., pp. 216 f.

24 This is also the opinion of Rubensohn, *AM*, XXIII (1898), 282.

25 According to Hans von Fritze, *EphArch*, 1897, col. 166.

26 According to D. Philios, *EphArch*, 1885, pl. 9: 8.

27 Cf. ibid., col. 173.

In general, classical texts are unlisted, especially when they are available in LCL or the Teubner editions. With a few exceptions, the texts listed are editions other than these (whether specified in the notes or not) and sources of quotations or translations.

For abbreviations, see the list on pages 189 f.

AESCHYLUS (AISCHYLOS). Fragments. In: *TGF*. (Fr. 363, 386.)

AILIOS ARISTEIDES. See ARISTIDES, AELIUS.

AISCHYLOS. See AESCHYLUS.

ALFÖLDI, ANDREAS. "Zur Kenntnis der Zeit der römischen Soldatenkaiser: 2. Das Problem des 'verweiblichten' Kaisers Gallienus." *Zeitschrift für Numismatik,* XXXVIII (1928), 156–203.

ALKIPHRON. *Alciphronis rhetoris Epistularum libri IV.* Edited by M. A. Schepers. (T.) Leipzig, 1905.

ANDOKIDES. *On the Mysteries* [*De mysteriis*]. Edited by Douglas MacDowell. Oxford, 1962.

ANTIPHANES. Fragment. In: THEODOR KOCK (ed.). *Comicorum atticorum fragmenta.* Leipzig, 1880–98. 3 vols. (II, 31 ff.)

APOLLONIOS RHODIOS. *Scholia in Apollonium Rhodium vetera.* Edited by Karl Wendel. (Bibliothecae graecae et latinae auctarium Weidmannianum, IV.) Berlin, 1935.

ARATUS OF SOLI. Scholia. In: ERNST WILHELM THEODOR MAASS. *Commentariorum in Aratum reliquiae.* Berlin, 1898.

ARISTIDES, AELIUS (ARISTEIDES, AILIOS). *Aelii Aristidis Smyrnaei quae supersunt omnia.* Edited by Bruno Keil. Berlin, 1898. New edn., Berlin, 1958. (Only II published.)

ARISTOPHANES. Scholia. In: FRIEDRICH DÜBNER (ed.). *Scholia graeca in Aristophanem.* Paris, 1842.

ARISTOTLE. *Works.* Translated into English under the editorship of W. D. Ross, Oxford, 1908–52. 12 vols. (XII, 87.)

ARNOBIUS. *Adversus nationes libri VII.* Edited by A. Reifferscheid. (CSEL, 4.) Vienna, 1875.

ARTEMIDOROS DALDIANOS. *Onirocriticon libri V.* Edited by Rudolf Hercher. Leipzig, 1864.

ASTERIOS, Bishop of Amasea. *Homilia X in SS. Martyres.* In: MIGNE, PG, XL, cols. 313–34.

BACHOFEN, JOHANN JAKOB. *Die Sage von Tanaquil.* In: *Gesammelte Werke.* Edited by Karl Meuli. Basel, 1943–58. 7 vols. [publication incomplete]. (VI.)

BEAZLEY, JOHN DAVIDSON. *Attic Black-Figure Vase Painters.* Oxford, 1956.

BERNAYS, JACOB. *Gesammelte Abhandlungen.* Edited by H. Usener. Berlin, 1885. 2 vols. (I.)

BEULÉ, CHARLES ERNEST. *Les Monnaies d'Athènes.* Paris, 1858.

BLAKE, WILLIAM. "A Descriptive Catalogue of Pictures . . . by William Blake . . . for Public Inspection . . ." (1809). In: *The Writings of William Blake.* Edited by Geoffrey Keynes. London, 1925. 3 vols. (III.) Also: *The Complete Writings of William Blake with All the Variant Readings.* Edited by Geoffrey Keynes. New York, 1957.

BÖTTICHER, KARL. *Der Baumkultus der Hellenen: Nach den gottesdienstlichen Gebräuchen und den überlieferten Bildwerken dargestellt.* Berlin, 1856.

BRUZZA, LUIGI. "Bassorilievo con epigrafe greca proveniente da Filippopoli." *Annali dell'Istituto di correspondenza archeologica* (Rome), XXXIII (1861), 380–88.

BUSCHOR, ERNST. "Zum Weihrelief von Mondragone." *AM,* LIII (1928), 48–51.

CALLIMACHUS. See KALLIMACHOS.

CAMPBELL, JOSEPH. *The Masks of God: Primitive Mythology.* New York, 1959; London, 1960.

CARCINUS. In: *TGF.* (Pp. 619–22.)

Catalogue des manuscrits alchimiques grecs. Edited by Joseph Bidez, Franz Cumont, et al. Brussels, 1924–30. 7 vols. (VI.)

CENSORINUS. *De die natali liber.* Edited by Friedrich Hultsch. (T.) Leipzig, 1867.

CICERO, MARCUS TULLIUS. *The Laws.* In: *De re publica; de legibus.* With an English translation by Clinton Walker Keyes. (LCL.) 1949.

CLAUDIANUS. *Claudii Claudiani de raptu Proserpina.* In: *Claudii Claudiani*

Carmina. Recension of Theodore Birt. (Monumenta Germaniae historica. Auctorum antiquissimorum, X.) Berlin, 1892. (Pp. 347–93.)

CLEMENT OF ALEXANDRIA. *Protrepticus.* In: [*Works*]. Edited by Otto Stählin. (GCS.) Leipzig, 1905–36. 4 vols. (I, 3–86.)

――――. *Stromata.* Ibid. (II, III.)

COOK, ARTHUR BERNARD. *Zeus: A Study in Ancient Religion.* Cambridge, 1914–40. 3 vols. in 5. (III: 1.)

Corpus inscriptionum graecarum. Edited by August Boeckh et al. Berlin, 1828–77. 4 vols. (II.)

COUVE, LOUIS. "Kernos," DarSag, III: 2, 822–25.

CUMONT, FRANZ. "Le Culte égyptien et le mysticisme de Plotin." *Monuments et mémoires publiés par l'Académie des inscriptions et belles-lettres . . .* (Fondation Eugène Piot) (Paris), XXV (1921–22), 77–92.

――――. *Les Religions orientales dans le paganisme romain.* 4th edn., Paris, 1929.

――――. *La Stèle du danseur d'Antibes et son décor végétal: Etude sur le symbolisme funéraire des plantes.* Paris, 1942.

DELATTE, ARMAND. *Le Cycéon: Breuvage rituel des mystères d'Eleusis.* (Collection des études anciennes.) Paris, 1955.

DEUBNER, LUDWIG. *Attische Feste.* Berlin, 1932.

――――. *Bemerkungen zu einigen literarischen Papyri aus Oxyrhynchos.* (Sitzungsberichte der Heidelberger Akademie der Wissenschaften, Philosophisch-historische Klasse, XVII.) Heidelberg, 1919.

DIELS, HERMANN. *Sibyllinische Blätter.* Berlin, 1890.

DIETERICH ALBRECHT. *Eine Mithrasliturgie.* 3rd edn., Leipzig and Berlin, 1923.

DIONYSIUS PERIEGETES. *Periegesis vel Orbis descriptio.* In: KARL MÜLLER (ed.) *Geographi graeci minores.* Paris, 1855–61. 2 vols. (II, 103–76.)

DIONYSIUS (of Philadelphia; or perhaps Periegetes). *Ixeuticon seu De aucupio libri tres.* Recension by Anton Garzya. (T.) Leipzig, 1963.

DITTENBERGER, WILHELM (ed.). *Sylloge inscriptionum graecarum.* 3rd edn., Leipzig, 1915–23. 4 vols. (III.)

Dodds, E. R. *The Greeks and the Irrational.* (University of California. Sather Classical Lectures, 25.) Berkeley and Los Angeles, 1951. (2nd paperbound edn. Berkeley and Los Angeles, 1964.)

Dragumis, S. N. "Μυστικὴ προστροπὴ Δήμητρος καὶ Περσεφόνης." *AM*, XXVI (1901), 38–49.

Eitrem, Samson. "Eleusinia—les mystères et l'agriculture." *SymbO*, XX (1940), 133–51.

———. "Les Epidauria." *Mélanges d'archéologie et d'histoire offerts à Charles Picard.* [A special issue of *Revue archéologique* (Paris), ser. 6, XXIX–XXXII (1948).] 2 vols. (XXIX–XXX, 351–59.)

Epiphanios. *Panarion.* In: *Ancoratus und Panarion.* Edited by Karl Holl. (GCS, XXV, XXXI, XXXVII.) Leipzig, 1915–33. 3 vols. (I, 153 ff.; II, III.)

Euboulos. In: John M. Edmonds. *Fragments of Attic Comedy.* Leiden, 1957–61. 3 vols. in 4 parts. (II, 82–145.)

Eupolis. Ibid. (I, 310–446.)

Euripides. Fragments. In: *TGF.*

———. *Phaëthon,* fragment. In: *Supplementum Euripideum.* Edited by Hans von Arnim. Bonn, 1913. (P. 77, 59/60.)

Eusebios. *Praeparatio evangelica.* Edited by Karl Maas. In: *Eusebius Werke*, VIII: 1, 2. (GCS, XL: 1, 2.) Berlin, 1954–56. 2 vols.

Foucart, Paul François. "Les Empereurs romains initiés aux mystères d'Eleusis." *Revue de philologie*, XVII (1893), 197–207.

———. *Les Mystères d'Eleusis.* Paris, 1914.

Fränkel, Ernst E. S. *Geschichte der griechischen Nomina agentis auf* -τήρ, -τωρ, -της [-τ-]. (Untersuchungen zur indogermanischen Sprach- und Kulturwissenschaft, 1, 4.) Strasbourg, 1910–12. 2 vols.

Freeman, Kathleen (tr.). *Ancilla to The Pre-Socratic Philosophers.* Cambridge, Mass., and London, 1948. (A complete translation of the Fragments in Diels, *Fragmente der Vorsokratiker.*)

———. *The Pre-Socratic Philosophers.* 2nd edn., Oxford, 1949. (A companion to Diels, *Fragmente der Vorsokratiker.*)

Fritze, Hans von. "Συμβολὴ εἰς τὸ τυπικὸν τῆς ἐν Ἐλευσῖνι λατρείας." *EphArch*, 1897, cols. 163–74.

GÀBRICI, ETTORE. "Cuma." *Monumenti antichi (Accademia dei Lincei)*, XXII (1913), cols. 6–766.

GERSTER, GEORG. "Ostern in Jerusalem." *Neue Zürcher Zeitung*, 31 March 1961, p. 5.

GIANNELLI, GIULIO. "I Romani ad Eleusi." *Atti della Reale Accademia della scienze di Torino*, L (1915), 319–33, 369–87.

GOETHE, JOHANN WOLFGANG VON. "Epirrhema" to "Die Metamorphose der Pflanzen." In: *Werke*. Edited by Erich Trunz, Wolfgang Kayser, and others. Hamburg, 1948–1960. 14 vols. (I.)

———. "Maximen und Reflexionen." Ibid. (XII.)

GRAINDOR, PAUL. *Athènes de Tibère à Trajan*. (Université Égyptienne. Recueil de travaux publiés par la Faculté des Lettres, 8.) Cairo, 1931.

HARPOKRATION. *Lexicon in decem oratores Atticos*. Edited by Wilhelm Dindorf. Oxford, 1853. (Only I published.)

HEMBERG, BENGT. *Die Kabiren*. Uppsala, 1950.

HERZOG, RUDOLF L. *Heilige Gesetze von Kos*. (Abhandlungen der Preussischen Akademie der Wissenschaften, 1928, Philosophisch-historische Klasse, no. 6.) Berlin, 1928.

HESIOD. Scholia. In: THOMAS GAISFORD (ed.). *Poetae minores graeci*. Oxford, 1814–20. 3 vols. (II.)

HESYCHIOS OF ALEXANDRIA. *Hesychii Alexandrini Lexicon post Joannem Albertum*. Edited by Moritz Schmidt. Jena, 1858–68. 5 vols.

HILLEBRANDT, ALFRED. *Der freiwillige Feuertod in Indien und die Somaweihe*. (Sitzungsberichte der [Königlich] Bayerischen Akademie der Wissenschaften, Philosophisch-, philologisch- und historische Klasse, 1917, no. 8.) Munich, 1917.

HILLER VON GÄRTRINGEN, FRIEDRICH. " 'Ανταγόρου 'Ροδίου." *Hermes*, XXVIII (1893), 469–71.

HIMERIOS. *Declamationes et orationes*. Edited by Aristides Colonna. (Scriptores graeci et latini.) Rome, 1951.

HIPPOLYTOS. *Elenchos* [or *Refutatio omnium haeresium*]. Edited by Paul Wendland. In: *Hippolytus' Werke*, III. (GCS, XXVI.) Leipzig, 1916. (For an English version, see *Philosophumena: or, The Refutation of all Heresies*.

Translated by Francis Legge. [Translations of Christian Literature.] London and New York, 1921. 2 vols.)

HIPPONAX. In: *Anth. lyr.* (III.)

HOMER. Scholia. In: EUSTATHIUS. *Eustathii commentarii ad Homeri Iliadem: ad fidem exempli Romani editi.* Leipzig, 1827–30. 4 vols.

―――. Scholiast T. In: W. DINDORF (ed.). *Scholia graeca in Homeri Iliadem . . . , V: Scholia graeca in Homeri Iliadem Townleyana.* Oxford, 1875–78. 6 vols. (V: 1.)

Homeric Hymns, The. Edited by Thomas W. Allen, W. R. Halliday, and E. E. Sikes. 2nd edn., Oxford, 1936.

HORNA, K. See MESOMEDES.

HYGINUS. *Astronomica.* Edited by Bernhard Bunte. Leipzig, 1875.

―――. *Fabulae.* Edited by Moritz Schmidt. Jena, 1872.

IAMBLICHOS. *De mysteriis.* Edited by Gustav Parthey. Berlin, 1857.

Inscriptiones graecae. Consilio et auctoritate Academiae Litterarum Regiae Borussicae editum. Berlin, 1873 ff. 14 vols. (Especially VII, XI, XII.)

―――. Editio minor. Berlin, 1913 ff. 4 vols. published. (Especially I, II, designated in notes as I² and II², respectively.)

Inscriptiones latinae selectae. Edited by Hermann Dessau. Berlin, 1892–1916. 3 vols. in 5 parts. (I.)

Inscriptions de Délos. Edited by F. Durrbach, Pierre Roussel, and Marcel Launay. Paris, 1926–37. 3 vols. in 5 parts. (V.)

JACOBY, FELIX. *FGrHist.* See KLEIDEMOS.

―――. *Das Marmor Parium.* Berlin, 1904.

JAEGER, WERNER. *Aristoteles: Grundlegung einer Geschichte seiner Entwicklung.* Berlin, 1923. 2nd edn., Berlin, 1955.

JAN, KARL VON. See MESOMEDES.

JENSEN, ADOLF ELLEGARD. *Die drei Ströme: Züge aus dem geistigen und religiösen Leben der Wemale, einem Primitiv-Volk in den Molukken.* (Ergebnisse der Frobenius-Expedition 1937–38 in die Molukken und nach Holländisch Neu-Guinea, II.) Leipzig, 1948.

———— and HERMANN NIGGEMEYER. *Hainuwele: Volkserzählungen von der Molukken-Insel Ceram.* (Ibid., I.) Frankfort on the Main, 1939.

————. *Das religiöse Weltbild einer frühen Kultur.* (Studien zur Kulturkunde, IX.) Stuttgart, 1948.

JONG, KAREL HENDRIK EDUARD DE. *Das antike Mysterienwesen in religionsgeschichtlicher, ethnologischer und psychologischer Beleuchtung.* Leiden, 1909.

JUNG, CARL GUSTAV, and C. KERÉNYI. *Einführung in das Wesen der Mythologie: Das göttliche Kind; Das göttliche Mädchen.* Amsterdam and Leipzig, 1941; new edn., Zurich, 1951. (For the English translation, see *Essays on a Science of Mythology*, below. For earlier versions of these essays, see the monograph *Das göttliche Kind* and KERÉNYI, "Kore," below.)

————. *Essays on a Science of Mythology: The Myth of the Divine Child and the Mysteries of Eleusis.* Translated by R. F. C. Hull. (Bollingen Series XXII.) New York, 1950; London, 1951 (titled *Introduction to a Science of Mythology*). (New edn., with different pagination, in: Tor., 1963.) (For the original text, see *Einführung in das Wesen der Mythologie*, above.)

————. *Das göttliche Kind in mythologischer und psychologischer Beleuchtung.* (Albae Vigiliae, 6, 7.) Amsterdam and Leipzig, 1940. (For the beginning of these studies, see KERÉNYI, "Zum Urkind-Mythologie," below. For the sequels to the 1940 versions, see *Einführung in das Wesen der Mythologie* and *Essays on a Science of Mythology*, above.)

————. *Das göttliche Mädchen: Die Hauptgestalt der Mysterien von Eleusis in mythologischer und psychologischer Beleuchtung.* (Albae Vigiliae, 8, 9.) Amsterdam and Leipzig, 1941. (For the beginning of these studies, see KERÉNYI, "Kore," below. For the sequels to the 1941 versions, see *Einführung* and *Essays*, above.)

KAIBEL, GEORG. "Zu den griechischen Künstlerinschriften." *Hermes,* XXII (1887), 151–56.

KALLIMACHOS. Scholia. In: *Callimachus.* Edited by Rudolf Pfeiffer. Oxford, 1949–53. 2 vols. (II.)

KERÉNYI, C. [in some publications KARL]. *Abenteuer mit Monumenten.* Olten, 1959.

————. *Apollon: Studien über antike Religion und Humanität.* 3rd edn., Düsseldorf, 1953. (Partly in *Werke*, I, q.v.)

KERÉNYI. "Dramatische Gottesgegenwart in der griechischen Religion." *EJ 1950*, XIX (1951), 13–39.

———. *Eleusis: De heiligste mysterien van Griekenland*. Translated into Dutch by Johan Anton Schröeder. The Hague [1960].

———. "Zum Fries des Ilissostempels." *AM*, LXXVI (1961), 22–24.

———. *Der frühe Dionysos*. (Universitetet i Oslo, Klassisk institutt. Eitremforelesninger, 2.) Oslo [1961].

———. *Die Geburt der Helena*. (Albae Vigiliae, N.S. 3.) Zurich, 1945.

———. "Über das Geheimnis der eleusinischen Mysterien." *Paideuma*, VII (1959), 69–82.

———. *The Gods of the Greeks*. Translated by Norman Cameron. London and New York, 1951. (Reprinted with different pagination in Pelican Books, Harmondsworth, 1958.)

———. *Griechische Grundbegriffe*. (Albae Vigiliae, N.S. 19). Zurich, 1964.

———. *Griechische Miniaturen*. Zurich, 1957.

———. *Hermes der Seelenführer: Das Mythologem vom männlichen Lebensursprung*. (Albae Vigiliae, N.S.1.) Zurich, 1944.

———. *The Heroes of the Greeks*. Translated by H. J. Rose. London, 1959.

———. " 'Herr der Wilden Tiere'?" *SymbO*, XXXIII (1957), 127–34.

———. *Die Jungfrau und Mutter in der griechischen Religion: Eine Studie über Pallas Athene*. (Albae Vigiliae, N.S. 12.) Zurich, 1952.

———. "Kore: Zum Mythologem vom göttlichen Mädchen." *Paideuma*, I (1940), 341–80.

———. On Kroll, Josef, "Gott und Hölle: Der Mythos vom Descensuskampfe. . . ." *Gnomon*, IX (1933), 363–71.

———. *Labyrinth-Studien: Labyrinthos als Linienreflex einer mythologischen Idee*. 2nd edn. (Albae Vigiliae, N.S. 10), Zurich, 1950. (*Werke*, q.v.)

———. "Miti sul concepimento di Dioniso." *Maia: Rivista di letterature classiche* (Messina), IV (1951), 1–13.

———. *Die Mysterien von Eleusis*. Zurich [1962.]

———. "Parva realia." *SymbO*, XXXVI (1960), 5–16.

———. "Persephone und Prometheus: Vom Alter griechischer Mythen." *Fest-*

schrift für Hans Oppermann. [A special issue of *Jahrbuch der Raabe-Gesellschaft* (Braunschweig), 1965.]

———. *Prometheus: Archetypal Image of Human Existence.* Translated from the German by Ralph Manheim. (Archetypal Images in Greek Religion, I.) New York (Bollingen Series LXV) and London, 1963. (Original: *Prometheus: Die menschliche Existenz in griechischer Deutung.* Hamburg, 1959.)

———. *Pythagoras und Orpheus: Präludien zu einer zukünftigen Geschichte der Orphik und des Pythagoreismus.* 3rd edn. (Albae Vigiliae, N.S., 9.), Zurich, 1950. (*Werke,* q.v.)

———. *The Religion of the Greeks and Romans.* London, 1962. (A translation by Christopher Holme of *Die antike Religion,* 3rd edn., revised, Düsseldorf, 1952.)

———. *Streifzüge eines Hellenisten, von Homer zu Kazantzakis.* Zurich, 1960.

———. *Umgang mit Göttlichem.* Göttingen, 1955. 2nd edn. (Kleine Vandenhoeck-Reihe, 18.) Göttingen, 1961.

———. "Zum Urkind-Mythologem." *Paideuma,* I (1940), 241–78.

———. "Zum Verständnis von Vergilius Aeneis B. VI." *Hermes,* 66 (1931), 413–41.

———. "Voraussetzungen der Einweihung in Eleusis." *Initiation: Contributions to the Theme of the Study-Conference of the International Association for the History of Religions, Held at Strasburg, September 17th to 22nd 1964.* (Studies in the History of Religions. Supplements to *Numen.* X.) Leiden, 1965. (Pp. 59–64.)

———. *Werke in Einzelausgaben,* I: *Humanistische Seelenforschung.* Munich, 1966.

KERN, OTTO. "Δημητήρ–Σελήνη." *EphArch 1892,* 1893, cols. 113–18.

———. *Die griechischen Mysterien der klassischen Zeit.* Berlin, 1927.

———. "Mysterien." In: *RE,* XVI, cols. 1209–1314.

———. (ed.). *Orph. fr.*

———. *Der Religion der Griechen.* Berlin, 1926–38. 3 vols. (II.)

KLEIDEMOS. Fragments. In: *FGrHist.* (Pt. III B.)

KONTOLEON, N. M. "Μέγαρον." In: *Mélanges offerts à Octave et Melpo Merlier.* Athens, 1952.

KÖRTE, ALFRED. "Zu den eleusinischen Mysterien." *ArchRW*, XVIII (1915), 116–26.

―――. "Eleusinisches." *Glotta*, XXV (1936), 134–42.

―――. See PHILIKOS.

KRETSCHMER, PAUL. "Zur Geschichte der griechischen Dialekte." *Glotta*, I (1909), 9–59.

KRINAGORAS. In: *Anth. Pal.* Also: *The Greek Anthology.* With an English translation by W. R. Paton. (LCL.) 1948–56. 5 vols. (IV.)

KUIPER, CONRAD. "De Euripidis Supplicibus." [Translated from Dutch into Latin by I. I. Hartman.] *Mnemosyne*, N.S. LI (1923), 102–28.

KURUNIOTIS, KONSTANTINOS. "Ἐλεσινιακὴ δαῖδουχία." *ArchEph*, 1937: 1, 223–53.

LACTANTIUS, LUCIUS CAELIUS FIRMIANUS. *Institutionum epitome.* In: *Opera omnia.* Edited by Samuel Brandt and Georg Laubmann. (CSEL, 19, 27.) Prague, Vienna, Leipzig, 1890–93. 2 vols. (I, 675–761.)

LEHMANN, KARL. *Samothrace: A Guide to the Excavations and the Museum.* (Institute of Fine Arts, New York University.) 2nd revised edn., New York, 1960.

LENORMANT, CHARLES. "Mémoire sur les représentations qui avaient lieu dans les mystères d'Eleusis." *Mémoires de l'Académie d'inscriptions et de belles-lettres* (Paris), XXIV: 1 (1861), 343–445.

LENORMANT, FRANÇOIS. "Eleusinia." In: DarSag, II, 544–81.

LEONARD, R. "Kernos." In: *RE*, XI, cols. 316–26.

LEVI, DORO. "A Magnificent Crater and Rich Pottery from the Crete of 4000 Years Ago: New and Vivid Light on the Earliest Palace of Phaistos." *The Illustrated London News*, 6 Oct. 1956, pp. 548–50.

LOBECK, CHRISTIAN AUGUST. *Aglaophamus; sive de theologiae mysticae graecorum causis libri tres . . . idemque poetarum Orphicorum dispersas reliquias collegit.* Regiomontii Prussorum (Königsberg, now Kaliningrad), 1829. 2 vols. (continuously paged).

LOEFF, A. RUTGERS VAN DER. "De formula quadam Eleusinia." *Mnemosyne*, XLV (1917), 361–66.

LUCIAN. Scholia. In: H. RABE (ed.). *Scholia in Lucianum.* Leipzig, 1906.

LYKOPHRON. *Alexandra.* Edited by Gottfried Kinkel. Leipzig, 1880.

———. *Scholia.* Ibid.

MAAS, PAUL. *Epidaurische Hymnen.* (Schriften der Königsberger Gelehrten Gesellschaft, Geisteswissenschaftliche Klasse, IX, 5). Halle, 1933. (Pp. [127]–61.)

MAASS, ERNST. "Segnen Weihen Taufen." *ArchRW,* XXI (1922), 241–86.

——— (ed.). See ARATUS.

MÉAUTIS, GEORGES. *Les Mystères d'Eleusis.* Neuchâtel, 1934.

MEILLET, (PAUL JULES) ANTOINE. *Aperçu d'une histoire de la langue grecque.* Paris, 1913.

MERRIAM, A. C. "Inscribed Sepulchral Vases from Alexandria." *AJA,* I (1885), 18–33.

MESOMEDES. Hymn to the Muse. In: KONSTANTIN HORNA. *Die Hymnen des Mesomedes.* (Sitzungsberichte der Akademie der Wissenschaften in Wien, Philosophisch-historische Klasse, CCVII, Abhandlung 1.) Vienna and Leipzig, 1928. Also in: KARL VON JAN (ed.). *Musici scriptores graeci.* (T.) Leipzig, 1895–99. (Reprinted 1962.)

MEYER, EDUARD. *Geschichte des Altertums.* Stuttgart, 1884–1902. 5 vols. Revised and enlarged, with some vols. in differing edns., Basel, 1953–58. 5 vols. in 8. (IV of 1st edn.; IV: 2, 4th edn.)

MINGAZZINI, PAOLINO. "Rilievo eleusinio rinvenuto in territorio de Mondragone (Sinuessa)." *NS,* LII (ser. 6, III) (1927), 309–15.

MONTUORO, PAOLA ZANCANI. See ZANCANI MONTUORO, PAOLA.

MYLONAS, GEORGE E. *Eleusis and the Eleusinian Mysteries.* Princeton, 1961 [actually 1962].

Mysteries, The. (Papers from the Eranos Yearbooks, 2; ed. Joseph Campbell.) New York (Bollingen Series XXX) and London, 1955.

NAUCK, AUGUST. See under AESCHYLUS; CARCINUS; EURIPIDES.

NÉROUTSOS, TASSOS DEMETRIOS. *L'Ancienne Alexandrie: Étude archéologique et topographique.* Paris, 1888.

NEUMANN, ERICH. *The Great Mother.* Translated by Ralph Manheim. New York (Bollingen Series XLVII) and London, 1955; 2nd edn., 1963. (Also: *Die grosse Mutter.* Zurich, 1956.)

NICANDER (NIKANDROS). *Alexipharmaca*. In: *The Poems and Poetical Fragments*. Edited with a translation and notes by A. S. F. Gow and A. F. Scholfield. Cambridge, 1953.

————. ————. Scholia. In: *Nicandrea: Theriaca et Alexipharmaca*. Revised and emended by Otto Schneider. Leipzig, 1856.

NIKOMACHOS OF GADARA. In: PHOTIOS. *Bibliotheca*, q.v.

NILSSON, MARTIN PERSSON. *The Dionysiac Mysteries of the Hellenistic and Roman Age*. (Skriften utgivna av Svenska institutet i Athen, ser. 2, 5.) Lund, 1957.

————. "Die eleusinischen Gottheiten." In: *Opuscula selecta*, II. (Ibid., ser. 2, 2.) Lund, 1952.

————. *Geschichte der griechischen Religion*. (Handbuch der Altertumswissenschaft, sec. 5, part 2, I, II.) Munich, 1941–50. 2nd edn., Munich, 1961. 2 vols. (II.) (An English version, in paperback, with different pagination: *A History of Greek Religion*. [Translated by F. J. Fielden.] 2nd edn., New York [1964].)

NISTLER, JOHANNA. "Vettius Agorius Praetextatus." *Klio: Beiträge zur alten Geschichte* (Leipzig), X (1910), 462–75.

NOACK, FERDINAND. *Eleusis: Die baugeschichtliche Entwickelung des Heiligtumes; Aufnahmen und Untersuchungen*. Berlin, 1927.

OKELLOS LUKANOS. *De universi natura*. Edited by Richard Harder. (Neue philologische Untersuchungen.) Berlin, 1926.

OLIVER, JAMES H. "Greek Inscriptions." *Hesperia: Journal of the American School of Classical Studies at Athens* (Cambridge, Mass.), IV (1935), 5–70.

Orphic Hymns. In: QUANDT, q.v.

OTTO, WALTER FRIEDRICH. "Apollon." *Paideuma*, VII (1959), 19–34.

————. *Dionysos: Mythos und Kultus*. (Frankfurter Studien zur Religion und Kultur der Antike, 4.) Frankfort on the Main, 1933.

————. "Der Sinn der eleusinischen Mysterien." *EJ 1939*, VII (1940), 99–106. (An English version, "The Meaning of the Eleusinian Mysteries," in: *The Mysteries*, 83–112, q.v.).

Oxyrhynchus Papyri 1381, 1612. In: *POxy*, XI, XIII.

Papiri della R. Università di Milano. Edited by Achille Vogliano with the collaboration of various scholars. (Pubblicazioni della R. Università di Milano.) Milan, 1937. (Only I published.)

PHANODEMOS. Fragments. In: *FGrHist.* (Pt. III B.)

PHILIKOS. Hymn. In: ALFRED KÖRTE. "Der Demeter-Hymnos des Philikos." *Hermes*, LXVI (1931), 442–54.

PHILIOS, A. "Κεφαλὴ ἐξ ᾿Ελευσῖνος." *EphArch*, 1886, cols. 257–66.

PHILIOS, D. " ᾿Αρχαιολογικὰ εὑρήματα τῶν ἐν ᾿Ελευσῖνι ἀνασκαφῶν." *EphArch*, 1885, cols. 169–84.

PHOTIOS. *Bibliothèque [Bibliotheca].* Edited and translated into French by René Henry. (Collection Byzantine publiée sous le patronage de l'Association Guillaume Budé.) Paris, 1959–62. 3 vols. (III.)

————. *Lexicon.* Edited by S. A. Naber. Leiden, 1864–65. 2 vols.

PICARD, CHARLES. "Les Bûchers sacrés d'Eleusis." *RHR*, CVII (1933), 137–54.

————. "L'Eleusinisme au Rome au temps de la dynastie julio-claudienne." *Revue des études latines* (Paris), XXVIII (1950), 77–80.

————. "L'Episode de Baubô dans les mystères d'Eleusis." *RHR*, XCV (1927), 220–55.

————. "La Patère d'Aquileia et l'éleusinisme à Rome aux débuts de l'époque impériale." *L'Antiquité classique* (Brussels, etc.), XX (1951), 351 ff.

PINDAR. *Carmina cum fragmentis.* Edited by Cecil Maurice Bowra. (Oxford Classical Texts.) 2nd edn., Oxford, 1947.

PLATO. *Phaedrus.* Translated by Reginald Hackforth. Cambridge, 1952.

————. *Phaedrus, Ion, Gorgias, and Symposium, with Passages from the Republic and the Laws.* Translated by Lane Cooper. London and New York, 1938.

PLUTARCH. *De profectu in virtute.* In: *Moralia.* With an English translation by Frank Cole Babbitt and others. (LCL.) Cambridge (Mass.) and London, 1927 ff. 15 vols. (I.)

POLEMO ILIENSIS. In: KARL MÜLLER. *Fragmenta historicorum graecorum.* Paris, 1841–84. 5 vols. (III, 108–48.)

PRINGSHEIM, HEINZ GERHARD. *Archäologische Beiträge zur Geschichte des eleusinischen Kults.* Munich, 1905.

PROKLOS. See HESIOD. Scholia.

PROTT, JOHANNES DE, and L. ZIEHEN. (eds.). *Leges graecorum sacrae e titulis collectae.* Leipzig, 1896–1906. 2 vols.

PRUDENTIUS. Hymn for the Burial of the Dead. In: *Aurelii Prudentii Clementis Carmina.* Recension by J. Bergman. (CSEL, LXI.) Leipzig, 1926. (An English version in: JOHN MASON NEALE. *Collected Hymns, Sequences and Carols.* London and New York, 1914.)

PSELLOS, MICHAEL. *Graecorum opiniones de daemonibus* (Τίνα περὶ δαιμόνων δοξάζουσιν "Ελληνες). In: *De operatione daemonum* (in Greek). Edited by Jo[hann] Fr[anz] Boissonade. Nuremberg, 1838. (Pp. 36–43.) Also in: MIGNE, *PG*, CXXII, 875–81.

———. "Ad Johannem Climacum" (in Greek). In: *Catalogue des manuscrits alchimiques grecs*, VI, q.v. (An English translation in ARISTOTLE, Works, XII, q.v.)

QUANDT, WILHELM (ed.). *Orphei hymni.* 2nd edn., Berlin, 1955.

REITZENSTEIN, RICHARD (ed.). *Etymologicum Vaticanum.* (Index lectionum in Academia rostochiensi . . . 1891–1892.) Rostock [1893?].

ROSENBACH, MANFRED. *Galliena Augusta: Einzelgötter und Allgott im gallienischen Pantheon.* (Aparchai: Untersuchungen zur klassischen Philologie und Geschichte des Altertums, 3.) Tübingen, 1958.

ROUSSEL, PIERRE. *Les Cultes égyptiens à Delos, du IIIe au Ier siècle avant Jésus-Christ.* (Annales de l'Est.) Paris, 1916.

RUBENSOHN, OTTO. "Demeter als Heilgottheit." *AM*, XX (1895), 360–67.

———. "Kerchnos." *AM*, XXIII (1898), 271–306.

———. "Das Weihehaus von Eleusis und sein Allerheiligstes." *JDAI*, LXX (1955), 1–49.

SÄFLUND, GÖSTA. *Aphrodite Kallipygos.* (Acta Universitatis Stockholmensis. Studies in Classical Archaeology, 3.) Stockholm, 1963.

Sanhedrin. Translated by Jacob Schachter and H. Freedman. 2 vols. In: *The Babylonian Talmud.* Edited by Isidore Epstein et al. London, 1935–48. 34 vols. (Seder Nezikin, V, VI.)

SCHÄFER, HANS. "Poros." *RE*, XXII, cols. 1225–28.

SCHAUENBURG, KONRAD. "Pluton und Dionysos." *JDAI*, LXVIII (1953), 38–72.

————. "Zur Symbolik unteritalischer Rankenmotive." *RM*, LXIV (1957), 198–221.

————. "Die Totengötter in der unteritalischen Vasenmalerei." *JDAI*, LXXIII (1958), 48–78.

SCHIFF, ————. "Eleusis." In: *RE*, V, col. 2342.

SERVIUS MAURUS HONORATUS. *Servii Grammatici qui feruntur in Vergilii carmina commentarii.* Edited by Georg Thilo and Hermann Hagen. Leipzig, 1881–1902; reprinted 1961. 3 vols. (I.)

SIMON, ERIKA. "Zum Fries der Mysterienvilla bei Pompeji." *JDAI*, LXXVI (1961), 111–72.

SKIAS, ANDREAS N. " Ἐλευσινιακαὶ κεραμογαφίαι." *EphArch*, 1901, cols. 1–50.

SOGLIANO, A. Quoted in "Notizie degli scavi: Febbrario." *NS*, 1883, pp. 25–54. (Especially 49 f.)

SOPATER (SOPATROS). Διαίρεσις ζητημάτων. In: CHRISTIAN WALZ (ed.). *Rhetores graeci.* Stuttgart, 1832–36. 9 vols. (VIII.)

SOPHOKLES. Fragments. In: *Fragmenta.* Edited by Alfred Chilton Pearson. Cambridge, 1917. 3 vols. (III.)

————. ————. In: *TGF.* (Fr. 760.)

————. *Oedipus at Colonus.* An English version by Robert Fitzgerald. In: SOPHOCLES. *The Oedipus Cycle: An English Version.* (A Harvest Book.) New York, n. d. (Pp. 79–181.) (Earlier editions, with different pagination: New York, 1939, 1941; London, 1957.)

————. *Triptolemos*, fragment. In: *Fragmenta*, ed. Pearson, above.

STATIUS, PUBLIUS PAPINIUS. *Achilleid.* Edited with introduction, apparatus criticus and notes by O. A. W. Dilke. Cambridge, 1954.

STEINER, PAUL. "Antike Skulpturen an der Panagia Gorgoepikoos zu Athen." *AM*, XXXI (1906), 325–41.

STEPHEN OF BYZANTIUM. *Ethnicorum quae supersunt.* Edited by A. Meineke. Berlin, 1849. (Only I published.)

STOBAEUS, JOANNES. *Anthologium.* Edited by K. Wachsmuth and Otto Hense. Berlin, 1884–94. 5 vols. (V.)

SUIDAS (SUDA). *Suidae Lexicon.* Edited by Ada Adler. (Lexicographi graeci recogniti et apparatu critico instructi, I.) Leipzig, 1928–38. 5 vols. (II.)

SVORONOS, J. N. " Ἑρμηνεία τοῦ ἐξ Ἐλευσῖνος μυστηριακοῦ πίνακος τῆς Νιιννίου." *Diethnes ephemeris tes nomismatikes archaiologias: Journal international d'archéologie numismatique* (Athens), IV (1901), 169–91.

TERTULLIAN. *Ad nationes.* In: MIGNE, *PL*, I, cols. 559–608.

THEODORETOS. *Graecarum affectionum curatio.* Edited by Johann Raeder. Leipzig, 1904.

THEOKRITOS. Scholia. In: CARL WENDEL. *Scholia in Theocritum vetera.* Leipzig, 1914.

THEON OF SMYRNA. *Expositio rerum mathematicarum.* Recension by E. Hiller. (T.) Leipzig, 1878.

THIMME, JÜRGEN. "Die religiöse Bedeutung der Kykladenidole." *Antike Kunst* (Olten), VIII (1965), 72–86.

TOEPPFER, JOHANN ALEXANDER FERDINAND. *Attische Genealogie.* Berlin, 1889.

TRAVLOS, IOANNES N. "Τὸ 'Ανάκτορον τῆς 'Ελευσῖνος." *ArchEph*, 1950–51, pp. 1–16.

―――. "'Ελευσίς." *Archaiologikon Deltion 1960*, XVI (1962), 46–59.

―――. In: Τὸ ἔργον τῆς 'Αρχαιολογικῆς 'Εταιρείας κατὰ τὸ *1957, 1960–62.* [Athens. Société archéologique.] Athens, 1958, 1961–63.

TRESP, ALOIS. *Die Fragmente der griechischen Kultschriftsteller.* Translated into German by C. B. Gluck. (Religionsgeschichtliche Versuche und Vorarbeiten, XV: 1.) Giessen, 1914.

ULPIAN. *Digest.* In: *Corpus juris civilis.* Edited by T. Mommsen and P. Krueger. Berlin, 1954.

VELLEIUS PATERCULUS. . . . *Res gestae divi Augusti.* With an English translation by Frederick W. Shipley. (LCL.) 1955.

VENTRIS, MICHAEL GEORGE FRANCIS, and JOHN CHADWICK. *Documents in Mycenaean Greek: Three Hundred Selected Tablets from Knossos, Pylos, and Mycenae.* Cambridge, 1956.

WIDENGREN, GEO. "Aspetti simbolici dei templi e luoghi di culto del vicino oriente." *Numen* (Leiden), VII (1960), 1–25.

WILAMOWITZ-MOELLENDORFF, ULRICH VON. *Der Glaube der Hellenen.* Berlin, 1931–32. 2 vols.

————. *Griechische Verskunst.* Berlin, 1921.

————. "Lesefrüchte." *Hermes,* LXIII (1928), 369–90.

WOLTERS, PAUL HEINRICH AUGUST. *Das Kabirienheiligtum bei Theben.* Arranged by Gerda Bruns. Berlin, 1940. (Only I published.)

WÜNSCH, RICHARD. *Das Frühlingsfest der Insel Malta.* Leipzig, 1902.

ZANCANI MONTUORO, PAOLA. "Il Rapitore di Kore nel mito Locrese." *Rendiconti della Accademia di archeologia, lettere, e belle arti., Napoli* (Naples), XXIX (1955), 79–86.

ZOSIMOS. *Historia nova.* Edited by Ludwig Mendelssohn. Leipzig, 1887.

INDEX

An asterisk indicates an illustration on the page cited; a superior figure (e.g., 194 [4]), a note likewise on the page cited. The abbreviation *q.* indicates a quotation.

Index

238

Apulian vase, 131 & *, 142 & 143 *
Arabia, 136
Aratus, 208 [39]
Arcadia, 27, 31, 32, 70
archaeological research/archaeology/excavation, xviii, xix, xxi, xxxiv–xxxvi, 18, 20, 21, 71, 82, 97, 105, 108–112 200 [12]
archaic, xx, xxv, xxvi, 13, 16, 28, 35, 37 *, 70, 71, 72, 80, 84, 127, 128, 134, 137
arche, xxxiii
archetypal images/archetypes, xvii, xxvi–xxxiii, 136, 145, 147
Areopagos (Athens), 204 [71]
Ares, 126
Argos, 138
Ariadne, 93, 161, 195 [26], 202 [45]
Aristides, Aelius, 203 [64], 207 [15]
Aristophanes: *Acharnenses*, 197 [30]; *Aves*, 204 [67]; *Nubes*, 91–92 *q.*, 200 [23], 201 [32]; *Pax*, 180 *q.*, 197 [29]; *Plutus*, 65, 199 [64 69]; *Ranae* (*The Frogs*), 9, 99, 194 [28], 197 [32], 198 [43], 199 [61 65], 200 [11], 202 [48], 204 [68 *q.* 69], 212 [151], 213 [156]; *Vespae*, 134, 209 [71]
Aristotle, 45, 113–114; *Athenaion politeia*, 198 [50]; *Ethica Nichomachea*, 204 [71]; *On Philosophy*, 113, 114 *q.*; *Poetics*, 113 *q.*
"Ark of Kypselos," 134
Arnobius, 177, 178 *q.*, 199 [8], 208 [35], 214 [2], 215 [14]
arrheton, 24, 26, 28, 42, 121, 126
arrhetos koura, 26, 97, 132, 133
Arrian, *Anabasis*, 205 [79 80]; *see also* Epiktetos
Artemidoros, 210 [93 101]
Artemis, xx, 49, 123; A. Agrotera, 49; A. Propylaia, 70; *see also under* Kallimachos
ascetic/asceticism, 100, 101, 119
Asia Minor, 34, 115
Asklepios/Asklepiad, 5, 61, 62, 93, 96, 119, 203 [56]
Aspasia, 121
Assisi, 90
Asterios, 117 *q.*

Athena, xx, 149, 159, 162, 164, 167 & *; A. Hygieia, 96–97; A. Nike, 137
Athenaios, 195 [13 29], 209 [78 79 90], 210 [113], 215 [18]
Athens/Athenians, xviii, 5–12, 17, 22, 25, 28, 36, 38, 42, 45, 48, 50, 51, 53, 62, 65–67, 72, 79, 80, 85, 93, 94, 98, 99, 101, 105, 110, 113, 115, 121, 122, 132, 137, 138, 141, 149, 155, 156, 158, 167, 171, 178, 182, 202 [50], 207 [15], 212 [141 145]
athletes/athletics, 101
Attica, 5, 8, 29, 50, 62, 92, 115–119, 121, 125, 132, 141, 149, 154, 201 [36], 207 [12], 124 [1]
Atticus, 18
Attis, 134, 135, 136, 184
Augustus, Emperor, 100, 101
aule (courtyard), 42, 79
autopsia, 114
autumn, *see* seasons of the year

B

Babbitt, F. C., tr., 201 [31 *q.*]
bacchantes, 59
Bachofen, J. J., 7 *q.*, 193 [3]
Bakchos, 25
barbarian, 25
barley, 40, 62, 121, 127, 130, 177–180, 184, 192 [1]
basket, 32, 57, 58, 63, 66, 75, 80, 106, 110, 151, 153, 181, 199 [8], 206 [6]; see also *cista mystica*
bath (ritual), 54, 60, 61, 88
Baubo, 40, 65, 171, 178, 181
beans, 184, 193 [1]
beatific vision, see *visio beatifica*
beatification, 95–96, 101, 119, 147
beatitude/happiness, 13–16, 44, 95, 96, 105
Beatitudes of Christ, 14
Beazley, J. D., 195 [26]
begetting, 31, 119, 135
Bernays, J., 204 [71]
betrayal of the Mysteries, xxxv, 82, 83–84, 108
Beulé, C. E., 215 [7]
beverage, see *kykeon*

Library of Congress Cataloging-in-Publication Data

Kerényi, Karl, 1897–1973.

Eleusis : archetypal image of mother and daughter/Carl Kerényi;
translated from the German by Ralph Manheim.

p. cm.

Reprint. Originally published: New York: Bollingen Foundation, 1967.
(Bollingen series; 65, v. 4) (Archetypal images in Greek religion; v. 4).
"First paperback printing, in the Mythos series, 1991"—T.p. verso.
Includes bibliographical references and index.

ISBN 0-691-01915-0

1. Eleusinian mysteries. 2. Eleusis (Greece)—Religion.
I. Title.   II. Series: Kerényi, Karl, 1897–1973.
Archetypal images in Greek religion; v. 4.
III. Series: Bollingen Series; 65-4.
IV. Series: Mythos (Princeton, N.J.)

BL795.E5K413   1991   90-20823 CIP

292.9—dc20

MYTHOS: *The Princeton/Bollingen Series in World Mythology*